PRONOIA

Is the Antidote for Paranoia

*How the Whole World Is Conspiring
to Shower You with Blessings*

ROB BREZSNY

and the Beauty and Truth Laboratory

Frog, Ltd.
BERKELEY, CALIFORNIA

Published by Frog, Ltd.

and

Televisionary Publishing
P.O. Box 150247
San Rafael, CA 94915
www.beautyandtruth.com

Frog, Ltd. books are distributed by North Atlantic Books,
P.O. Box 12327, Berkeley, California 94712

Cover design by Catherine Campaigne
Printed in the United States of America
Distributed to the book trade by Publishers Group West

North Atlantic Books' publications are available through most bookstores.
For further information, call 800-337-2665 or visit our website
at www.northatlanticbooks.com

Substantial discounts on bulk quantities are available to corporations, professional associations, and other organizations. For further details and discount information, contact our special sales department.

Library of Congress Cataloging-in-Publication Data

Brezsny, Rob.
    Pronoia is the antidote for paranoia : how the whole world is
conspiring to shower you with blessings / by Rob Brezsny.
        p.   cm.
    Summary: "In this how-to book, Rob Brezsny builds a case for
cagey optimism, a perspective which engages rather than
represses difficulty and views the universe as inherently
friendly"—Provided by publisher.
    ISBN 1-58394-123-1 (pbk.)
    1. Optimism.   2. Life.   3. Blessing and cursing. I. Title.
B829.B74 2005
149'.5—dc22

                                                    2005002872
1 2 3 4 5 6 7 8 9 Data 09 08 07 06 05

Instructions

1.

Start at the beginning of this book and read it in a sequential fashion
straight through to the end;
OR
start in the middle of the book and read here and there, trusting your instincts
to find exactly what you need, exactly when you need it;
OR
ignore the above suggestions and improvise your own approach.

2.

Commune with the book as if it were made of music as well as writing.
Let the recurring melodic and rhythmic themes guide your passage.

3.

Regard yourself as my coauthor.
Keep a pen or pencil with you as you read,
and add your comments and drawings with abandon.
There are numerous questions and assignments to spark you.
Chapter 16 is entirely yours,
and you'll find lots of empty space for your use in the 14 "Pronoia Therapy" pieces.
But feel free to scrawl and doodle anywhere.

4.

I invite you to begin your contribution to our collaboration on this page.
You could tell a good and beautiful lie, or brag about how smart you are in the way you love,
or describe the circumstances in which you were most dangerously alive.
Jot down the five things you most want to accomplish in the next 20 years.
Name the people you'd like to see naked.
Write the first two sentences of your 500-page autobiography.

Table of Contents

Chapter 5
Let's go wash some water

Chapter 6
"I vow to interpret every experience as a direct dealing of the Goddess with my soul"

Chapter 7
Everyone's a nobody—and nobody's perfect

Chapter 8
When did you first realize you are the rain's teacher?

Chapter 9
Visualize _____ at the moment of orgasm
        Put your deity's name here

Chapter 10
Only you can prevent the genocide of the imagination

Chapter 11
Stronger than hate, wetter than water, deeper than the abyss, more exotic than trust

Chapter 12
This language prevents crime.
This engineering moves you to sing.
These advertisements make you smart.
These rhythms free all prisoners of childhood.

Chapter 13
The 11th Commandment: Thou Shalt Not Bore God
The 12th Commandment: Thou Shalt Not Bore Thyself

☼

Chapter 14
You Are a Fucking Lucky Plucky Good-Sucking Genius

☼

Chapter 15
"Ever since I learned to see three sides of every story, I'm finding much better stories"

☼

Chapter 16
You Are My Coauthor <------[or whiteout "You Are My Coauthor" and create your own chapter title]

1

Bravo
Viva
Kudos
Whoopee
Eureka
Hallelujah
Abracadabra

This is a Perfect Moment

This is a perfect moment.

It's a perfect moment for many reasons, but especially because you and I are waking up from our sleepwalking, thumb-sucking, dumb-clucking collusion with the masters of illusion and destruction.

Thanks to them, from whom the painful blessings flow, we are waking up.

Their wars and tortures,
their crimes against nature,
extinctions of species
and brand new diseases.

Their spying and lying
in the name of the father,
sterilizing seeds and
trademarking water.

Molestations of God,
celebrations of shame,
stealing our dreams and
changing our names.

Their cunning commercials
and blood-sucking hustles,
their endless rehearsals
for the end of the world.

Thanks to them, from whom the awful teachings flow, we are waking up.

Their painful blessings are cracking open more and more gashes in the shrunken and crippled mass hallucination that is mistakenly called "reality." And through the fractures, ripe eternity is flooding in; news of the soul's true home is pouring in; our allies from the other side of the veil are swarming in, inspiring us to become smarter and wilder and kinder and trickier.

We are waking up.

As heaven and earth come together, as the dreamtime and daytime merge, we register the shockingly exhilarating fact that we are in charge of creating a brand new world. Not in some distant time or faraway place, but right here and right now.

As we stand on this brink, as we dance on this verge, we can't let the ruling fools of the dying world sustain their curses. We have to rise up and fight their insane logic; defy, resist, and prevent their tragic magic; unleash our sacred rage and supercharge it.

But overthrowing the living dead is not enough. Protesting the well-dressed monsters is not enough. We can't afford to be consumed with our anger; we can't be obsessed and possessed by their danger. Our mysterious bodies crave delight and fertility. Our boisterous imaginations demand fresh tastes of infinity.

In the new world we're gestating, we need to be suffused with lusty compassion and ecstatic duty, ingenious love and insurrectionary beauty. We've got to be teeming with radical curiosity and reverent pranks, voracious listening and ferocious thanks.

So I'm curious, my fellow creators. Since you and I are in charge of making a new world—not just breaking the old world—where do we begin? What stories do we want at the heart of our experiments? What questions will be our oracles?

Here's what I say: We will ignore the cult of doom and gloom and embrace the cause of zoom and boom. We will laugh at the stupidity of evil and hate, and summon the brilliance to praise and create. No matter how upside-down it all may temporarily appear, we will have no fear because we know this secret: Life is crazily in love with us—wildly and innocently in love with us. The universe always gives us exactly what we need, exactly when we need it.

Pronoia is our word of power, the spell we cast to shake ourselves awake again and again. It's the antidote for paranoia. It's the brazen perception that all of creation is conspiring to shower us with blessings.

Pronoia means that even if we can't see and don't know, primal benefactors are plotting to emancipate us. The winds and tides are on our side, forever and ever, amen. The fire and rain are scheming to steal our pain. The sun and moon know our real names, and the animals pray for us while we're dreaming. Do you believe in guardian angels and divine helpers? Whether you do or not, they're always wangling to give you the gifts you don't even realize you want. Can you guess how many humble humans are busy making things for you to use and enjoy?

I'm allergic to dogma. I thrive on the riddles. Any idea I believe, I reserve the right to disbelieve as well.

But more than any other vision I've ever tested, pronoia describes the way the world actually is. It's wetter than water, stronger than death, and truer than the news. It smells like cedar smoke in early spring rain, and if you close your eyes right now, you can feel it shimmering like the aurora borealis in your organs and muscles. Its song is your blood's song.

Some people argue that life is strife and suffering is normal. Others swear we're born sinful and only heaven can provide us with the peace that passes understanding. But pronoia says that being alive on the rough green and brown earth is the highest honor and privilege. It's an invitation to work wonders and perform miracles that aren't possible in any nirvana, promised land, or afterlife.

I'm not exaggerating or indulging in poetic metaphor when I tell you that we are already living in paradise. Visualize it if you dare. The sweet stuff that quenches all of our longing is not far away in some other time and place. It's right here and right now.

Poet Elizabeth Barrett Browning knew the truth: "Earth's crammed with heaven."

You're alive because of love. You're *made* of love.

Primordial Gossip

GLORY IN THE HIGHEST

Thousands of things go right for you every day, beginning the moment you wake up. Through some magic you don't fully understand, you're still breathing and your heart is beating, even though you've been unconscious for many hours. The air is a mix of gases that's just right for your body's needs, as it was before you fell asleep.

You can see! Light of many colors floods into your eyes, registered by nerves that took God or evolution or some process millions of years to perfect. The interesting gift of these vivid hues comes to you courtesy of an unimaginably immense globe of fire, the sun, which continually detonates nuclear reactions in order to convert its body into light and heat and energy for your personal use.

Did you know that the sun is located at the precise distance from you to be of perfect service? If it were any closer, you'd fry, and if it were any further away, you'd freeze. Here's another one of the sun's benedictions: It appears to rise over the eastern horizon right on schedule every day, as it has since long before you were born.

Do you remember when you were born, by the way? It was a difficult miracle that involved many people who worked hard on your behalf. No less miraculous is the fact that you have continued to grow since then, with millions of new cells being born inside you to replace the old ones that die. All of this happens whether or not you ever think about it.

On this day, like almost every other, you have awoken inside a temperature-controlled shelter. You have a home! Your bed and pillow are soft and you're covered by comfortable blankets. The electricity is turned on, as usual. Somehow, in ways you're barely aware of, a massive power plant at an unknown distance from your home is transforming fuel into currents of electricity that reach you through mostly hidden conduits in the exact amounts you need, and all you have to do to control the flow is flick small switches with your fingers.

You can walk! Your legs work wonderfully well. Your heart circulates your blood all the way down to replenish the energy of the muscles in your feet and calves and thighs, and when the blood is depleted it finds its way back to your heart to be refreshed. This blessing recurs over and over again without stopping every hour of your life.

Your home is perhaps not a million-dollar palace, but it's sturdy and gigantic compared to the typical domicile in every culture that has preceded you. The floors aren't crumbling, and the walls and ceilings are holding up well, too. Doors open and close without trouble, and so do the windows. What skillful geniuses built this sanctuary for you? How and where did they learn their craft?

In your bathroom, the toilet is functioning perfectly, as are several other convenient devices. You have at your disposal soaps, creams, razors, clippers, tooth-cleaning accessories: a host of products that enhance your hygiene and appearance. You trust that unidentified scientists somewhere tested them to be sure they're safe for you to use.

Amazingly, the water you need so much of comes out of your faucets in an even flow, with the volume you want, and either cold or hot as you desire. It's pure and clean; you're confident no parasites are lurking in it. There is someone somewhere making sure these boons will continue to arrive for you without interruption for as long as you require them.

Look at your hands. They're astounding creations that allow you to carry out hundreds of tasks with great force and intricate grace. They relish the pleasure and privilege of touching thousands of different textures, and they're beautiful.

In your closet are many clothes you like to wear. Who gathered the materials to make the fabrics they're made of? Who imbued them with colors, and how did they do it? Who sewed them for you?

In your kitchen, appetizing food in secure packaging is waiting for you. Many people you've never met worked hard to grow it, process it, and get it to the store where you bought it. The bounty of tasty nourishment you get to choose from is unprecedented in the history of the world.

Your many appliances are working flawlessly. Despite the fact that they feed on electricity, which could kill you instantly if you touched it directly, you feel no fear that you're in danger. Why? Your faith in the people who invented, designed, and produced these machines is impressive.

It's as if there's a benevolent conspiracy of unknown people that is tirelessly creating hundreds of useful things you like and need.

There's more. Gravity is working exactly the way it always has, neither pulling on you with too much or too little force. How did that marvel ever come to be? By some prodigious, long-running accident? It doesn't really matter, since it will continue to function with astounding efficiency whether or not you understand it.

Meanwhile, a trillion other elements of nature's miraculous design are expressing themselves perfectly. Plants are growing, rivers are flowing, clouds are drifting, winds are blowing, animals are reproducing. The weather is an interesting blend of elements you've never before experienced in quite this combination. Though you may take it for granted, you relish the ever-shifting sensations of light and temperature as they interact with your body.

There's more. You can smell odors and hear sounds and taste tastes, many of which are quite pleasing. You can think! You're in possession of the extraordinary gift of self-awareness. You can feel feelings! Do you realize how improbably stupendous it is for you to have been blessed with that mysterious capacity? And get this: You can visualize an inexhaustible array of images, some of which represent things that don't actually exist. How did you acquire this magical talent?

By some improbable series of coincidences or long-term divine plan, language has come into existence. Millions of people have collaborated for many centuries to cultivate a system for communication that you understand well. Speaking and reading give you great pleasure and a tremendous sense of power.

Do you want to go someplace that's at a distance? You have a number of choices about what machines to use in order to get there. Whatever you decide—car, plane, bus, train, subway, ship, helicopter, or bike—you have confidence that it will work efficiently. Multitudes of people who are now dead devoted themselves to perfecting these modes of travel. Multitudes who are still alive devote themselves to ensuring that these benefits keep serving you.

Maybe you're one of the hundreds of millions of people in the world who has the extraordinary privilege of owning a car. It's a brilliant invention made by highly competent workers. Other skilled laborers put in long hours to extract oil from the ground or sea and turn it into fuel so you can use your car conveniently. The roads are drivable. Who paved them for you? The bridges you cross are potent feats of engineering. Do you realize how hard it was to fabricate them from scratch?

You're aware that in the future shrinking oil reserves and global warming may impose limitations on your ability to use cars and planes and other machines to travel. But you also know that many smart and idealistic people are diligently striving to develop alternative fuels and protect the environment. And compared to how slow societies have been to understand their macrocosmic problems in the past, your culture is moving with unprecedented speed to recognize and respond to the crises spawned by its technologies.

As you travel, you might listen to music. Maybe you've got an MP3 player, a fantastic invention that has dramatically enhanced your ability to hear a stunning variety of engaging sounds at a low cost. Or maybe you have a radio. Through a process you can't fathom, music and voices that originate at a distance from you have been converted into invisible waves that bounce off the ionosphere and down into your little machine, where they are transformed back into music and voices for you to enjoy.

Let's say it's 9:30 a.m. You've been awake for two hours, and a hundred things have already gone right for you. If three of those hundred things had not gone right—your toaster was broken, the hot water wasn't hot enough, there was a stain on the pants you wanted to wear—you might feel that today the universe is against you, that your luck is bad, that nothing's going right. And yet the fact is that the vast majority of everything is working with breathtaking efficiency and consistency. You would clearly be deluded to imagine that life is primarily an ordeal.

Secrets of Pronoia

The Experiment

OBJECTIVE: To explore the secrets of becoming a wildly disciplined, fiercely tender, ironically sincere, scrupulously curious, aggressively sensitive, blasphemously reverent, lyrically logical, lustfully compassionate Master of Rowdy Bliss.

DEFINITION: Pronoia is the antidote for paranoia. It's the understanding that the universe is fundamentally friendly. It's a mode of training your senses and intellect so you're able to perceive the fact that life always gives you exactly what you need, exactly when you need it.

HYPOTHESES: Evil is boring. Cynicism is idiotic. Fear is a bad habit. Despair is lazy. Joy is fascinating. Love is an act of heroic genius. Pleasure is our birthright. Receptivity is a superpower.

PROCEDURE: Act as if the universe is a prodigious miracle created for your amusement and illumination. Assume that secret helpers are working behind the scenes to assist you in turning into the gorgeous masterpiece you were born to be. Join the conspiracy to shower all of creation with blessings.

GUIDING QUESTION: "The secret of life," said sculptor Henry Moore to poet Donald Hall, "is to have a task, something you devote your entire life to, something you bring everything to, every minute of the day for your whole life. And the most important thing is—it must be something you cannot possibly do." What is that task for you?

UNDIGNIFIED MEDITATIONS TO KEEP YOU HONEST: Brag about what you can't do and don't have. Confess profound secrets to people who aren't particularly interested. Pray for the success of your enemies while you're making love. Change your name every day for a thousand days.

MYTHIC ROLE MODELS: Prometheus and Pronoia. In Greek mythology, Pronoia was the consort of Prometheus, the divine rebel who pilfered a glowing coal from his fellow gods so that he could slip the gift of fire to humans.

TOP-SECRET ALLIES: Sacred janitors, benevolent pranksters, apathy debunkers, lyrical logicians, ethical outlaws, aspiring masters of curiosity, homeless millionaires, humble megalomaniacs, hedonistic midwives, lunatic saints, sly optimists, mystical scientists, dissident bodhisattvas, macho feminists, and socialist Libertarians who possess inside information about the big bang.

DAILY PRACTICE: Push hard to get better, become smarter, grow your devotion to the truth, fuel your commitment to beauty, refine your emotional intelligence, hone your dreams, negotiate with your shadow, cure your ignorance, shed your pettiness, heighten your drive to look for the best in people, and soften your heart—even as you always accept yourself for exactly who you are with all of your so-called imperfections.

POSSIBLE REWARDS: You will be able to claim the rewards promised you at the beginning of time—not just any old beauty, wisdom, goodness, love, freedom, and justice, but rather exhilarating beauty that incites you to be true to yourself; crazy wisdom that immunizes you against the temptation to believe your ideals are ultimate truths; outrageous goodness that inspires you to experiment with irrepressible empathy; generous freedom that keeps you alert for opportunities to share your wealth; insurrectionary love that endlessly transforms you; and a lust for justice that's leavened with a knack for comedy, keeping you honest as you work humbly to liberate everyone in the world from ignorance and suffering.

USAGE NOTE: We employ the adjectival form "pronoiac" rather than "pronoid." That way, it rhymes with "aphrodisiac" and resonates with "paradisiacal" instead of being conditioned by "paranoid."

DISCLAIMER: Material in this book may be too intense and controversial for some readers. It contains graphic scenes of peace, love, joy, passion, reverence, splendor, and understanding. You will not find any references to harsh, buzzing fluorescent lights in a cheap hotel room where an Arab American heroin dealer plots to get revenge against the teachers at his old high school by releasing sarin gas into the teachers' lounge. There are no reports of Nazi skinheads obsessed with recreating the 14th-century Tartars' war strategy of catapulting plague-ridden corpses into an enemy's citadel. Completely absent from these pages are any stories about a psychotic CEO of a Fortune 500 company who has intentionally disfigured his face to help him elude the CIA, which wants to arrest him for the treasonous sale of his company's nanotech weapons technology to the Chinese.

You should therefore proceed with caution if you are a jaded hipster who is suspicious of feeling healthy and happy. Ask yourself: "Am I ready to stop equating cynicism with insight? Do I dare take the risk that exposing myself to uplifting entertainment might dull my intelligence?" If you doubt your ability to handle relaxing breakthroughs, you should close the book now.

Dionysian Manifesto

8   **The Experiment**

♡Dear Gorgeous Genius

While you and I are together here:

Your favorite phrase is *flux gusto*

The colors of your soul are sable, vermilion, ivory, and jade

Your magic talisman is a thousand-year-old Joshua tree whose flowers blossom
just one night each year and can only be pollinated by the yucca moth

Your holiest pain comes from your yearning to change yourself in the exact way
you'd like the world around you to change

Your soil of destiny is peat moss

Your mythic symbol is a treasure chest dislodged from its hiding place
in the earth by a flood

Your lucky number is 13 to the 13th power

Your sweet spot is in between the true believers and the scoffing skeptics

A clutch of frog eggs from an unpolluted river is your auspicious hair-care product

The anonymous celebrity with whom you have most in common is the jester
who followed Buddha around and kept him loose

The question that perks you up when your routine becomes too rote is this:
What possesses the bar-tailed godwit to migrate annually from Alaska to New
Zealand by hitching rides on gale-force winds?

PRONOIA THERAPY

Practice in becoming a Master of Rowdy Bliss

On this page, write your own version of "Glory in the Highest." Describe the everyday miracles you take for granted, the uncanny powers you possess, the small joys that occur so routinely you forget how much they mean to you, and the steady flow of benefits bestowed on you by people you know and don't know.

2.

When they say
"Be yourself,"
which self
do they mean?

BABY WIPE COMMUNIQUÉ

Right before Labor Day every year, the temporary nation of Burning Man (www.burningman.com) sprouts up for a week in the Nevada desert. A mix of festival, survivalist challenge, outdoor museum, and performance art spectacle, it is populated by the world's largest concentration of half-naked freaks. They're *practical* half-naked freaks, though. Since water and food and electricity are absent in that barren landscape, the determined revelers have to bring their own. The dangerous celebration culminates on a Saturday night, when fire-dancers bearing torches ignite a 60-foot-tall wooden and neon effigy—the Burning Man.

During my maiden voyage there in 2001, I got sunburned in 100-degree heat, rarely slept for more than five hours a night, ate mostly canned tuna and dried fruit, had to drink water constantly to avoid dehydration, collected blowing dust in my ears, nose, and eyes— and had the best time of my life. Forget Maui and the south of France and Florence, Italy: Burning Man was the closest I'd ever come to living in heaven on earth.

Its most deeply relaxing element was the absence of money, advertisements, and commerce. The community was run as a *gift economy.* Nothing was for sale. You couldn't buy anything except ice and coffee. When goods and services were exchanged, it was because they were given freely. This was beyond bartering. You didn't trade your treasure for another's treasure; you just handed yours over, no strings attached.

A second utopian feature of the festival was protection from media assault. There may have been some hopeless TV addicts among my 26,000 fellow citizens, but I never spied a single telltale rectangular glow ema-

nating from a tent or RV. Corporate logos and advertising were banished, too, as well as all signs of America's other best and brightest brainwashers, like *The Wall Street Journal, USA Today,* and *The New York Times.* Nor did any of Clear Channel's 130 radio stations infect me with their fake music and zombie newscasts. Within 24 hours of slipping into the safe haven of Burning Man's propaganda-free zone, I felt as if I had come home.

But my sense of sanctuary was not merely built on the absence of America's toxic culture. My new power spot was filled with things I loved: allies as smart and interesting as me, most of whom were committed to being creators rather than spectators; car-free streets filled with bicyclists and pedestrians; gold top hats and green silk pantaloons and blue velvet frock coats and bras made of rubber shark masks; good, often surprising music and lots of places to dance; the Born-Again Pagan Church of Lascivious Feminism, the Polyester Pagoda of the Palpitating Pulpit, and countless other homemade religions that included divine mischief in their ceremonies.

Everywhere I wandered I encountered exuberant, large-scale works of art. The elegant and improbable "Mausoleum: Temple of Memory" was made entirely of recycled dinosaur puzzles. It hosted a steady flow of visitors, many in tears, who came to write messages on the walls, mourning or honoring their departed friends and loved ones.

Not far from the Mausoleum was the "Plastic Chapel," a two-story-high church whose facade was a mosaic of brightly colored pieces of plastic salvaged from dumps and junkyards all over Nevada and

California. Here, priests and priestesses of every variety presided over roguish, rowdy, and puckish weddings. A few of the ceremonies were legal in the eyes of the state. But many joined together conclaves of polyamorous experimentalists for whom a two-person union was not inclusive enough. I myself officiated a mass ritual in which everyone in a crowd of 300 got married to himself or herself.

Of the hundreds of sculptures and installations and murals and labyrinths and decorated vehicles packed into the eight-square-mile expanse, not all were sublime works of art. But some were, and many others were at least provocative, amusing, and aesthetically pleasing, even to a tough critic like me. My imagination was in a constant state of delighted arousal.

Adding to my pleasure was the fact that the gallery was the desert itself, an ancient lake bottom beneath a towering sky. Every creation had to be built to withstand dust storms, gale-force winds, downpours, and extremes of temperature.

Back in America, far from the independent republic of Burning Man, teams of Tibetan Buddhist monks have become famous for bringing their sand paintings to museums. Painstakingly laying out colored grains in precise designs on large platforms, they work for weeks. But the masterpiece survives only a short time. Then its makers sweep it up and dispose of the sand, exhibiting their freedom from attachment and demonstrating the transitoriness of life.

Many of the works of art at Burning Man had a similar fate in 2001, as they do each year: to be dismantled or even destroyed at the end of the festival. As a creative artist who has had to resort to all manner of spiritual trickery to prevent my ego from appropriating what my soul makes, I regard this as a celebration of my deepest values.

When I visited Toronto in July 2000, astrologer Richard Geer asked me, "What are the conditions you'd need in your world in order to feel like you were living in paradise?"

"Let me get back to you on that," I said at the time. It seemed too abstract and remote a fantasy to entertain.

But 13 months later, during my sojourn at Burning Man, I had a practical answer: Many of the conditions I'd need to feel as if I were living in paradise already existed at Burning Man.

The idea for the Beauty and Truth Laboratory hatched there at the Burning Man festival in 2001. The birth occurred officially around 6 p.m. on Friday, the day before the Man burned.

Refuse to dehumanize anyone, even those who dehumanize you.

Five of us were squatting in a circle under a 20-foot by 20-foot canopy. We yakked and free-associated as we sipped vials of Red Bull, an energy drink containing legal but stimulating ingredients that I liked to imagine were the more sensible equivalent to poet William Butler Yeats having monkey testicles sewn to his chest back in the 1920s.

With me were two other members of my band, Sacred Uproar, guitarist George Earth (Burning Man "superhero" name: Maniacal Miracle Maker) and chanteuse Jessica Rice (Burning Man superhero name: Lush Confuser). Our group was rounded out by two new friends we'd met when they'd participated in our "Brag Therapy Rite" during our first gig some days before.

Firenze Matisse was a young literature professor (from Massachusetts who was writing a science fiction book about a gang of radical leftist Peruvian shamans conspiring to cast spells on American political leaders. Thirza Guest was a thirty-something German journalist who claimed to have scored candid interviews with a range of political celebrities from Russia's President Vladimir Putin to India's "Bandit Queen," though she had not yet found any mainstream media willing to publish them.

All five of us had succumbed to the alchemy of Burning Man. Our skins had drunk so deeply of the desert sun and wind that we'd turned translucent brown. If I stared hard enough, I swear I could catch glimpses of the blood rushing along beneath the see-through outer layer of my arm. The mist-like white dust had caked permanently in every body crevice, especially the corners of our eyes and up our nostrils. Though now and then each of us had stumbled upon some prodigal and improbable feast—one night the camp next to ours had given away fresh sushi served on the nude bodies of human "platters," for instance—more often we had forgotten to eat or else munched on ephemera as we trekked to the next party. Our dry, cooked bodies had become thinner.

And then there was the matter of our altered relationship with sleep. So as not to deny ourselves any of

Medicine Story

the inexhaustible variety of playtime activities spread over Burning Man's eight square miles, none of us had lain down for longer than five or six hours on any night since we arrived. Weariness was not the result, though. Instead, we'd been transformed into liminal creatures who dwelt in an in-between realm that was composed of equal portions dreamtime and waketime. We were having lucid dreams with our eyes open.

It was in this setting that the Beauty and Truth Laboratory announced itself.

Thirza nudged me in the right direction. "Hey, Rob," she said to me, "you know how in your 'Crimes That Don't Break Any Laws' shtick you imitate that pompous German guy? Do it for me. I'll give you some pointers on refining your German accent."

She was referring to a passage in one of Sacred Uproar's performance art pieces, in which I mockingly imitate Udo Kier, a German film actor who specializes in playing villains.

I obliged her. Born and raised in Berlin and the daughter of a linguist, she could no doubt provide me with dialect tips. I puffed up my chest like a swaggering braggart, then repeated, in my best German accent, the statement Kier had made in an interview I'd heard.

"Evil has no limit! Evil has no limit! Good, on the other hand, *does* have a limit. It is nowhere near as interesting. It is boring! It is dull! Good is not worthy of my artistry!"

"You've got the 'evil has no limit' part down," Thirza mused. "If I close my eyes, I could picture it coming out of the mouth of my ex-husband. But when you said 'good does have a limit,' you lapsed into a kind of Cockney twang."

Before I could enlist her to correct my diction, Firenze interrupted me. "I like that 'evil has no limit' bit," he said, "but my favorite part is the rant you go into right after that. What is it? 'How dare the editors of *The New York Times* act as if good has a limit?!' Or something. Do that one."

I launched into the rap he was talking about. In contrast to the pretentious pose of my previous riff, now I spoke in a low, conspiratorial tone. "I hate to admit it, but I have to say that most everyone everywhere seems

to agree with Udo Kier. And I am in a tiny minority in my belief that evil is a fucking bore. But how dare Udo Kier, or for that matter Dan Rather and Stephen King and Eminem and Ridley Scott and the editors of *The New York Times*—how dare they proceed on the assumption that 'good has a limit' and that 'good isn't as interesting' when there are so few smart artists and thinkers who are brave and resourceful enough to explore the frontiers of beauty and truth and joy and compassion?"

Ending with a flourish, I blew a kiss in the direction of the sky.

"You know I'm a fanatical new convert to you and Sacred Uproar, Rob," Firenze said after a pause, "but if I have any problem at all with your stuff, it's that you're a bit heavy on bitching about the old world and a bit light about imagining the new world. I mean, you talk about how newspapers are obsessed with reporting bad news, but you never actually say what the alternative would be."

"He's got a point," chimed in Jessica, offering me a fresh bottle of Red Bull to replace the one I'd downed. "You say that the hypothetical good news should be just as entertaining as the bad news that everyone seems to think is so fascinating. It can't be ho-hum stuff like, 'Two thousand planes took off from American airports yesterday and every one landed safely.' But you really don't give many examples of what that entertaining good news would be."

Suddenly I felt like a pregnant woman who hadn't known she was pregnant until the labor pains kicked in. Which they had just done. I felt a big ripe creation pushing to get out.

"Are you or are you not one of those smart artists who's brave enough to explore the frontiers of beauty and truth?" asked Firenze with mock solemnity.

"I am," I said. "I want to be." I winced as something like a contraction shuddered through my mind's eye.

"You really should start a think tank," Thirza said. "A place to brainstorm about interesting kinds of sweetness and light. Not the fluffy, glazed-eyed New Age junk or the withered, sentimental Christian crap."

"Only trouble is," I said, "most smart, educated people wouldn't be caught dead near a discussion of sweetness and light, no matter how interesting it might be. Me and you guys might be the only fools I can round up for our think tank."

"Hard-core sweetness and light!" George spouted. "Kick-ass joy and peace! Razor-edged harmony!"

"Aren't you forgetting that you are right now in the thick of the most concentrated assemblage of mutated brains on the planet?" Firenze said. "If the North Koreans, or for that matter the ass-souls in Washington, D.C., wanted to ensure a future enslaved to anachronistic modes of consciousness, all they'd have to do is nuke Burning Man."

"Unfortunately, I don't think there's enough time to get a decent recruitment drive going here this year," I said. "Most everyone's leaving on Sunday."

"I once dreamed I worked as a corporate head-hunter," Jessica offered. "I'm ready to get started as your recruitment chief immediately."

"I'm on the team," Thirza said.

"Me, too," said Firenze.

It was then that my new creation popped out. I'd given birth. I looked at my watch. It was 6:16 p.m. P.D.T., August 31, 2001. I wondered what its horoscope would be.

Its name was immediately clear: Beauty and Truth Laboratory. It would be a tribe of hope fiends. A hotbed of loving geniuses. A gang of lunatic saints and emotional giants and crafty optimists. A think tank of sacred agents and scientific poets and dissident bodhisattvas and virtuoso bliss-invokers.

The Beauty and Truth Laboratory would be an actual place, or maybe a web of places, where compassionate masters of rowdy bliss gathered to explore the frontiers of beauty, truth, love, justice, integrity, goodness, pleasure, fun, redemption, and emotional intelligence. Part of it would serve as a real laboratory, a matrix where we could conduct actual experiments. Our purpose would not be merely to make our own lives richer, but also to offer inspiration to others through the books, music, performances, and films we'd generate in the course of our work.

"Where are you going, Rob?" Jessica asked, seeing that I had risen out of my squat and was walking away. "Your gang's ready to launch a crusade. Give us some direction."

"I will return shortly with a plan," I said. "But right now I'm being urgently called on to carry out an emergency walking meditation."

I veered out onto the dirt road adjoining our camp and headed toward the edge of town. A happy cacoph-

Combustion luster verve blaze
Luminous flourish lucid mojo
Lightning splendor wake-up fuel

ony of live and recorded music poured in on me from every direction. I could make out at least four different styles. This profusion, which streamed every hour of the night and day, was one of the elements about Burning Man I loved and hated best. It meant I could always find a place to dance, even at 7 a.m., to pretty much any kind of beat I was in the mood for. But it also meant that the only possible way to sleep was armed with a defense of earplugs and the kind of sound-canceling headphones worn by jackhammer operators.

I passed a camp where four men wearing leather skirts were playing a punk version of klezmer music. One camp had bleachers where people sat and called out for passers-by to entertain them. Then there was the Inner Demon Rodeo, where you were encouraged to mime the action of hog-tying your inner demon.

My nascent musings about the Beauty and Truth Laboratory had hit a snag. How could I justify calling it a laboratory for beauty and truth? Those two terms alone didn't cover anywhere near the total territory I was concerned with. To be accurate, shouldn't it be something like the Beauty and Truth and Love and Bliss and Goodness and Justice and Liberation Laboratory?

And another thing. I wasn't interested in just any old beauty and truth. The words themselves have been so grossly overused by so many people to promote such widely different agendas that they've been gutted of meaning. Say them aloud and you're likely to provoke a numbing sensation in your listeners' imaginations.

It would be at best a half-truth to say that the laboratory was a sanctuary to explore "beauty." That dead arrangement of letters could be invoked to describe everything from a supermodel flouncing down a Milan runway in a faux fur bikini to a sleek high-tech tank gleaming in hateful splendor on the deck of a carrier battleship. Our lab would have a sacred duty to ignore fraudulent pretenders to beauty like that. It would aspire to investigate wild beauty that awakens radical curiosity, convulsive beauty that potentiates the longing for freedom, fierce beauty that rouses lusty compassion, and shocking beauty that mobilizes healing mischief.

All the other virtues needed rehabilitation, too, having been similarly paralyzed through overuse and exploitation. Shouldn't our laboratory specify that what we were really interested in studying was not "truth," a

Medicine Story

concept that was long ago stripped of its meaning and vitality, but rather crazy wisdom that makes you allergic to dogma? Not just "liberation," but ingenious liberation that is never permanent but must be reinvented and reclaimed every day? Not merely justice, but a boisterous justice that schemes and dreams about tricks to diminish the suffering and increase the joy of every sentient being?

I thought of the possibility of coining new words to replace the used-up old husks. "Beauty" could become, maybe, "allurabliss," for instance. "Truth" might be "swirloluminous."

The Allurabliss and Swirloluminous Laboratory?

Nah. That wasn't right. Too esoteric. Though our lab would never hire marketing experts to advise us how to manipulate our message so it would reach the widest possible demographic, neither would we want to ignore the reality of what people are entertained by. We needed a name that was simple and catchy.

My walking meditation was taking me past the camp of the Burning Scouts of America. I hadn't visited them yet, but I'd read their spiel somewhere. They were dedicated to teaching the love of chaos and hedonism. If you signed up for one of their programs, you could earn Demerit Badges in "Unfocused Rage," "Spitting Into the Wind," and "Gender Mutation." Drunken scoutmasters might take you on a naked tour of all the theme camps that were doling out free massages, and foul-mouthed Burning Girl Scouts would serve you charred cookies and ripe peaches.

As much as I was tempted to stop and partake, the urge to keep trekking was stronger. I'd begun to feel more contractions. Labor had resumed. Was there still another creation in me? Was I going to have twins?

That's when the word "pronoia" popped into my wide-open mind.

I wasn't initially sure of all the implications of its appearance, but I could see how it might be useful for the Beauty and Truth Laboratory. I loved the term and had been using it gleefully for several years, though it had never made it into any dictionary. It had been coined

in the mid-1970s by Grateful Dead lyricist and co-founder of the Electronic Frontier Foundation, John Perry Barlow, who defined it as the opposite of paranoia: "the suspicion that the universe is a conspiracy on your behalf."

The Scottish psychologist Fraser Clark revived the word in the 1990s. He referred to pronoia as "the sneaking hunch that others are conspiring behind your back to help you." Once you have contracted this benevolent virus, he said, the symptoms include "sudden attacks of optimism and outbreaks of goodwill." Working with the Zippies, a group of gypsy ravers, Clark organized the Zippy Pronoia Tour to America in 1994. With a boost from a cover story by *Wired* magazine, the tour's parties and performances spread the word.

Shortly thereafter, a website devoted to pronoia appeared on the Web at www.pronoia.net. It has mostly been devoted to telling the story of the Zippies.

So why exactly had the concept shown up in my intuition at exactly this moment, in the midst of my walking meditation at Burning Man? I knew my creative process well enough to understand that it was a crucial clue about how to proceed. Did it mean I should call our research center the "Pronoia Laboratory"?

No. My logical mind couldn't buy that. While "pronoia" was a euphonious coinage with a built-in association to the well-known word "paranoia," it was unfamiliar to most people. As the name of an organization that aspired to provide a populist alternative to the mainstream media's toxic stories, it would be too limiting.

But it *was* euphonious and evocative. Couldn't it be useful as long as it was not the first thing that newcomers encountered? Maybe the name of our think tank would be "The Beauty and Truth Laboratory," with pronoia featured prominently in our benevolent propaganda and artistic products.

I had reached the edge of the formal city of Burning Man. Now the wilderness began. This was not a picturesque desert dotted with cacti, scrub, and lizards. It was barren playa for as far as the eye could see. As I stepped out into the emptiness, the wind came up, blasting me head-on with a dusty whirlwind.

An urge to write overtook me. The number of good ideas welling up threatened to exceed what I could hold in my short-term memory. I wanted to commit them to paper. But reaching in the back pocket of my shorts, I found nothing where I usually kept my small spiral-bound notebook. Damn! How could I have gone out on a walking meditation without something to take notes on?

At least there was a felt-tip marker in my vest pocket. I supposed I could try scrawling notes on my skin. But I quickly realized that would be problematic. I was sweating. Though it was getting on toward 7 p.m., the temperature seemed still to be in the 90s. I made an attempt to inscribe "pronoia" on my left forearm, but the ink barely penetrated the moisture.

Then I spied a possible solution. In the distance, lying on the sand, was an open box of baby wipes—the moist towelettes most commonly employed to clean the butts of infants who've pooped in their diapers. Out here in the middle of the desert, where there was no running water and you had to import every drop you used, many adult denizens of Burning Man regarded the baby wipes as indispensable aids to maintaining their personal hygiene.

It was unusual to see a box of wipes reduced to litter, though. "Leave no trace" is a central tenet of the Burning Man commitment to ecological impeccability, and most burners live up to it.

I ran to the potential treasure. It was the "Quilted Northern" brand, antibacterial and scented. Not my personal favorite—I hated wipes with cloying perfumes—but I wasn't in a position to be picky. And other than that problem, I was in luck. The open box meant that all the wipes had lost their moisture. They would be easy to write on.

Using the plastic box as my writing surface, I jotted down notes as I continued to walk. "But hold on," I wrote. "Wait a minute. Is pronoia a big enough concept for the Beauty and Truth Laboratory? Is it poetic enough?" So began my "Baby Wipe Communiqué."

In Asian myth, snakes and birds are often portrayed as adversaries. Their eternal struggle symbolizes humanity's difficulty in coordinating the agendas of heaven and earth. Is morality inherently at odds with desire? Noble intentions in opposition to unconscious motivations? Bright rationality at war with dark poetry? Pronoia is the cure for their strife—the medicine that harmonizes snake and bird.

I was having doubts about pronoia. I mused on how neither John Perry Barlow nor Fraser Clark had developed the notion beyond their brief one- and two-line definitions. They'd given us little to go on. Pronoia was "the suspicion that the universe is a conspiracy on your behalf." It was "the sneaking hunch that others are conspiring behind your back to help you." Not exactly a well-developed philosophy.

Despite periodic searches of the Web with Google, I'd come across only three other analogs of the pronoia meme over the years. All were very brief and none invoked the word "pronoia." In his book, *Raise High the Roof Beam, Carpenters,* J.D. Salinger had the character Seymour Glass write in his diary, "Oh, God, if I'm anything by a clinical name, I'm a kind of paranoiac in reverse. I suspect people of plotting to make me happy." Then there was philosopher Terence McKenna, who had once said: "I believe reality is a marvelous joke staged for my edification and amusement, and everybody is working very hard to make me happy." Philosopher Robert Anton Wilson had uttered advice that also sounded pronoiac: "You should view the world as a conspiracy run by a very closely-knit group of nearly omnipotent people, and you should think of those people as yourself and your friends."

As I ruminated now on how unripe the concept of pronoia still remained, I was dumfounded. I'd vaguely thought about the paucity of discussion before, but for the first time I wondered if there were some collective blind spot that had prevented it from flourishing. In an ironic burst of paranoia, I even entertained the possibility that there was a conspiracy to prevent pronoia from catching fire in the collective imagination.

How else to explain why it hadn't spread with contagious glee, at least through bohemian and underground culture? It wasn't just another generic version of the "positive thinking" movement. It didn't have the cult-like associations of teachings like "The Course in Miracles." Pronoia was snappy and seductive, a feel-good yet saucy meme just begging to be turned into a pop philosophy for hipsters. The New Age movement alone should have seized upon it long ago. How many wannabe gurus might have made fortunes selling self-help books like *Embracing Pronoia: Fifty Ways to Live as If the Whole World Is Conspiring to Help You?*

Even I myself had displayed a curious passivity in relation to pronoia. When I first happened upon the term years ago, I recognized that it echoed the spiritual teachings of Hermeticism, which I had been studying for two decades. This tradition, taught in the mystery schools of the West for centuries, is a synthesis of Qabala, astrology, alchemy, tarot, and magick. One of its core principles is that despite superficial appearances to the contrary, all of creation is on our side; that the very structure of reality ensures our eventual liberation from suffering; that life is a divine conspiracy to awaken us to our god-like nature and become co-administrators of the divine plan for evolution.

Pronoia was a more simplistic and pop culture-worthy meme for expressing this same set of ideas: seemingly a perfect fit for me. I had long been an aspiring Hermetic magician disguised as a rock musician and horoscope columnist. I'd built my entire career on translating esoteric spiritual themes into entertaining forms that could be enjoyed by people who'd never heard of a mystery school. Pop culture was my milieu.

So why didn't I start writing a book about pronoia when I first encountered the meme? In *The Televisionary Oracle,* the 486-page book I worked on from 1991–1999 and published in 2000, there was only one small reference to pronoia in the last chapter. And why hadn't I at least made pronoia a regular theme in my syndicated weekly astrology column? (Later I determined that between 1989 and 2001, I'd mentioned pronoia in my column only three times.) I had never invoked pronoia by name in a single song I'd written.

If there was a cultural blind spot that prevented pronoia from flourishing, I had suffered from it as much as anyone.

By now my walking-and-writing meditation had taken me far from the babble of music flooding from Burning Man's hundreds of generators. I was surrounded by pure desert. Memories of the glorious past few days, accompanied by the emotions they roused, rushed into my awareness with an intensity akin to what I imagined would happen during the instantaneous life review that comes with a near death experience.

I remembered arriving at the gates to Burning Man about 2 a.m. on Sunday night after the day-long drive from my home in Northern California. As I climbed down out of the RV to check in, three dusty-skinned women wearing white turbans, white silk bikinis, and black work boots danced around me, their faces aglow in the torch-light. One sang, "Welcome home, Rob. We've been waiting for your return since the Big Bang." (How did she know my name?) They converged upon me with swarming hugs and kisses. Each whispered a secret in my ear.

"Your Burning Man superhero name is 'Friendly Shocker.'"

"You're like the chrysanthemum, which needs long hours of darkness to bloom."

"In my dream, you were a good trickster who did healing mischief to defuse the terrible mischief committed by the evil tricksters in Washington, D.C."

That was just one of a score of recent memories that flooded through me as I stood transfixed with gratitude in the vast white desert wasteland. I recalled Sunyatta, a classically trained ballet dancer, teaching me how to do a professional pirouette as we danced inside a circle of flames . . . globe-trotting activist Pax, who'd been arrested during demonstrations in 17 different countries, regaling me with the story of the idealistic 18-year-old woman who initiated events that led to the overthrow of the repressive Bulgarian government in 1996 . . . my band Sacred Uproar conducting a "Chaotic

Meditation" ceremony in which hundreds of reverently irreverent bohemians kicked their own asses, bragged about what they could not do and did not have, mimed throwing rocks toward heaven as they sent complaining messages to God, simulated the sounds they would make as they gave birth, and cast love spells on themselves.

During the six days I'd been at Black Rock City, I glided through the streets without a taint of fear, no matter what the hour. I had eaten fresh sushi off naked bellies while dancing to the funky Arab Celtic music of the best band I'd never heard of; had played a giant game of billiards using bowling balls; had taken a joyride on a wheeled version of Captain Hook's schooner as it swayed with scores of sweaty dancers dressed like characters from my dreams; had enjoyed numerous no-strings-attached gifts from magnanimous strangers, including a free foot rub, free homemade organic beer, free palm reading, free portrait-painting, free skydiving lesson, and free kisses. I had also sampled a variety of soulmates at the Costco Soulmate Trading Outlet, a clearinghouse for soulmates that offered "quality name-brand and private-label soulmates at substantially lower prices than can be found through conventional wholesale sources."

The values I held most dear were reflected back to me wherever I wandered: generosity, playfulness, luxurious conviviality, a relaxed attitude about sexuality, spirituality that didn't take itself too seriously, frequent celebration, and love of creative ritual. I've been in love with more than a few women in my life, but this was the first time I'd become infatuated with a time and place.

As the rush of memories subsided, I turned my attention to my surroundings. The full moon was rising over the black mountains in the east. Maybe because there was so little humidity in the air, the silver globe looked closer and more spherical than usual. It had an intimate presence--wasn't as flat and lifeless as it seemed back in the civilization that burners called Babylon. I fantasized that it was a sentient creature gazing back at me.

I swiveled around to bear witness to the setting sun at the other side of the sky. It, too, had lost its blank, two-dimensional veneer. It was no longer far away and abstract. It had swooped down very close. I couldn't help but register a detail that did not normally reach my conscious awareness: It was a ball of fire. And more than that: It was alive. It was a conscious and intelli-

gent being, clearly not just a mass of soulless matter or a natural machine running on automatic.

I searched for a groove in my awareness where I could tune in to the thoughts of the living, sentient sun. Abracadabra! Suddenly I was flooded with its consciousness—as if we had slipped into telepathic communion. Not that I could immediately translate the sun's language into English.

Then I awakened to an even more amazing perception: The sun was acutely aware of me. It knew me intimately. It was beaming specific thoughts, made for me, directly into me.

Break open the forbidden happiness.

Well, "thoughts" was not the right term. There was a fierce, musical, lilting quality to whatever the sun was beaming into me. As if a great deal of intelligent emotion were coming along for the ride. Lush, hot emotion. Delightful, surprising, demanding emotion. The more I allowed it in, the happier I became.

It was no metaphor. I wrote on one of my baby wipes: "The sun is singing its love into me." Not just my imagination, but my entire body was awash in a flood of erotic sensation. A contrapuntal weave of haunting melodies massaged me on the inside, leaving trails of sweet warmth. Flashes of unfamiliar longing arose and were instantly satiated by floods of pleasure, as if the sun were both the source of and answer to a primal desire I was feeling for the first time. To note merely that my cock was hard would be trivial: My entire body had an erection.

I became absolutely certain that the sun loved me personally. Its love was not just incidental or careless, provided because I happened to be within range of the radiance it showered down on everything unconditionally. No, the great eternal God known outwardly as the sun was beaming into me now, as she (or he?) had always done, a unique torrent of beneficence that was specially designed for me alone. And she did the same for every human soul, too! I knew beyond a doubt that each and every one of us receives a singular flow of the Sun Goddess's intimate blessings without end. Whether we appreciate, register, or take advantage of the blessings is another thing.

In the spiritual system I've studied for more than two decades, I've been taught to bring my analytical intelligence with me everywhere: into sleep and dreams, into meditation, into shamanic journeys, into all unusual states of awareness. There are many realms of creation outside of what normal waking consciousness can perceive, but the data encountered while visiting those places is not necessarily more reliable than what can be gleaned on the material plane. Be discriminating, I've been cautioned, even in the midst of mystical rapture. Beware of illusion even when seemingly talking with a deity.

Under my own power, I've developed a corollary to this sensible advice: Never take myself too seriously, even when I seem to be talking to a deity. Along with keeping my skepticism in gear, nursing a giggling mockery of my own earnestness is a foolproof protection against being deceived on any plane of existence.

Fortunately, one of the perks of my spiritual training is that my discriminating, self-mocking mind does not feel a need to tear down all other modes of awareness. It knows it's a servant, not an omnipotent master above which there must be no other masters. I am able, therefore, to bring my Chuckling Kibitzer with me into interludes of mystical rapture without fear that I'll lose my grip on the mystical rapture. I'm psychologically double-jointed.

Right on schedule, the Chuckling Kibitzer appeared in the midst of my mystical rapture in the desert. "Fucking the sun, eh?" was its first comment. "Doing the nasty with the Goddess herself?"

I broke into a cackle, but the joke didn't disrupt my tantric communion in the least. If anything, it intensified my full-body hard-on. It's often the case that the Chuckling Kibitzer's humor helps me relax more fully into an experience I'm on the verge of taking too seriously.

"It's not too much for you, right?" the Chuckling Kibitzer continued after a pause. "You sure you're up for this much mojo? You're not going to get fucked to death, I trust."

That jab had a bite to it.

"I just want to make sure you're not going to have a stroke," C.K. pressed on. "As we know from the case of Semele and Zeus, gods aren't always careful about protecting fragile humans from their sublime blasts. Pindar said, 'Long-haired Semele died in the roar of the thunderbolt.'"

That made two quick mentions of death: unusual for C.K. What was he driving at? Ever so slightly, I slowed the acceleration of my expansive opening to the sun's gifts.

"Even if the sun wants nothing but the best for you," C.K. continued, "even if the sun literally lusts to shower you with blessings that are meant to activate your highest potential, maybe you're not ready for them yet. Maybe you need to be your neurotic self for a few more years—or lifetimes."

With the introduction of this doubt, the ecstasy I had been feeling abated a bit, but not much. On the other hand, a new emotion sprouted: terror. Soon I'd learned a new thing about myself: I was capable of feeling rapture and terror at the same time.

And this was honest, intelligent terror. It wasn't rooted in an archaic, superstitious guilt about feeling good; I'd shed the Judeo-Christian mistrust of pleasure fairly early on in my spiritual work.

No, this was terror of a higher order, a terror I'd sometimes faced during my many years of meditation and spiritual work on myself: What are the risks of seeking face-to-face communion with Divine Intelligence? What treasured illusions must be sacrificed? What part of me has to die?

All the best teachings I'd encountered agreed that in order for one's Higher Self to be born—and it was only the Higher Self that could endure direct communion with the Creator—the little self had to die. Hermetic philosophy asserted that there is an immortal part of each of us, an adamantine uniqueness that was never born and will never die; but our awareness can't inhabit that immortal part until we dissolve our attachments to the hodgepodge of conditioning that most of us mistake as our precious, fascinating, unique self.

And that dissolution can be excruciating, especially if a slew of attachments expire in one sudden swoop.

There in the Nevada desert, I was as scared as I had ever been. What if I opened myself so completely to the sun's raging blessings that I would be transformed into something I no longer recognized as me?

I understood that the gift was beyond my understanding. As brilliant and hot and sweet as it was, it was also dark. Majestic and intimate and perfect, but also wild. I was invigorated by the stabbing vortex of divine love, and I was annihilated by it. I wrote on my baby wipe: "What if the Sun Goddess is annihilating me with her staggering beneficence?"

I was not on drugs at this time. In fact, I had not ingested (and still have not, as of this writing) a single mind-altering substance, even marijuana, since 1985. And while the vision in the desert was an extreme state, the gnosis it climaxed had been building in me for years. I had long been a connoisseur of the mysterious interplay of dark and light. *The Televisionary Oracle,* the book I worked on for so long, was a reverent exploration of the riches to be gleaned from hanging out with the chthonic embodiment of the Goddess.

My awareness that there can be no yang without yin, and vice versa, explained one of my problems with pronoia—a reason why it had not yet bloomed in me and generated a New Age bestseller. The bare-bones version of pronoia promulgated by Barlow and Fraser and McKenna and Wilson was a cute cartoon. It was suitable for framing as a pop culture icon, but was not sufficiently true to the complex poetry of real life to take root in me.

In the past few years, I had felt like a fraud every time I invoked pronoia. People had loved me for introducing the idea to them; they saw me as a bright light giving them permission to be optimistic. But I'd always been slightly embarrassed, aware that I was hiding my some of my true feelings.

If I had ever said what I meant, I'd have told them that *my* pronoia has got to be a pronoia for the soul, not for the ego. *My* pronoia, if it ever took root, would overthrow your ego and my ego and everyone's ego,

would overthrow the status quo, the government, and even reality itself.

But I had remained forever coy, never playing with pronoia to make it more aesthetically and ethically appealing to myself. I'd written nothing beyond the same one-sentence formulations that my predecessors had been content with. Questions like, "What does pronoia have to say to someone who has just been widowed or been in a car crash?" or "If I believe in pronoia, will I get my dream job and find my perfect lover this week?" had never won my attention; let alone the subtler inquiries, like, "What would a psychology based on pronoia look like?" or "Does pronoia require a belief in God?"

There at Burning Man, the Goddess of the sun finally thunderstruck me, forcing me to escape my lazy rut. I realized with a burst of rebellious joy that there was no reason I had to be loyal to the meaning of pronoia as promulgated by its originators. Pronoia didn't belong to them or anyone. I could use it any way I wanted. I could stretch it and bend it to fit my extravagant needs.

My benefactor, the sun, slowly dipped beneath the horizon. The sky's zenith had turned from purple to indigo. I sat down on the grey playa, facing the rising moon, and wrote for a long time on my baby wipes. The Beauty and Truth Laboratory had been born. The last line I wrote before trekking back to my camp to find my co-conspirators was a quote from the mathematician Ralph Abraham: "Heart physiologists find more chaos in the healthy heart than in the sick heart."

Sacred
Advertisement

The healthy chaos of the heart has been brought to you by Rigel 3200 Pro Night Vision Goggles and Sharon Doubiago's The Book of Seeing With One's Own Eyes.

GUERRILLA ORACLE

Clues to the Rebel Grail

Your Inalienable Right to Fresh Omens

Factual information alone isn't sufficient to guide you through life's labyrinthine tests. You need and deserve regular deliveries of uncanny revelation. One of your inalienable rights as a human being should therefore be to receive a mysteriously useful omen every day of your life. Unfortunately, our culture conditions us to be overly receptive to bogus superstitious portents and hostile to the real thing. It's hard to get our minimum daily requirement. In this spirit we present "Guerrilla Oracles: Clues to the Rebel Grail," a recurring feature designed to help you reclaim your birthright. Here's one for you now.

Burn, Baby, Burn

Try this meditation: Imagine that you are both the wood and the fire that consumes the wood. When you focus your awareness on the part of you that is the wood, you hurt; it's painful to feel your sense of solidity disintegrating. But as you shift your attention to the part of you that is the fire, you exult in the wild joy of liberation and power.

It may be tempting to visualize yourself more as the fire than the wood. But if you'd like to understand pronoia in its fullness, you've got to be both wood and fire simultaneously.

FREE PRONOIA THERAPY

Practice in becoming a modest Master of Brilliant Happiness

Do one of the following assignments:

1. Talk about the time a force beyond your understanding reached down and altered your course in one tricky, manic swoop.

2. Make up a dream in which you violate a big taboo without hurting anyone.

2. Describe the difference, if any, between what your ego needs and what your soul needs.

3

We're searching
for the answers
so we can
destroy them
and dream up
better questions

LUMINOUS TEASE

Meditate naked under a waterfall.

Relive the last day of your childhood.

Sip the tears of someone you love.

Rebel against your horoscope.

Create a luxurious orphanage in Romania.

Pick blackberries in the rain.

Feel sorry for a devious lawyer.

See how far you can spit a mouthful of beer.

Give yourself another chance.

Dream of stealing the peaches of immortality from a dragon guarding Plato's cave.

Write a love letter to your evil twin during a lunar eclipse.

Sing the first song you ever heard.

EVIL IS BORING

When an old tree in the rain forest dies and topples over, it takes a long time to decompose. As it does, it becomes host to new saplings that use the decaying log for nourishment.

Picture yourself sitting in the forest gazing upon this scene. How do you describe it? Would you dwell on the putrefaction of the fallen tree while ignoring the fresh life sprouting out of it? If you did, you'd be imitating the perspective of many modern storytellers, especially the journalists and novelists and filmmakers and producers of TV dramas.

They devoutly believe that tales of affliction and mayhem and corruption and tragedy are inherently more interesting than tales of triumph and liberation and pleasure and ingenuity. Using the machinery of the media and entertainment industries, they relentlessly propagate this covert dogma. It's not sufficiently profound or well thought out to be called nihilism. *Pop nihilism* is a more accurate term. The mass audience is the victim of this inane ugliness, brainwashed by a multibillion-dollar propaganda machine that in comparison makes Himmler's vaunted soul-stealing apparatus look like a child's backyard puppet show.

At the Beauty and Truth Laboratory, we believe that stories about the rot are not inherently more captivating than stories about the splendor. On the contrary, given how predictable and omnipresent the former have become, they are actually quite dull. Obsessing on evil is boring. Rousing fear is a hackneyed shtick. Wallowing in despair is a bad habit. Indulging in cynicism is akin to committing a copycat crime.

Most modern storytellers go even further in their devotion to the rot, implying that breakdown is not only more interesting but far more common than breakthrough. We reject this assumption as well. We don't believe that entropy dominates the human experience. Even factoring in the prevailing misery in the Middle East and Africa, we doubt that the Global Bad Nasty Ratio ever exceeds 50 percent. And here in the West, where most of you reading this live, the proportion is lower.

Still, we're willing to let the news media fill up half their pages and airwaves and bandwidths with poker-faced accounts of decline and degeneration. We can tolerate a reasonable proportion of movies and novels and TV dramas that revel in pathology. But we also demand EQUAL TIME for stories about integrity and joy and beauty and bliss and renewal and harmony and love. That's all we ask: a mere 50 percent.

I vividly recall a shock I had in April 2000. While perusing the front page of my local daily newspaper, I found a tiny oasis of redemptive news amidst the usual accounts of reeling turmoil. It reported that inner cities all over America were undergoing a profound renaissance. From Los Angeles to New Orleans to Boston, the poorest sections of town were becoming markedly safer. New businesses were opening, capital was flowing in, neighborhood clean-ups were proliferating, drug sales were decreasing, and people were relaxing on their front porches again.

I was amazed that such an uplifting story had cracked the media's taboo against good news. And yet its anomalous presence as an exception to the rule proved that the rule is virtually ironclad.

At this late date in the evolution of pop nihilism, the problem is not merely the media's relentless brainwashing. We of the mass audience have become thoroughly converted to the sadomasochistic vision of the world: so much so that we've almost lost the power even to *perceive* evidence that contradicts that vision. The good news is virtually invisible.

Even those of us whose passion it is to champion the cause of beauty and truth are in the early stages of fighting our blindness. We are retraining our eyes to see the emancipating truth about the nature of reality.

What would it be like to fight tenderly for beauty and truth and love without despising those who spread ugliness and lies and division?

As we gather the secret stories of the human race's glories and success, the Beauty and Truth Laboratory doesn't spend much time on ho-hum data like, "Two thousand planes took off yesterday and all landed safely." We leave that to others with more patience. Our preferred evidence emphasizes the triumphs that have entertainment value equal to the bad nasty stuff.

We also want our good news to consist of more than reports about hurts being healed and disasters being averted. We celebrate the family of the deceased Israeli girl who gave her heart to be transplanted into a sick Palestinian boy, but we also want a front-page story about physicist Paul Ginsparg, who has revolutionized scientific communication by creating a free service for publishing and reading research reports on the Internet.

We cheer forest protection activist Odigha Odiga's successful campaign to preserve Nigeria's last remaining rain forests, but we want to hear more about George Soros, whose philanthropy has provided billions of dollars in support for intellectual freedom and democratic societies in more than 30 countries.

We honor West Virginia's Julia Bonds, who has made headway in her campaign to halt mountaintop coal mining before it turns more river valleys into waste dumps, but we also want sensational acknowledgment for Ruth Lilly, who donated $100 million of her fortune to *Poetry* magazine, even though its editors had rejected all the poems she had submitted for possible publication over the years.

I invite you to share with us the *interesting* good news you come across in your travels. Not sentimental tales of generic hope; not "Chicken Soup for the Soul;" not life imitating the faux Hollywood art of contrived happy endings; but rather crafty, enigmatic, lyrical eruptions of the sublime; unpredictable outbreaks of soul that pass Emily Dickinson's test for poetry: She said she always knew when she was reading the real thing because it made her feel like the top of her head was about to come off.

Feel free, too, to take up the cause of zoom and boom as you resist the practitioners of doom and gloom in your own sphere. Demand equal time for news about integrity and joy and beauty and pleasure and renewal and harmony and love. In your personal life, be alert for stories that tend to provide evidence for the fact that all of creation is conspiring to give us exactly what we need, exactly when we need it.

P.S. Part of our task is to hunt down and identify the interesting good news that's going on now. But we've also been charged with the job of *creating* the good news that's coming.

SACRED
ADVERTISEMENT

The cabal of zoom and boom
is brought to you in part by
Erwin S. Strauss's book
How to Start Your Own Country.
It's also sponsored
by the website
"Footnotes to History,"
(www.buckyogi.com/footnotes),
which provides data on
micro-nations, secessionist states,
sovereign enclaves, liberated
territories, and temporary
autonomous zones.

Subvert Colonialism

Six miles from Maui is a Hawaiian island that tourists never visit—Kaho'olawe. The U.S. Navy seized it in 1941 and used it as a target range for decades. After years of protests by Native Hawaiians, the Navy finally stopped bombing and began a clean-up campaign. In November, 2003, it formally turned control of the island over to the rightful owners.

"You can get a feel on Kaho'olawe of what it was like to live on Hawaii at the time of our ancestors," says Native Hawaiian Davianna McGregor. "We can practice our traditions there without it being a tourist attraction. It's one place we can go to be in communion with our natural life forces."

Each of us has a personal version of Kaho'olawe: a part of our psyche that has been stolen or colonized by hostile forces. To grow bolder in exploring pronoia, you'll need to take back yours.

SLAM

If you've ever been to a poetry slam, you know that sensitive lyrics in praise of love and beauty are rare. Far more common are vehement diatribes that curse injustice and hypocrisy.

I'm not putting that stuff down; I've been known to unload some dark rants myself. But at this perfect moment, the Beauty and Truth Laboratory is more interested in pragmatic idealism. We're thirsty for streams of visionary consciousness, fountains of lustrous truth, and floods of feisty hope.

Therefore, we propose that instead of a poetry slam, you participate in our "I Have a Dream" Slam. To get in the mood, read or listen to the speech that Martin Luther King Jr. made at the Lincoln Memorial in Washington, D.C., on August 28, 1963. The text, as well as an MP3 of King giving the speech, is available on the Web at: www.americanrhetoric.com/speeches/Ihaveadream.htm.

Here's an excerpt:

I have a dream that one day this nation will rise up and live out the true meaning of its creed: We hold these truths to be self-evident that all men are created equal.

I have a dream that one day on the red hills of Georgia the sons of former slaves and the sons of former slave owners will be able to sit down together at the table of brotherhood.

I have a dream that one day even the state of Mississippi, a state sweltering with the heat of injustice, sweltering with the heat of oppression, will be transformed into an oasis of freedom and justice.

I have a dream that my four little children will one day live in a nation where they will not be judged by the color of their skin but by the content of their character. I have a dream today!

I have a dream that one day, down in Alabama, with its vicious racists, with its governor's lips dripping with the words of interposition and nullification; one day down in Alabama little black boys and black girls will be able to join hands with little white boys and white girls as sisters and brothers. I have a dream today!

I have a dream that one day every valley shall be exalted, and every hill and mountain shall be made low, the rough places will be made plain, and the crooked places will be made straight, and the glory of the Lord shall be revealed and all flesh shall see it together.

Maybe King's plea will inspire you to create your own personal "I Have a Dream" manifesto. To be part of the "I Have a Dream" Slam, send your offering to rebelgrail@yahoo.com or P.O. Box 150628, San Rafael, CA 94915.

Now here's my "I Have a Dream" speech.

I HAVE A DREAM

I have a dream.

I have a dream that in the New World, there will be a new Bill of Rights. The first amendment will be, "Your daily wage is directly tied to how much beauty and truth and love you provide."

I have a dream that in the New World, childbirth will be broadcast in prime time on a major TV network every night.

I have a dream that the New World will have rapturists, and they'll vastly outnumber the terrorists. The rapturists will be performance artists with a conscience . . . charismatic improvisers who love to spring fun surprises. They'll commit unexpected interventions and unscheduled spectacles that delight hordes of strangers.

I have a dream that in the New World, we will add an eleventh commandment to the standard ten: *Thou shalt not bore God.*

I have a dream of a week-long annual holiday called the Bacchanalia. Work and business will be suspended so that all adults can explore their ripe mojo with frothy erotic experiments. Tenderly orgiastic marathons will rage unabated. Reverential ecstasy and grateful generosity will rule.

I have a dream that when anchormen report tragedies on their nightly TV shows, they'll break down and cry and let their emotions show. No more poker faces.

In the New World, you'll be a fascinating enigma worthy of a best-selling unauthorized biography and I'll be an inscrutable genius whose every move is packed with symbolic meaning—and vice versa. That will be the law in the New World—far different from the Old World, where schadenfreude is epidemic and your distinctive flair is supposed to make me feel worshipful or diminished.

I have a dream that in the New World, the word "asshole" will be a term of endearment rather than abuse. Plutocracy will be a felony. April Fool's Day will come once a month. There'll be scientific horoscopes and mystical logic. Every one of us will have at least one imaginary friend. Compassion will be an aphrodisiac.

In the New World, we'll launch an affirmative action program that ultimately makes most of us celebrities. Buddhist real estate developers will build a chain of sacred shopping centers in the heartland. The CEOs of the Fortune 500 companies will be required by law to enjoy once-a-week sessions with Jungian psychotherapists. Pioneers in artificial intelligence research will develop computers that can talk to God.

In the New World, same-sex marriages will be fully sanctioned, of course. But why stop there? We'll also legalize wedding bonds among threesomes, foursomes, fivesomes, and large groups of people who are in love with each other. I have a dream that we will expand the meaning of love beyond anything our ancestors imagined.

In the New World, our children will study singing and dancing and meditation and dream work with as much diligence as they now devote to math and science. They'll learn to see with their own eyes and think with their own minds and feel with their own hearts, studying those subjects as intently as they do spelling and grammar and social studies. Beginning in seventh grade, they'll get lessons in the art of creating successful intimate relationships. And we'll teach them why it's only fair that for the next 3,000 years we use "her" for the generic singular pronoun instead of "him."

I have a dream that we will take everything we need and give everything we have. We'll be both selfish altruists and generous braggarts, Llibertarian socialists and capitalist humanitarians. That'll be the law in the New World—different from the Old World, where you can blindly serve your own interests or devote yourself to the needs of others, but not both.

I have a dream that in the New World, Oprah Winfrey will buy up all the Pizza Huts on the planet and convert them into a global network of menstrual huts, where for a few days each month, every one of us, men and women alike, can resign from the crazy-making 9–5—drop out and slow down, break trance and dive down into eternal time.

We will sleep eight and a half hours every night and practice our lucid dreams . . . sing love songs from the future while soaking in steamy herb baths . . . feast on chocolate as we converse with the little voices in our heads . . . research the difference between stupid suffering and wise suffering until we finally get it right . . . wear magic underwear made from eagle feathers, spider webs, and 100-year-old moss . . . and conjure up bigger, better, more original sins and wilder, wetter, more interesting problems.

In the New World, you'll kick your own ass and I'll wash my own brain. I'll be my own parents and you'll be your own wife. And vice versa. That'll be normal in the New World—different from the Old World, where everyone except me is to blame for my ignorance and you call on everyone except yourself to give you what you need.

I'll push my own buttons and right my own wrongs. You'll wake yourself up and sing your own songs.

I'm the president now . . . and so are you. I am the Supreme Commander of the United Snakes of the Blooming HaHa . . . and so are you. And what we proclaim is that in the New World, we will love our neighbors as ourselves, even if our neighbors are jerks. We will never divide the world into us against them. We will search for the divine spark even in the people we most despise, and we will never dehumanize anyone, even those who dehumanize us.

I have a dream that sooner or later every one of us will become a well-rounded, highly skilled, incredibly rich master of rowdy bliss—with lots of leisure time and an orgiastic feminist conscience.

Pyrokleptomania refers to a Promethean compulsion to steal fire.

Primordial Gossip

DREAMY PRONOIA THERAPY

Practice in becoming a doggedly visionary Master of Freaky Purity

Write your own "I Have a Dream" poem, story, essay, or manifesto here.

The Missing Everything

The force of gravity is omnipresent, even though it can't be seen, heard, or touched, and almost no one can explain it.

There wasn't even a word for it until the 17th century, when the seminal scientist Isaac Newton discovered it and named it after the Latin term *gravitas,* meaning "heaviness" or "seriousness."

As you deepen your inquiries into pronoia, you may enjoy a similar breakthrough. Can you imagine what it would feel like to become aware of an omnipresent ocean of wild divine love that has always been a secret to you in the same way that the sea is invisible to a fish?

WHAT IS THE BEAUTY AND TRUTH LABORATORY?

The Beauty and Truth Laboratory is an ever-expanding web of think tanks and mystery schools devoted to exploring pronoia. Since I launched the prototype in October 2001, 12 other branches have sprung up in basements, barns, and bedrooms all over the world: eight in North America and others in Amsterdam, London, Florence, Italy, and Sydney, Australia.

All of these, including my own in Marin County, California, are similar in spirit to pirate radio stations. They're not registered, incorporated, or licensed, and Goddess forbid that they should ever become the canonical hubs of a franchise.

That doesn't mean I eschew power, authority, and wealth. My own branch of the Beauty and Truth Laboratory is stationed in a garage next to the house I rent on the seedy outskirts of suburbia, but I'd have no problem moving to a more expansive location, like say, a conference center on a 100-acre compound in an idyllic place that the original inhabitants of this continent regarded as a power spot. And I'd love it if this book sold a million copies, or if Beauty and Truth Laboratories were as common as 7-Elevens in 10 years.

On the other hand, I'm happy with whatever blessings life conspires to bring me. If it's to my and your ultimate benefit that this book reaches no more than 2,000 wise guys and riot grrrls, I will celebrate that outcome. And my garage-based laboratory is fine just the way it is, with its sloping floor and row of tiny windows darkened by the exuberant persimmon tree outside. The modesty of its structure is a constant reminder that the most important aspect of my work is building the Beauty and Truth Laboratory within me. As I prod my imagination to nurture ever-more detailed visions of love, compassion, joy, freedom, beauty, and truth, I'm better able to spot and name all those good things in the world around me. I also become more skilled at creating them.

My humble headquarters brings another advantage. It encourages me to regard everywhere I go as a potential extension of the Beauty and Truth Laboratory. My experiments aren't confined to the hours I spend in the solitude of my ivory tower, but also spill out into the fertile chaos of daily life.

On one epiphanic occasion, an eight-lane highway at rush hour turned into a temporary Beauty and Truth Laboratory. It was just a few days after my return from the Burning Man festival where the dream of the Laboratory had hatched. I was driving on 101, the artery that bisects Marin County.

As I cruised at 65 mph between Larkspur and Corte Madera, a blonde in a Jaguar convertible with the top down passed me on the right. Perhaps distracted by the chat she was enjoying on her cell phone, she suddenly zipped in front of me. After hitting my brakes to avoid rear-ending her, I honked my horn to express my annoyance. In response, she careened back over to the lane she'd been in before cutting me off, then slowed down and waited for me to catch up. I avoided eye contact at first, but finally looked over. Quaking with agitation, she was flashing me a middle-finger salute and a mad face as fierce as a Tibetan demon. Her car was veering closer to mine. Might she actually crash into me on purpose?

I was quaking with agitation myself. My adrenaline surged, threatening to explode to mushroom cloud-proportions. Curses were rising from my gut to throat. At the same time, I resisted it all. I didn't want to be possessed by stupid rage because of the carelessness of a bad driver. Such a trivial eruption of my fight-or-flight instinct was against my religion.

Then a miracle happened. As if through divine intervention, without any prompting from my will, fond memories of Burning Man surged into my imagination. I was back there squatting on the ancient lake bed with my stack of baby wipes, intimately conversing with the Goddess of the sun. I could hear the thump of music in the distance and feel the desert breeze on my cheeks.

The stabbing rage that had filled my abdomen dissipated. In its place, a whirlpool of warmth spiraled around my heart. It was a luxurious, sensual feeling, almost erotic. Then came a prick like a needle popping a water balloon, followed by a gush of sweet release. A heart orgasm? I was suffused with a sense of well-being. All was right with the world, and I felt a cheerful affection for everything, even the mad woman in the Jaguar.

As urgent as my wrath had been just a few moments before, so now was my tenderness. I felt triumphant. For the first time in my life, I had conquered an adrenaline rush of anger *as it was happening.* In comparable situations in the past, I had always needed a cooling-off period before I could soften my heart.

It was as if I had succeeded at a difficult game that required all my macho prowess, only the prowess in this case was demonstrated through love instead of strength and cleverness.

I looked over at the crazed monster in the car that was on the verge of sideswiping mine. She was still glaring at me as if transfixed. Her demeanor had not lost any of its obscene savagery. Had she even glanced at the road in front of her recently?

I rolled down my window and leaned my head out. Less than ten feet now separated our faces. She looked as if she were about to leap out of her seat and pounce on me. Just in time, I smiled and blew her three kisses. Then, summoning my ample powers of vocal projection, I boomed out the words, half-singing, "I love you. I have always loved you. And I will love you until the end of time." I put my hands together in the gesture of prayer, using my knees to steady the steering wheel, and bowed my head in her direction.

I was utterly sincere. There was not a speck of sarcasm or irony in the mix. At that moment, I was a bodhisattva linked directly to the undulating love of the Goddess. I had no doubt that a radiant beam of divine sweetness was emanating from me, bathing the mad woman in a palpable ray of lusty compassion. She had to be feeling it.

There was one more gift I longed to deliver: the talisman I kept on my dashboard. It was a spectacular piece, meticulously constructed by my friend Calley, who was an adept in a Qabalistic mystery school as well as an expert in origami, the Japanese art of paper-folding. She had taken eight one hundred-dollar bills—real legal tender—and folded them into the shape of an eight-pointed star. Golden threads, small rubies, fragments of a meteorite, and the 400 million-year-old fossilized penis of a daddy longlegs were the other essential elements. Everything was mounted on a circular disk

As formulated by Hakim Bey, a Temporary Autonomous Zone (TAZ) is any event that liberates the imaginations of everyone present, thereby making it possible for life to be penetrated by the Marvelous.

of gold, six inches in diameter.

I treasured the piece. Calley had made it for me at a time in my life when I was purging myself of old, ingrained desires that were no longer in harmony with my evolving ideals. The kind of fame that I had coveted in my early years of being a rock musician, for instance, no longer interested me. Nor did my former fascination with having an endless variety of sexual partners. Calley invoked her sophisticated understanding of Qabalistic and astrological principles to design the talisman so that it would supercharge my ability to change my life in accordance with my will.

This was the gift I wanted to bequeath to my former adversary, Jaguar Woman. Her convertible top was down and our cars were nearly touching, so the risk of missing my target was small. Taking my beloved power object in my right hand, I reached out the window and flung it. She swerved away but not out of range. It fell into the front seat of her car.

I returned my gaze to the road ahead, checking to see if the divine guidance that had been pouring through me had extended to keeping my car on track. It had. A few seconds later, I returned my gaze to Jaguar Woman. She was holding up the talisman as she stared at me. Her face had turned innocent and awed, almost reverent, as if she had seen the Ghost of Christmas Future arm-in-arm with a long-lost loved one. I guessed that her demons had withdrawn.

After that her car slowed, quickly falling behind my pace. In my rearview mirror, I observed her making her way to the far right lane. She drove carefully, using her turn signal. She got off at the next exit.

In the midst of my exuberant oneness with all of creation, a tinge of sadness crept in. I mused on how I'd never know if my victory over the angry devil within me would produce any lasting effect on Jaguar Woman. Would she fully appreciate the love I invoked in response to her attack? If nothing else, surely the gift of the talisman would change her life forever, right?

As I sped toward the Golden Gate Bridge, I remembered a quote I'd once heard attributed to basketball coach John Wooden: "You can't have a perfect day without doing something for someone who'll never be able to repay you." I mused on the fact that while this *was* a relatively selfless approach to giving gifts, it was still imperfect: Maybe the recipient of your largesse couldn't literally pay you back, but he or she could think wonderful thoughts about you; your ego would benefit. No, a more ultimate expression of generosity, an improvement on Wooden's formulation, would be to give *anonymously* to someone who couldn't repay you.

Which was what I had just done. Rather than bemoaning the fact that I'd never know whether or how Jaguar Woman would benefit from my gift, I realized I should celebrate.

At this point in my impromptu Beauty and Truth Laboratory experiment, I had settled into full meditation mode. Though I was barreling along a crowded freeway at high velocity, my brain was enjoying an expansive perspective made possible by an abundance of alpha waves. I embodied the definition of meditation offered by the Hindu sage Patanjali: "an unbroken flow of knowledge on a particular object."

My stream of consciousness flowed on to the next clue, advice I'd once heard articulated by the Dalai Lama. He said you should work as hard as you can to fight for justice and reduce suffering—even as you accept with equanimity that all of your efforts may come to absolutely nothing in the end. My translation: Give your best beauty and live your highest truth without expecting any rewards.

My unbroken flow of knowledge glided on to the next thought, this one planted in me by the author Rachel Pollock. "We cannot predict the results of healing, either our own or the world around us," she said. "We need to act for the sake of a redemption that will be a mystery until it unfolds before us."

I looked around my car for something to write on. At the end of my drive I'd be meeting a potential investor in San Francisco, and I wanted to record the results of my spontaneous Beauty and Truth Laboratory experiment before having to hand myself over to the business part of my brain.

There was only one surface available to take notes on: a piece of junk mail lying on the floor in the backseat. Poorly designed, it had a lot of empty space on one page. I balanced it on my thigh as I recorded the notes that became the basis for what you've just read.

A half hour later I was at 16th Street and Portrero in San Francisco, where I scored a parking space in record time. Before getting out to go to my meeting, I sat in my car and composed the last few paragraphs of this report. They read as follows:

First there was the "Baby Wipe Communiqué," and now there's the "Blank Space on a Piece of Junk Mail Communiqué." I prophesy that the future will bring the "Bar Napkin Communiqué," the "Grocery Bag Communiqué," the "Mulberry Leaf Torn Off the Tree Next to the Library While I'm Walking by Communiqué," and many others.

A new tradition is announcing itself. It reveals I've got to be ready to conjure up the Beauty and Truth Laboratory at a moment's notice, whenever a pressing experiment needs to be done—even if it's in my car, a sports bar, the check-out line at Safeway, or on a stroll downtown.

This is not to say that some future Beauty and Truth Laboratory breakthroughs won't also unfold on the beach after midnight on the winter solstice or on my meditation pillow after three days of fasting and praying.

But I vow to be vigilant for the possibility that any place and any time may become the holy ground where I can commit radical acts of pronoia or gather revelations that will change my mind every which way about the mysterious, ever-deepening meanings of pronoia. I promise to seize the pregnant pauses, leap into the empty spots, and squeeze through the cracks in the system.

SACRED
ADVERTISEMENT

The work of the Beauty and Truth Laboratory is sponsored by hand-loomed Turkish shower curtains trimmed with emeralds and rubies, mud-cloth journals crafted from Ghanaian textiles and Italian paper, wool patchwork ottomans made from the traditional ground covering used by shepherds in Kyrgyzstan, and ceramic spice jars containing ten million-year-old salt from the Himalayas.

This space has been
liberated for your use

Everyone
who believes
in the devil
is the devil

Drowning in Love

The sage and her student were standing by a pool discussing longing and ambition.

"What do you want more than anything else?" the sage asked.

"To perfect my ability to love all of creation the way I love myself," the young man replied.

At that moment, the sage tackled the student and shoved his head beneath the water. Accustomed to letting his teacher shape the unpredictable contours of his education, he did not resist.

One minute went by. Then another. The student began to struggle and kick. His teacher was strong.

Finally she released her grip and the student surfaced, fighting for breath.

"What did you want more than anything else during these last few minutes?" the sage inquired.

"Nothing else was in my mind except the desire for air," gasped the student.

"Excellent," beamed the sage. "As soon as you are equally single-minded in your desire to perfect your ability to love all of creation the way you love yourself, you will achieve your goal."

The Universe Is Made of Stories

The poet Muriel Rukeyser said the universe is composed of stories, not of atoms. The physicist Werner Heisenberg declared that the universe is made of music, not of matter.

And we believe that if you habitually expose yourself to toxic stories and music, you could wind up living in the wrong universe, where it's impossible to become the gorgeous genius you were born to be.

That's why we implore you to nourish yourself with delicious, nutritious tales and tunes that inspire you to exercise your willpower for your highest good.

"The only war that matters is the war against the imagination.
All other wars are subsumed by it."
—Diane DiPrima, "Rant," from *Pieces of a Song*

Astrologer Caroline Casey offers an apt metaphor to illustrate how crucial it is for us to hear and read good stories. She notes that if we don't have enough of the normal, healthy kind of iodine in our bodies, we absorb radioactive iodine, which has entered the food chain through nuclear test explosions conducted in the atmosphere. Similarly, unless we fill ourselves up with stories that invigorate us, we're more susceptible to sopping up the poisonous, degenerative narratives.

Novelist Ursula K. Le Guin decries the linear perspective that dominates modern storytelling. She says it's "like an arrow, starting here and going straight there and THOK! hitting its mark." Furthermore, she complains, plots are usually advanced through conflict, as if interesting action can't possibly arise from any other catalyst.

I invite you to rebel against these oppressive conventions. Wean yourself from tales that have reductive plot lines fueled primarily by painful events. Celebrate the luminous mysteries that have shaped your own life story: the meandering fascinations that didn't lead to tidy conclusions, the wobbly joys that fed your soul but didn't serve your ego's ambitions, the adventures whose success revolved around brain-teasing breakthroughs instead of exhausting triumphs over suffering.

"It is difficult
to get the news from poems
        yet men die miserably every day
                for lack
of what is found there." —William Carlos Williams,
"Asphodel, That Greeny Flower"

In *The White Goddess: A Historical Grammar of Poetic Myth,* Robert Graves tells us that "In ancient Ireland, the *ollave,* or master-poet, sat next to the king and was privileged, as none but the queen was, to wear six different colors in his clothes." The *ollave,* he adds, was also a judge and seer, and tutored the king in morality.

In contrast, our culture relegates poets to the margins of every debate. After the terrorist attack of September 2001, for example, only Maya Angelou, in an ephemeral appearance on ABC-TV's *Nightline,* and Robert Pinsky on *The MacNeil News Hour,* managed to crack the procession of pundits, politicians, and lawyers that dominated the airwaves and shaped our experience of what had happened. During the same period, leftist radio stations KPFA, WBAI, KPFK, KPFT, and KBOO, which define themselves as alternatives to the corporate news media, also offered newscasts monopolized by political analysis. It was rare to hear commentary from anyone who specialized in psychological, spiritual, or imaginal modes of perception.

If we of the rabble-rouser persuasion don't champion the *ollave,* how can we expect the culture of the living dead to do so?

"It's not until an event, institution, thought, principle, or movement, crosses the media threshold that it becomes real to us." —Todd Gitlin, *Media Unlimited: How the Torrent of Images and Sounds Overwhelms Our Lives*

"Though we don't have to believe what the media tell us, we can't know what they don't tell us." —Bernard McGrane, "The Zen TV Experiment," www.adbusters.org

How did it come to be that what we call the news is reported solely by journalists? There are so many other kinds of events besides the narrow band favored by that highly specialized brand of storytellers. Indeed, there are many phenomena that can literally not even

be perceived by journalists. Their training, their temperament, and their ambitions make vast areas of human experience invisible to them.

"Ninety-six percent of the cosmos puzzles astronomers." I loved reading that headline on the CNN website. It showed that at least some of our culture's equivalents of high priests, the scientists, are humble enough to acknowledge that the universe is made mostly of stuff they can't even detect, let alone study.

If only the journalists were equally modest. Since they're not, we'll say it: The majority of everything that happens on this planet is invisible to them.

The Beauty and Truth Laboratory is gathering a network of seers to report the news that journalists miss and ignore. We're tempted to call them "spies," since they've got to be on the lookout for what has become secret. They don't necessarily have to be covert in their operations, but they do have to be attentive to stories unfolding below the media threshold. Maybe it's better if we don't give them a title yet. That way we won't limit the kinds of people who can serve in this role.

In the early years of Christianity, there were hundreds of books interpreting the life and teachings of Jesus Christ. But by 325 A.D., a group backed by the political and military might of the Roman Empire had determined which few of the stories about Christ would thereafter be considered the canonical New Testament, and which would be regarded as heretical bilge. No better evidence exists for the saying, "History is a tale told by the victors." Keep this in mind as you strategize your way through your personal War of the Stories. Your account of events may have more truth in it than everyone else's conflicting tales, but that won't carry much weight unless you obtain the power to *enforce* your version.

"The world is composed of rival gangs of hypnotists, each competing for your entranced attention." —graffiti on the wall of a public restroom at Northgate Mall, San Rafael, California

"The news flies down its beam of dusted light." —Osip Mandelstam

WELCOME TO THE SHOW

You have tuned in to the premier broadcast of the Pronoia News Network.

We're coming to you live from your repressed memory of paradise, reminding you that you can have anything you want if you will just ask for it in an unselfish way.

The Pronoia News Network is brought to you by the state of mind that the philosopher Robert Anton Wilson inhabited when he said, "Reality is what you can get away with."

Welcome to the end of your nightmares, beauty and truth fans! The world is young, your soul is free, and a naked celebrity is dying to talk to you about your most intimate secrets right now.

Just kidding.

In fact, the world is young, your soul is free, and at any moment you will begin to feel horny compassion for salamanders, clouds, toasters, oak trees, and even the ocean itself.

I'm your host for the Pronoia News Network. My name is the Sacred Janitor at the Edge of Time, and I'm proud to announce that this is a perfect moment. Stay with us for the next million perfect moments, and we promise to overstimulate your imagination and convince you that all you have to do to achieve the impossible is attempt the absurd.

Why is it so important to the future of red-tailed hawks and daffodils and coral reefs that childbirth be broadcast live in prime time on one of the major TV networks every night? Stay tuned.

What is the best way for you to cancel the curses you've cast on yourself over the years? Stay tuned.

Why are we so sure that sooner or later every one of you will become a good-humored, vehemently compassionate, innocently wise master of pronoia, with a skill for lucid dreaming and a knack for being yourself even when you are beside yourself?

Stay tuned to the Pronoia News Network, and all will become bewilderingly clear. We will prove to you that life is a conspiracy to shower you with a nonstop feast of interesting experiences, all of which are designed to help you grow your intelligence, shed your pretensions, and master the art of ingenious love.

The Pronoia News Network is a tricky experiment designed to bring heaven all the way down to earth . . . if that's what you want. It's a holy advertisement based on the story of your life . . . if that's what you want.

The clues that will lead to the end of your ancient amnesia are all around you, beauty and truth fans . . . if that's what you want. You're ready to rediscover the 13 perfect secrets from the beginning of time . . . if that's what you want.

So what do you want, anyway?

The Immortalists Current human life expectancy, already at age 78 for Americans, is steadily increasing. Men now live an average of 27 years longer than they did a century ago, and women 31 years. Many scientists believe there is no absolute limit to the human life span. Some expect that by 2070, life expectancy will be 100.

Crime Declines Between 1973 and the end of 2002, the violent crime rate in the U.S. decreased by 52 percent, from 48 victims per 1,000 people to 23. During the same period, crimes against property shrank by 69 percent, from 520 victims per thousand to 159. Crime is now at its lowest level since it was first officially tracked. The report comes from the Bureau of Justice's "National Crime Victimization Survey."

"Despite our perceptions, based on television or chats around the water cooler, it is clear crime is on the decline in a significant way and has been for some years now," said Ralph Myers, a criminologist at Stanford University, speaking to *USA Today*.

Moose Luxury A Canadian moose can now walk in peace and safety all the way to South America, thanks to Harrison Ford. He and other celebrities with wealth and influence quietly worked together for years to purchase land along corridors that connect various wildlife refuges and national parks.

Meanwhile, Canadian government officials announced that their country, the second largest in the world, plans to create ten giant national parks and five marine conservation areas. The new sanctuaries, when added to the existing 39 national parks, will double the amount of protected land.

Conversation with Eternity Beauty and Truth Laboratory researcher Firenze Matisse traveled to Antarctica. On the first day, the guide took him and his group to a remote area and left them alone for an hour to commune with the pristine air and unearthly stillness. After a while, a penguin ambled up and launched into a ceremonial display of squawks and stretches. Firenze responded with recitals of his favorite memorized poems, imagining he was "engaged in a conversation with eternity." Halfway through his inspired performance of Thich Nhat Hanh's "Please Call Me by My True Names," the penguin sent a stream of green projectile vomit cascading against his chest, and shuffled away.

Though Firenze initially felt deflated by eternity's surprise, no harm was done. He soon came to see it as a first-class cosmic joke, and looked forward to exploiting its value as an amusing story with which to regale his friends back home.

Beauty and Truth Laboratory researcher Michael Logan was the first person to hear Firenze's tale upon his return from Antarctica. "You might want to consider this, Firenze," Michael mused after taking it all in. "Penguins nurture their offspring by chewing food—mixing it up with all God's enzymes—and then vomiting it into the mouths of the penguin babies. Perhaps you weren't the butt of a cosmic joke or some Linda Blair-esque bad review, but in fact the recipient of a very precious gift of love. Who knows?"

Now Firenze has two punch lines for his tale of redemptive pronoia.

PNN is made possible by Mary Oliver's poem about sunflowers, in which she writes that the long work of turning their lives into a celebration is not easy.

IMPOSSIBLE DREAM FULFILLED

The world's largest private bank, Citigroup, has agreed to stop financing projects that damage sensitive ecosystems. It has promised to invest more in projects that use renewable energy and to pursue policies that protect indigenous people. How did this impossible dream come to pass? The humble but dogged environmental group, Rainforest Action Network, creatively pestered Citigroup for years until the corporation gave in to its demands.

PNN is brought to you by this passage from Eknath Easwaran's book Gandhi, the Man: *"One of the most radical discoveries Gandhi was to make in a lifetime of experimentation: In order to transform others, you have to transform yourself."*

Sharing Your Breath

Quoting geneticists, Guy Murchie says we're all family. You have at least a million relatives as close as tenth cousin, and no one on Earth is any farther removed than your 50th cousin.

Murchie also describes our kinship through an analysis of how deeply we share the air. With each breath, you take into your body 10 sextillion atoms, and—owing to the wind's ceaseless circulation—over a year's time you have intimate relations with oxygen molecules exhaled by every person alive, as well as by everyone who ever lived. Right now you may be carrying atoms that were once inside the lungs of Malcolm X, Christopher Columbus, Joan of Arc, and Cleopatra. (Source: Guy Murchie, *The Seven Mysteries of Life*)

Fortune Cookie
You're like an arrow in flight. You're a half-cooked feast, the fifth month of pregnancy, the week before a big election. Have you ever mastered a second language? You resemble the time right before fluency arrives.

Greedy Giant Versus Generous Giant

Wal-Mart is famous for the stingy pay and benefits it offers its employees. But another giant chain store, Costco, takes a different approach. Full-time workers there average $15.97 per hour, which is almost 40 percent higher than their Wal-Mart counterparts, who earn $11.52. After four years, a Costco cashier's yearly salary can rise to $44,000. The company also covers 92 percent of most of its workers' health care costs. While the industry-wide turnover rate averages 66 percent, Costco's is just 23 percent.

Costco is so unusual in its benevolence that some business gurus disapprove. "From the perspective of investors, Costco's benefits are overly generous," says retail analyst Bill Dreher, quoted in *The Wall Street Journal*. He thinks that the company's largesse depresses its stock value because investors are afraid its profit margins aren't as high as they could be.

But the fact is that Costco is very successful. Its five-year growth rate has been 10.1 percent annually, better than Wal-Mart's 9.8 percent. Its annual earnings were expected to rise from $41.7 billion in 2003 to $47.2 billion in 2004.

Sacred Genius of Generosity
"The Sun, each second, transforms four million tons of itself into light, giving itself over to become energy that we, with every meal, partake of. For four million years, humans have been feasting on the Sun's energy stored in the form of wheat or reindeer, as each day the Sun dies as Sun and is reborn as the vitality of Earth. Every child of ours needs to learn the simple truth: She is the energy of the Sun. And we adults should organize things so her face shines with the same radiant joy.

"Human generosity is possible only because at the center of the solar system a magnificent stellar generosity pours forth free energy day and night without stop and without complaint and without the slightest hesitation. This is the way of the universe. This is the way of life. And this is the way in which each of us joins this cosmological lineage when we accept the Sun's gift of energy and transform it into creative action that will enable the community to flourish." —Brian Swimme, *The Hidden Heart of the Cosmos*, video

2 + 2 = 3.8 Sometimes two plus two does not equal four. For instance, if you combine two gallons of water with two gallons of ethyl alcohol, you get a mixture that's only 3.8 gallons.

It's in the Genes

Researchers at Emory University found that humans are biologically programmed to be nice. Their study used magnetic resonance imaging to scan the brains of women who were playing a game called the Prisoners' Dilemma. While seeking the goal of financial gain, the women could choose between collaborative or self-aggrandizing strategies. Whenever they opted for the former, the parts of their brains correlated with reward-seeking behavior lit up.

"The longer the women engaged in a cooperative strategy, the more strongly flowed the blood to the pathways of pleasure," wrote Natalie Angier in her account in *The New York Times*. (Source: Natalie Angier, *The New York Times*, July 23, 2002)

The Inner Voice Speaks

Scientists have confirmed what we all knew: You do indeed have a little voice in your head that warns you when you're about to do something dumb. It's called the anterior cingulate cortex, according to white-coated authorities at Carnegie-Mellon University. If you're receptive to it, it's as good as having a guardian angel. "Don't do it," the voice whispers when you're on the verge of locking your keys in your car or leaving the bar with the cute drunk you just met. "Go back," it murmurs as you start to walk away from a huge, though initially inconvenient, opportunity.

Better Than Cloning a Dinosaur

Aeschylus, the seminal playwright of ancient Greece, wrote more than 90 plays, but most did not survive. The evidence for his reputation as the "Father of Tragedy" has consisted of just seven works. Recently, however, archaeologists have discovered an eighth, *Achilles*. It was on a papyrus scroll stuffed inside an Egyptian mummy. In the summer of 2004, a theater company in Cyprus staged the ancient play for the first time in over 2,000 years.

"The secret of change is to focus all your energy not on fighting the old, but on building the new." —Socrates

"The basis of freedom is recognition of the unconscious; the invisible dimension; not yet realized; leaving a space for the new." —Norman O. Brown, *Love's Body*

"Never doubt that a small group of thoughtful, committed citizens can change the world. Indeed, it's the only thing that ever has." —Margaret Mead

"No work is more worthwhile than to be a sign of divine joy and a fountain of divine love." —Andrew Harvey

"If a man is called to be a street sweeper, he should sweep streets even as Michelangelo painted, or Beethoven played music, or Shakespeare wrote poetry. He should sweep streets so well that all the hosts of heaven and earth will pause to say, here lived a great street sweeper who did his job well.—Martin Luther King Jr.

Teen Angst Update

Crime committed by teenagers has plummeted to its lowest levels in more than two decades. Drunken teens are still killing themselves while driving cars, but the rate is half what it was 20 years ago. The overall teen death rate from accident, homicide, or suicide dropped 28 percent between 1990 and 2000.

In 60 years, there hasn't been a lower birth rate among teenage girls than there is now. The overall dropout rate among American high school students has declined by four percent in the last two decades, with an eight percent improvement among African Americans. Three-fourths of high school students say they get along very well or extremely well with their parents, and only three percent say they don't get along well.

Urban Renewal At a concert in California, devotional singer Krishna Das told a story of escorting his revered teachers, a frail old Indian couple, to an acupuncturist in New York. They had to walk through a neighborhood dominated by strip clubs, prostitutes, and drug dealers. Every few feet, a new salesperson approached with an offer of crack, weed, crank, or sexual adventures.

Krishna Das worried about subjecting his beloved guides to such a degrading experience, but they were unfazed. "This is heaven," said the woman. When a surprised Krishna Das asked what she meant, she replied, "Heaven is any place where one's needs can be met."

Early last century, marauding boll weevils devoured the cotton crop that was the main product of Enterprise, Alabama. Local farmers had no choice but to diversify the plants they grew. As a result, the town's per capita income tripled what it had been when cotton was king. In response, grateful citizens built a huge bronze monument to the insect that had forced them to grow richer.

✺

Leo Alard was the first Hispanic to become an Episcopalian bishop in the U.S. His pioneer spirit emerged early on. As a young priest in the 1960s, he headed a racially integrated parish in Cattahoochee, Florida. The bigots of the KKK didn't look favorably on his work, and on one occasion they burned a cross on the church lawn. Alard, who was supervising a youth group on that particular night, brought the class out and had everyone toast marshmallows over the fire.

MIRABILIA REPORT *Mirabilia* n. events that inspire wonder, marvelous phenomena, small miracles; from the Latin *mirabilia,* "marvels."

■ With every dawn, when first light penetrates the sea, many seahorse colonies perform a dance to the sun.

■ A seven-year-old Minnesota boy received patent number 6,368,227 for a new method of swinging on a swing.

■ As it thrusts itself into our Milky Way Galaxy, the dwarf galaxy Sagittarius is unraveling, releasing a thick stream of dark matter that is flowing right through the Earth.

■ A chemist in Australia finally succeeded in mixing oil and water.

■ Except among birds and land mammals, the females of most species are bigger than the males.

■ The South African version of TV's *Sesame Street* has an AIDS-positive Muppet named Kami.

■ In just two minutes, an ingenious octopus at the Bronx Zoo learned to unscrew the lid from a jar to get at the food inside, though it had never experienced a jar with a lid before.

■ Black sheep have a better sense of smell than white sheep.

■ There are about 60,000 miles of blood vessels in your body. Every square inch of your body has an average of 32 million bacteria on it.

*Here's a message from one of our spiritual underwriters, poet James Broughton.
"I never learned to distinguish between illusion and miracle. I didn't need to. I trusted in love's confusing joy."
—"Memento of an Amorist,"
from* Packing Up for Paradise: Selected Poems 1946–1996

The Benevolence of Pleasure The quest for chemical-induced erections has helped stem the extinction of endangered species. Since the advent of Viagra, demand for traditional aphrodisiacs like harp seal penises and reindeer antlers has plummeted in Asia. The wild animals in possession of the body parts in question are no longer hunted so relentlessly.

Blasphemous Optimism "The biggest event of the last 20 years—the collapse of the Soviet Union—occurred without violence: the first nonviolent revolution of that size in all of human history, extending from Berlin to Siberia.

"Nelson Mandela went from a prison cell to the President's office in a country that evolved from white supremacy to power-sharing in only seven years.

"The Internet more and more evolves toward the planetary brain once only imagined by visionary scientists like Tielhard de Chardin and Arthur Clarke.

"What some call my 'blasphemous cheerfulness' or my 'cockeyed optimism' just depends on my basic agnosticism. We don't know the outcome of the current worldwide transformation, so it seems sick and decadent (in the Nietzschean sense) when fashionable opinion harps on all the gloomy alternatives and

resolutely ignores the utopian possibilities that seem equally likely (and, on the basis of past evolution, perhaps a little more likely)." —Robert Anton Wilson, www.rawilson.com

Name Trends Emily, Madison, and Kaitlyn are among the most popular names for new baby girls, whereas Jacob, Ryan, and Nicholas are top choices for boys. On the other hand, Condescensia, Crumpet, and Bucket are some of the least popular girl names, and Beelzebub, Humpty, and Scratch the least favorite for boys.
—Thevoiceofreason.com

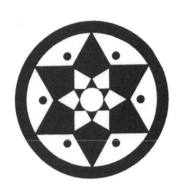

Gazing Into the Abyss of Happiness

More and more creative people find they do their best work when they're feeling healthy and secure. We know writers who no longer need to be drunk or in agony in order to shed the numbness of their daily routine and tap into the full powers of their imagination. We have filmmaker friends whose best work flows not from the depths of alienated self-doubt but rather from the heights of well-earned bliss. Singer-songwriter P.J. Harvey is the patron saint of this new breed. "When I'm contented, I'm more open to receiving a lot of inspiration," she has testified. "I'm most creative when I feel safe and happy."

At the Beauty and Truth Lab, we've retired the archetype of the tormented genius. We have zero attraction to books and movies and songs by depressed jerks whose work is celebrated but whose lives are a mess. Stories about supposedly interesting creeps don't rouse our perverse fascination because we've broken our addiction to perverse fascination. When hearing about illustrious creators who brag that they feel most stimulated when they're angry or miserable, we unleash the Official Beauty and Truth Lab Histrionic Yawn.

Sadly, many storytellers and artists are still addicted to the old delusions about the risks of good mental health. Even those who don't view peace of mind as a threat to their creative power often believe that it's a rare commodity attainable only through dumb luck. "One cannot divine nor forecast the conditions that will make happiness," said novelist Willa Cather. "One only stumbles upon them by chance, in a lucky hour, at the world's end somewhere."

There is another obstacle to overthrowing the status quo. Oppressively nice, indiscriminately optimistic, sentimental comfort-hoarders give happiness a bad name. They seem to justify Flaubert's mean-spirited observation that "To be stupid, selfish, and have good health are three requirements for happiness, though if stupidity is lacking, all is lost."

Here's a third blotch on the reputation of happiness: that it's mostly an absence of pain. In *The Tibetan Book of Living and Dying,* Sogyal Rinpoche frames the issue well: "Would you prefer the happiness of scratching a mosquito bite over the happiness of not having a mosquito bite in the first place?"

It's possible to define a more supple variety of happiness that does not paralyze the will or sap ambition. For the first clue about how to proceed, we turn to Buddhist researchers Rick Foster and Greg Hicks. In their book *How We Choose to Be Happy: The 9 Choices of Extremely Happy People,* they reveal that the number one trait of happy people is a serious determination to be happy. Bliss is a habit you can cultivate, in other words, not an accident that you stumble upon by chance, in a lucky hour, at the world's end somewhere.

For another clue about how to conjure up a kind of happiness that does not anesthetize the soul, we call on Kenneth Koch. Here's what he wrote about Nobel Prize-winning poet Saint-John Perse: "So many poets have the courage to look into the abyss. But Perse had the courage to look into happiness."

Your Awakening Tree

In her book *For the Time Being,* Annie Dillard says that while many people alive today think that our civilization is in a dark age and on the verge of collapse, similar beliefs have been common throughout history. Around 300 B.C., Hindus were convinced they lived in a "degenerate and unfortunate time" known as the Kali Yuga—the lowest point in the great cosmic cycle. In 426 A.D., the Christian writer Augustine mourned that the world was in its last days. In the 1800s, renowned Hasidic Rabbi Nachman grieved for the world's "widespread atheism and immorality."

Dillard goes on to offer more examples, concluding, "It is a weakening and discoloring idea that rustic people knew God personally once upon a time but that it is too late for us. There never was a more holy age than ours, and never a less. There is no whit less enlightenment under the tree by your street than there was under the Buddha's bo tree."

Go sit under that tree. The time for your awakening is at hand.

SACRED
ADVERTISEMENT

Here's a message from our spiritual patron,
Ralph Waldo Emerson:
"Make your own Bible. Select and collect all the
words and sentences that in your reading
have been like the blast of triumph out of Shakespeare,
Seneca, Moses, John and Paul."
—The Portable Emerson, *Carl Bode, editor*

This Sacred Advertisement has been brought to you by
the old Hawaiian word polikua, *which refers to the dip*
that lies just on the other side of the horizon, where the
eye can't quite reach.

UNABASHED PRONOIA THERAPY

Experiments and exercises in becoming a blasphemously reverent, lustfully compassionate, eternally changing Master of Rowdy Bliss.

Report your answers and research results below

1 Go to the ugliest or most forlorn place you know—a drugstore parking lot, the front porch of a crack house, a toxic waste dump, or the place that symbolizes your secret shame—and build a shrine devoted to beauty, truth, and love.

Here are some suggestions about what to put in your shrine: a silk scarf; a smooth rock on which you've inscribed a haiku or joke with a felt-tip pen; coconut cookies or ginger candy; pumpkin seeds and an origami crane; a green kite shaped like a dragon; a music CD you love; a photo of your hero; a votive candle carved with your word of power; a rubber ducky; a bouquet of fresh beets; a print of Van Gogh's *Starry Night*.

2 Late at night when there's no traffic, stride down the middle of an empty road that by day is crawling with cars. Dance, careen, and sing songs that fill you with pleasurable emotions. Splay your arms triumphantly as you extemporize prayers in which you make extravagant demands and promises. Give pet names to the trees you pass, declare your admiration for the workers who made the road, and celebrate your sovereignty over a territory that usually belongs to heavy machines and their operators.

3 What causes happiness? Brainstorm at length about this question. Map out the foundations of your own personal science of happiness. Get serious about defining what makes you feel good. To get you started, I will list a few experiences that might possibly arouse your deepest gratification: physical pleasure; seeking the truth; being a good person; contemplating the meaning of life; enjoying the fruits of your accomplishments; escaping your routine; purging pent-up emotion. Do any of these work for you? Name at least ten more.

4 Have you ever seen the game called "Playing the Dozens?" Participants compete in the exercise of hurling witty insults at each other. Here are some examples: "You're so dumb, if you spoke your mind you'd be speechless." "Your mother is so old, she was a waitress at the Last Supper." "You're so ugly, you couldn't get laid if you were a brick."

I invite you to rebel against any impulse in you that resonates with the spirit of "Playing the Dozens." Instead, try a new game, "Paying the Tributes." Choose worthy targets and ransack your imagination to come up with smart, true, and amusing praise about them. The best stuff will be specific to the person you're addressing, not generic, but here are some prototypes: "You're so far-seeing, you can probably catch a glimpse of the back of your own head." "You're so ingenious, you could use your nightmares to get rich and famous." "Your mastery of pronoia is so artful, you could convince me to love my worst enemy."

5 Salvador Dali once staged a party in which guests were told to come disguised as characters from their nightmares. Do the reverse. Throw a bash in which everyone is invited to arrive dressed as a character from the best dream they remember.

6 "The messiah will come when we don't need him any more," wrote Franz Kafka. Give your interpretation of his remark.

7 On a big piece of cardboard, make a sign that says, "I love to help; I need to give; please take some money." Then go out and stand on a traffic island while wearing your best clothes, and give away money to passing motorists. Offer a little more to drivers in rusty brown Pinto station wagons and 1976 El Camino Classics than those in a late-model Lexus or Jaguar.

8 In response to our culture's ever-rising levels of noise and frenzy, rites of purification have become more popular. Many people now recognize the value of taking periodic retreats. Withdrawing from their usual compulsions, they go on fasts, avoid mass media, practice celibacy, or even abstain from speaking. While we applaud cleansing ceremonies like this, we recommend balancing them with periodic outbreaks of an equal and opposite custom: the Bliss Blitz.

During this celebration, you tune out the numbing banality of the daily grind. But instead of shrinking into asceticism, you indulge in uninhibited explorations of joy, release, and expansion. Turning away from the

Unabashed Pronoia Therapy

mildly stimulating distractions you seek out when you're bored or worried, you become inexhaustibly resourceful as you search for unsurpassable sources of cathartic pleasure. Try it for a day or a week: the Bliss Blitz.

9 When many people talk about their childhoods, they emphasize the alienating, traumatic experiences they had. It has become fashionable to avoid reporting memories of the good times in one's past. This seems dishonest—a testament to the popularity of cynicism rather than a reflection of objective truth.

I don't mean to downplay the way your early encounters with pain demoralized your spirit. But as you reconnoiter the promise of pronoia, it's crucial for you to extol the gifts you were given in your early years: all the helpful encounters, kind teachings, and simple acts of grace that helped you bloom.

In Homer's epic tale, *The Odyssey,* he described *nepenthe,* a mythical drug that induced the forgetfulness of pain and trouble. Modern culture has turned the myth into reality: There are now many stimuli serving that purpose.

If Homer were alive today, we wonder if he'd write about a potion that stirs up memories of delight, serenity, and fulfillment? Imagine that you have taken such a tonic. Spend an hour or two remembering the glorious moments from your past.

10 Become a *rapturist,* which is the opposite of a terrorist: Conspire to unleash blessings on unsuspecting recipients, causing them to feel good.

Before bringing your work as a rapturist to strangers, practice with two close companions. Offer them each a gift that fires up their ambitions. It should not be a practical necessity or consumer fetish, but rather a provocative tool or toy. Give them an imaginative boon they've been hesitant to ask for, a beautiful thing that expands their self-image, a surprising intervention that says, "I love the way you move me."

11 "There are two ways for a person to look for adventure," said the Lone Ranger, a TV character. "By tearing everything down, or building everything up." Give an example of each from your own life.

12 To many people, "sacrifice" is a demoralizing word that connotes deprivation. Is that how you feel? Do you make sacrifices because you're forced to, or maybe because your generosity prompts you to incur a loss in order to further a good cause?

Originally, "sacrifice" had a different meaning: *to give up something valuable in order that something even more valuable might be obtained.* Carry out an action that embodies this definition. For instance, sacrifice a mediocre pleasure so as to free yourself to pursue a more exalted pleasure.

13 Are other people luckier than you? If so, psychologist Richard Wiseman says you can do something about it. His book *The Luck Factor* presents research that proves you can learn to be lucky. It's not a mystical force you're born with, he says, but a habit you can develop. How? For starters, be open to new experiences, trust your gut wisdom, expect good fortune, see the bright side of challenging events, and master the art of maximizing serendipitous opportunities.

Name three specific actions you'd like to try in order to improve your luck.

14 Conjure up an imaginary friend and have an intimate conversation with him and her for at least 10 minutes. Bear in mind that this talk can be a rational creative act, not an excursion into lunacy. Composer Robert Schuman had long dialogues with his imaginary friends, Florestan and Eusebius, who provided valuable ideas for his musical scores. W.S. Merwyn wrote a poem in which he recounted the surprising counsel of his teacher John Berryman: "He suggested I pray to the Muse/ get down on my knees and pray/ right there in the corner and he/ said he meant it literally."

15 Some scholars believe the original Garden of Eden was where Iraq stands today. Though remnants of that ancient paradise survived into modern times, many were obliterated during the American war on Iraq in 2003. A Beauty and Truth Laboratory researcher who lives near the confluence of the Tigris and Euphrates Rivers kept us posted on the fate of the most famous remnant: the Tree of the Knowledge of Good and Evil. Until the invasion, it was a gnarled stump near Nasiriyah. But today it's gone; only a crater remains.

Let this serve as an evocative symbol for you as you demolish your old ideas about paradise, freeing you up to conjure a fresh vision of your ideal realm.

16 The primary meaning of the word "healing" is "to cure what's diseased or broken." Medical practitioners focus on sick people. Psychotherapists wrestle with their clients' traumas and neuroses. Philanthropists donate their money and social workers contribute their time to helping the underprivileged. I am in awe of them all. The level of one's spiritual enlightenment, I believe, is more accurately measured by helping people in need than by meditation skills, shamanic shapeshifting, supernatural powers, or religious knowledge.

But I also believe in a second kind of healing that is largely unrecognized: to supercharge what is already healthy; to lift up what's merely sufficient to a sublime state. Using this definition, describe two acts of healing: one you would enjoy performing on yourself and another you'd like to provide for someone you love.

17 Is the world a dangerous, chaotic place with no inherent purpose, running on automatic like a malfunctioning machine and fundamentally inimical to your happiness? Or are you surrounded by helpers in a friendly universe that gives you challenges in order to make you smarter and wilder and kinder? Trick questions! The answers may depend, at least to some degree, on what you believe is true.

Formulate a series of experiments that will allow you to objectively test the hypothesis that the universe is conspiring to help you.

18 Those who explore pronoia often find they have a growing capacity to help people laugh at themselves. While few arbiters of morality recognize this skill as a mark of high character, I put it near the top of my list. In my view, inducing people to take themselves less seriously is a supreme virtue. Do you have any interest in cultivating it? How might you go about it?

19 "God offers to every mind its choice between truth and repose," wrote Ralph Waldo Emerson. "Take which you please; you can never have both." Give an example from your own life that refutes or proves Emerson's assertion.

20 "Creativity is like driving a car at night," said E. L. Doctorow. "You never see further than your headlights, but you can make the whole trip that way." I would add that life itself is like driving a car at night. You're often in the dark except for what's right in front of you. At least that's usually the case. But for a few shining hours sometime while you're communing with this book, I predict you'll be able to see the big picture of where you're headed. It will be as if the whole world is suddenly illuminated by a prolonged burst of light; as if you're both driving your car and also watching your journey from high above. Write about what you see.

Unabashed Pronoia Therapy

SACRED
ADVERTISEMENT

Here's a message from our sponsor, Tatsuya Ishida at www.sinfest.net: "All I ever wanted in life was to make a difference, be worshiped like a god, conquer the universe, travel the world, meet interesting people, find the missing link, fight the good fight, live for the moment, seize each day, make a fortune, know what really matters, end world hunger, vanquish the dragon, be super popular but too cool to care, be master of my own fate, embrace my destiny, feel as much as I can feel, give too much, and love everything."

Tatsuya says it's fine if you want to say that this is what you feel, too.

5

Let's go wash some water.

Beyond Goodness

" I used to have superpowers," the bumper sticker says, "but my therapist took them away." Does that describe you? Have you been overly normalized by the bland conventions of what constitutes psychological health? Has your spunk been sapped by the pressure to behave yourself in a civilized manner?

If so, I'll offer you three pieces of advice. They may have a sickening effect if you apply them too liberally, but they'll be a tonic if you use them in small doses.

Here's the first, courtesy of Henry David Thoreau: "Do not be too moral. You may cheat yourself out of much life. Aim above morality. Be not simply good; be good for something."

Here's the second, from Isaac Asimov: "Never let your sense of morals get in the way of doing what's right."

Here's another, formulated by William Irwin Thompson: "An overdose of an antidote becomes a poison in itself."

A DANGEROUS TABOO

This book is a conversation, not a dictation. It's an inquiry, not dogma. We're explorers in search of the ever-evolving truth, not authorities proclaiming doctrine from on high. We refuse to be salespeople intent on getting you to be like us or buy our ideas. In fact, let's look at the downsides of the perspectives we celebrate.

The first thing you should consider before leaping into a relationship with pronoia is that it is utterly at odds with conventional wisdom. The 19th-century poet John Keats said that if something is not beautiful, it is probably not true. But the vast majority of modern storytellers—journalists, filmmakers, novelists, talk-show hosts, and poets—assert the opposite: If something is not *ugly,* it is probably not true.

In a world that equates pessimism with acumen and regards stories about things falling apart as having the highest entertainment value, pronoia is deviant. It is a taboo so taboo that it's not even recognized as a taboo.

The average American child sees 20,000 murders on TV before reaching age 18. This is considered normal. Every community has video rental stores filled with hundreds of multimillion-dollar films that depict people doing terrible things to each other. If you read newspapers, you have every right to believe that Bad Nasty Things compose 90 percent of the human experience. The authors of thousands of books published this year will hope to lure you in through the glamour of murder, addiction, self-hatred, sexual pathology, shame, betrayal, extortion, robbery, cancer, arson, and torture.

But you will be hard-pressed to find more than a few novels, films, news stories, and TV shows that dare to depict life as a gift whose purpose is to enrich the human soul.

If you cultivate an affinity for pronoia, people you respect may wonder if you have lost your way. You might appear to them as naive, eccentric, unrealistic, misguided, or even stupid. Your reputation could suffer and your social status could decline.

But that may be relatively easy to deal with compared to your struggle to create a new relationship with yourself. For starters, you will have to acknowledge that what you previously considered a strong-willed faculty—the ability to discern the weakness in everything—might actually be a mark of cowardice and laziness. Far from being evidence of your power and uniqueness, your drive to produce hard-edged opinions stoked by hostility is likely a sign that you've been brainwashed by the pedestrian influences of pop nihilism.

Before the onset of pronoia, you may feel fine about the fact that you generate much of your dynamic energy through anger, agitation, discomfort, and judgmental scorn. But once the pronoia kicks in, you'll naturally want more positive feelings to be your high-octane fuel. That will require extensive retraining. The work could be arduous, delicate, and time-consuming.

Are you truly ready to shed the values and self-images that keep you locked into alignment with the dying civilization? Will you have the stamina and inspiration necessary to dream up bigger, better, more original sins and wilder, wetter, more interesting problems? Do you realize how demanding it will be to turn yourself into a wildly disciplined, radically curious, fiercely tender, ironically sincere, ingeniously loving, aggressively sensitive, blasphemously reverent, lustfully compassionate master of rowdy bliss?

In the future, judges will send criminals to holy spots where reverence-provoking beauty will overwhelm their addiction to hatred.

Try saying this aloud: "I die daily." It's one of our favorite formulas for success. Is it right for you? Say it again, using a different tone of voice this time. "I die daily." Chant it in a fake foreign accent. Sing it to the tune of the nursery rhyme, "Frère Jacques." Play with it in the voice of the cartoon character you loved best as a child. Repeat it 10 times in a row, or try other vocal experiments. Then muse on these questions.

What do you need to kill off in yourself in order to tune in to the beauty that's hidden from you? What worn-out shticks are blinding you to the blessings that life is conspiring to give you? Which of your theories may have been useful and even brilliant in the past but are now keeping you from becoming aware of the ever-fresh creation that unfolds before you?

"I die daily" means that it's not enough to terminate your stale mental habits just once. The price of admission into pronoia is a commitment to continual dying. You'll have to ask yourself rude questions and kick your own ass again and again. Today's versions of beauty, truth, love, goodness, justice, and liberation will pass away. To keep abreast of the latest developments—to cultivate tomorrow's versions of pronoia—you will have to immerse yourself regularly in the waters of chaos. Your relationship with pronoia will have to be a never-ending improvisation.

The dream of a steady-state utopia is anathema to Beauty and Truth Laboratory researchers. We're allergic to any paradise that resembles a spotless shopping mall within the walls of a gated community in heaven.

Pronoia is fueled by a drive to cultivate happiness and a determination to practice an aggressive form of gratitude that systematically identifies the things that are working well. But it is not a soothing diversion meant for timid Pollyannas strung out on optimistic delusions. It's not a feel-good New Age fantasy used to deny the harsh facts about existence. Those of us who perceive the world pronoiacally refuse to be polite shills for sentimental hopefulness.

On the contrary, we build our optimism not through a repression of difficulty, but rather a vigorous engagement with it. We understand that the best way to attract blessings is to grapple with the knottiest enigmas. Each fresh puzzle is a potential source of future bliss—an exciting teaching that may usher us to our next breakthrough.

Do you want to be a pronoiac player? Blend anarchistic rebelliousness with open-hearted exuberance. Root your insurrectionary fervor in expansive joy instead of withering hatred. Enjoy saying "no!" but don't make it the wellspring of your vitality. Be fueled by blood-red yeses that rip against the grain of comfortable ugliness.

A Spell to Commit Pronoia, by psychotherapist Jennifer Welwood:

Willing to experience aloneness,
I discover connection everywhere;
Turning to face my fear,
I meet the warrior who lives within;
Opening to my loss,
I am given unimaginable gifts;
Surrendering into emptiness,
I find fullness without end.

Each condition I flee from pursues me.
Each condition I welcome transforms me
And becomes itself transformed
Into its radiant jewel-like essence.
I bow to the one who has made it so,
Who has crafted this Master Game;
To play it is pure delight,
To honor it is true devotion.

Sacred
Advertisement

The generous dangers of pronoia are brought to you by the origin myth of the Iroquois' Thunderbird Clan: Earthmaker woke up to realize he was the only being in the universe. Out of the depths of his loneliness, he cried, unleashing a flood of tears that became the oceans and rivers and lakes of our world.

GUERRILLA ORACLE

Clues to the Rebel Grail

Lazy Work

Meditation teacher Wes Nisker helps students learn to calm the frenetic chatter of their minds. As earnest as he is in this heroic work, though, he also appreciates the importance of not trying too hard. As you pursue your pronoia practice, call on his influence now and then. It'll keep you honest and prevent your anal sphincter from getting too high-strung.

Here's the promo for one of his workshops. "This day will be of absolutely no use to you. Nothing will be furthered or accomplished by coming. Expect a time of effortlessness, relaxation, and poetry, hanging out, maybe a little mindfulness meditation—all for nothing. Some might understand this as a protest against our culture's speedy, goal-driven nature, but we know it won't amount to a hill of beans. Good intentions and purposefulness must be checked at the door."

ORIGINS OF THE
HOMEOPATHIC MEDICINE SPELLS

Being a devotee of pronoia doesn't mean you will never have another difficult or painful experience. It doesn't obligate you to pretend everything is perfectly right with the world. You don't have to cover your eyes whenever you come into proximity with a daily newspaper.

On the other hand, we're not going to waste our valuable space or your precious energy by giving equal time to stories of tragedy, failure, and tumult. They get far more than their fair share of attention everywhere else. Future historians might even conclude that our age suffered from a collective obsessive-compulsive disorder: the pathological need to repetitively seek out reasons for how bad life is.

Still, we feel the need to push a bit further in our acknowledgement of all the confusing evils of the world. We realize that what we've said so far may not be sufficient to satisfy the paranoid cynics, who include among their number many well-respected thinkers. Unless we demonstrate that we have some mastery of their ideology, they'll dismiss us as intellectual pussies. They will need proof that we're familiar with the data they favor.

We've decided, therefore, to launch a preemptive strike that will make it harder for the paranoids to dismiss us pronoiacs as naive optimists. On the next page and at four other places in this book, we've created Homeopathic Medicine Spells. They're designed to recognize the evils of the world, but in a controlled manner that prevents them from poisoning you. In this way, we can also practice what we preach, subverting any tendencies we might have toward fanaticism and unilateralism.

Each Homeopathic Medicine Spell consists of a contained space within which lies a recitation of Very Bad Things. The border around each space is a magical seal that we consecrated during a ritual invocation of the Cackling Goddess Who Eternally Creates Us Anew. Inspired through communion with Her fierce jokes, we also surrounded each seal with good mojo in the form of word charms and talismanic symbols.

As you gaze at the Homeopathic Medicine Spells, you'll be building up your protection against the dangers named inside the contained space. You'll also get intuitions about how to dissolve the pop nihilistic toxins within you that resonate with those dangers.

namaste

bravo

eureka

aloha

blessed be

viva

hallelujah

rowdy blessings

shalom

abracadabra

whoopee

In lak'ech—A lak'en

mitakuye oyasin

kudos

The earth is in the midst of the greatest mass extinction since the disappearance of the dinosaurs 65 million years ago. Half of all species may be exterminated by 2100. The Air Force has fighter planes with radar scopes that can detect the body heat of an infant from 20,000 feet. About 37 million Americans take antidepressants. Only 15 percent of the shoppers in a grocery store express line obey the ten-item limit. Heart disease is the worst epidemic since the medieval plague. By the time girls reach seventeen, 78 percent are unhappy with their bodies. Living within one's means is un-American; the economy would collapse if consumers did it. The U.S. is the biggest arms dealer in the world, having sold more than $142 billion of weaponry since 1992, much of it to non-democratic regimes whose soldiers regularly commit human rights abuses. Sperm counts are falling. Many clothes worn by Americans are made by youngsters working long hours in brutal conditions for paltry wages. Some of the biggest banks in the world turn a blind eye to money laundering. The average home is swimming in a noxious cocktail of chemicals that have been linked to allergies, cancers, and infertility. Three million children are abused and three million women are the victims of domestic violence. Blatantly totalitarian government is unnecessary because the mass audience eagerly participates in its own brainwashing. Studies show no relationship between an eyewitness's confidence and the accuracy of his testimony. The Red Cross says half of all war casualties are civilians caught in the crossfire. Aggressive advertising to children is increasing. True "personality" as we know it has begun to die out as more people perform imitations of celebrities they admire. The U.S. has the most overweight population and the highest infant mortality rate in the West, and is the only major industrialized nation besides South Africa without nationalized health care. The U.S. has the world's largest prison population and the highest rate of incarceration. Most pesticides on the market have not been tested for their ability to cause genetic damage. "People do not want God, people want to enslave God to their whim," says Da Avabhasa. Americans waste $12 billion of food a year. Many seemingly nice people cynically use honesty, cheerfulness, and openness to manipulate others into doing things their way. Over 80 million Americans live on incomes estimated by the U.S. Department of Labor as below a "comfortable adequacy," and 35 million of these live below the poverty level. The world's rain forests are disappearing at a rate of 80 acres per minute. He who dies with the most toys does NOT win. A million school children are treated with powerful mind control drugs for "hyperactivity" every year, with side effects like weight loss, growth retardation, and acute psychosis. Everyone tells at least one lie every day.

WORLD KISS

To love the Goddess the way she wants to be loved, we've got to be in love with all of her creation, not just the parts that we personally find beautiful and helpful and interesting. We've got to feel a burning, churning ache of holy longing for every single thing she has made. How, then, could any of us remain content with being mere heterosexuals? That would be a blasphemous limitation. The same is true about homosexuality and bisexuality. They're equally narrow and quaint.

Even bestiality doesn't go far enough. Nor does the flower boinking of the Essenes, or the sky copulations of the Illuminati, or the ritual fisting of the Mediterranean Sea by the ancient Sapphic cults.

If we want to commune with the world the way the Goddess does, we've got to be Pantheosexuals—adepts in the art of Polymorphous Perverse Omnidirectional Goddess Diddling. Anything less is a lie, an obscene limitation.

With this in mind, I invite you to perform the ritual of the World Kiss. Here's how: Summon your most expansive feeling of tenderness—similar to what you might experience when infatuated with a new lover—and then blow kisses to all of creation. Blow kisses to the oak trees and sparrows and cougars and weeds. Blow kisses to the wind and rain and rocks and machines. Blow kisses to the salesmen and nurses and clerks and hackers.

With each World Kiss you bestow, keep uppermost in your emotions a mood of irreverent adoration and horny compassion. And remember that it's not enough simply to perform the outer gesture; you've got to have a *heart-on* in each of your seven chakras.

As you unleash your barrage of World Kisses, you might also want to contemplate the love spells that history's greatest World Kissers have bequeathed to us. Try these:

Rainer Maria Rilke: "For one human being to love another is the most difficult task of all. It's the work for which all other work is mere preparation."

Teilhard de Chardin: "Someday after we have mastered the winds, the waves, and gravity, we will harness for God the energies of love; and then for a second time in the history of the world, human beings will have discovered fire."

Leo Tolstoy: "Love is life. All, everything that I understand, I understand only because I love. Everything is, everything exists, only because I love."

Blaise Pascal: "If you do not love too much, you do not love enough."

Emily Dickinson: "Until you have loved, you cannot become yourself."

To get you in the mood and to demonstrate the technique, I'm blowing World Kisses right now, as I sit in the garden in front of my house and write down these words.

I'm blowing World Kisses to the dirt below me and the hyacinths brushing my elbows. I'm blowing World Kisses to the persimmon tree near my front door and to the neighbor's cat gazing up into the persimmon branches. I'm blowing World Kisses to the ants snaking along the cracked sidewalk across the street and to the orange butterfly perched on the tip of the antenna of my Honda Accord.

My World Kisses fly further, reaching where I can't go right now. I blow World Kisses to you, wherever you are, and to your loved ones. I blow World Kisses to the Norwegian widower working as a welder on an offshore oil rig near Nigeria, and to the poet playing cards with her nine-year-old granddaughter in the bus station in Quetzaltenango, Guatemala, and to the head cook at the Hotel de la Sûre in Esch-sur-Sûre, Luxembourg.

I'm not afraid of running out of love. The more I give, the more I have to give.

I blow World Kisses to what some people (not me) call inanimate objects: to the Black Hills of South Dakota, and to Picasso's *Guernica* in the Reina Sofía National Museum in Madrid, and to the rolls of blue Saxony Plush carpet in the Carpeteria store on East Tropicana Avenue in Las Vegas. I blow World Kisses to all the stone walls in Ontario, and to the tornado outside the city of Suhumi on the Black Sea coast, and to the 15-year-old backhoe rusting in a junkyard in Montevideo, Uruguay.

I blow World Kisses to the woman who fooled me into thinking she loved me, and to the rich old white politicians in Washington, D.C., who hate everything I stand for, and to the two gunmen who shot me one night many years ago in Durham, North Carolina.

Everything and everyone deserve my love.

On you and me and all of everything, I bestow my ripe blessings and boisterous bliss, and hereby declare that since my particles and your particles were ripped asunder at the Big Bang, I have fantasized obsessively of the rapturous reunion in which we now exult.

I love you more than it's possible to love anyone. I love you more than love itself.

Here's more from history's renowned World Kissers:

Ralph Waldo Emerson: "He who is in love is wise and becoming wiser, sees newly every time he looks at the object beloved, drawing from it with his eyes and his mind those virtues which it possesses."

Wolfgang Amadeus Mozart: "Love, love, love: That is the soul of genius."

André Gide: "Any thought that is not filled with love seems unholy."

Krishnamurti: "The problem, if you love it, is as beautiful as the sunset."

Henry David Thoreau: "There is no remedy for love but to love more."

Erica Jong: "Love is everything it's cracked up to be. It really is worth fighting for, being brave for, risking everything for. And the trouble is, if you don't risk everything, you risk even more."

Pablo Neruda: "Love is like a well in the wilderness where time watches over the wandering lightning."

You're hungry for the infinite, and the infinite is hungry for you

VOLCANIC PRONOIA THERAPY

Experiments and exercises in becoming a mercurial but loyal Master of Rowdy Bliss.

Write a love splurge to the person you love best or to the person you want to love best.

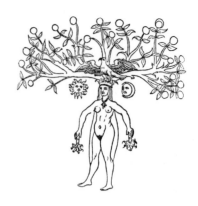

Continue your love splurge to the person you love best or to the person you want to love best.

Sacred Advertisement

"World Kiss" and your love splurge are brought to you by the state of mind the poet William Blake was enjoying when he wrote these words:

He who bends to himself a joy
Does the winged life destroy;
But he who kisses the joy
as it flies
Lives in eternity's sunrise.

LET'S MAKE MORALITY FUN

Are you turned off by the authoritarian, libido-mistrusting perversity of the right-wing moral code, but equally reluctant to embrace the atheism embedded in the left wing's code of goodness?

Are you hungry for a value system rooted in beauty, love, pleasure, and liberation instead of order, control, politeness, and fear, but allergic to the sophistry of the New Age?

Are you apathetic toward the saccharine goodness evangelized by sentimental, superstitious fanatics, but equally bored by the intellectuals who worship at the empty-hearted shrine of scientific materialism?

It may be time for you to whip up your very own moral code.

If you do, you might want to keep the following guidelines in mind:

1. A moral code becomes immoral unless it can thrive without a devil and enemy.

2. A moral code grows ugly unless it prescribes good-natured rebellion against automaton-like behavior offered in its support.

3. A moral code becomes murderous unless it's built on a love for the fact that EVERYTHING CHANGES ALL THE TIME, and unless it perpetually adjusts its reasons for being true.

4. A moral code will corrupt its users unless it ensures that their primary motivation for being good is because it's fun.

5. A moral code deadens the soul of everyone it touches unless it has a built-in sense of humor.

Do not share deep secrets with convicted felons. Do not put handfuls of dead ants in envelopes and mail them to people you're mad at. Do not wolf down greasy burgers alone in a dirty bathtub while fantasizing about making love to an inaccessible idol. Do not wake up drunk on a pool table with strange symbols painted on your body. Do not romance the neglected spouse of a corporate executive in order to pry loose insider stock tips. Do not steal something that already belongs to you or pine for people who are sitting right next to you.

HOW PRONOIA WORKS

There was once a poor farmer who could afford to own just one horse. He cared well for the animal, but one summer night, it escaped through a weak fence and ran away.

When his neighbors discovered what had happened, they visited to offer their condolences. "What bad luck!" they exclaimed. The farmer replied, "Maybe. Maybe not."

A week later, the fugitive horse sauntered back to the homestead, accompanied by six wild horses. The farmer and his son managed to corral all of them. Again the neighbors descended. "What great luck!" they exclaimed. "Maybe," the farmer replied. "Maybe not."

Soon the farmer's son began the work of taming the new arrivals. While attempting to ride the roan stallion, he was thrown to the ground and half-trampled. His leg was badly broken. The neighbors came to investigate. "What terrible luck!" they exclaimed. The farmer replied, "Maybe. Maybe not."

The next day, soldiers visited the farmer's village. Strife had recently broken out between two warlords, and one of them had come to conscript all the local young men. Though every other son was commandeered, the farmer's boy was exempted because of his injury. The neighbors gathered again. "What fantastic luck!" they exclaimed. "Maybe," the farmer said. "Maybe not."

(Source: an old Taoist folk tale)

This space has been liberated for your use

6

"I vow
to interpret every experience
as a direct dealing of the Goddess
with my soul"

What's the Most Important Question for You to Ask Today?

You are potentially a genius. Maybe not in the same way that
Einstein and Beethoven were, but still: You possess some exceptional capacity
that is absolutely unique. You're a masterpiece unlike any other that has ever lived
in the history of the world.

Furthermore, the precise instructions you need to ripen into your genius
have always been with you, even from the time before you were born. In the words
of psychologist James Hillman, you have a *soul's code.*

You might also call it the special mission you came to Earth to carry out;
the divine blueprint that contains the open secret of how to be perfectly, unpredictably
yourself; the master plan that is your heart's deepest desire.

Would you like help in deciphering it? The Divine Intelligence Formerly Known as God is
always on call, ready to help. It's your birthright to ask Her a specific question every day
about what you need to do next to express your soul's code; it's also your birthright to
receive a response.

The divine revelation may not be as unambiguous as a little voice in your head. It might
appear in the form of a TV commercial, an odd dream, or an encounter with a stranger. It
could be demanding and difficult, delivering information you'd rather not have to deal with.
Or it might show up as a clear and simple feeling of knowing exactly what to do, and it
could be easy and fun.

What question will you ask the Divine Wow today?

P.S. "There is a vitality, a life force, a quickening that is translated through you into
action, and because there is only one of you in all time, this expression is unique. If
you block it, it will never exist through any other medium. It will be lost.
The world will not have it.

"It is not your business to determine how good it is, nor how valuable it is, nor how it
compares with other expressions. It is your business to keep it yours clearly and
directly, to keep the channel open." —Martha Graham, quoted by Agnes de Mille,
Dance to the Piper and Promenade Home

Bigger, Better, More Interesting Problems

Is there anything more dangerous than getting up in the morning and having nothing to worry about, no problems to solve, no friction to heat you up? That state can be a threat to your health. If untreated, it incites an unconscious yearning for any old dumb trouble that might rouse some excitement.

Acquiring problems is a fundamental human need. It's as crucial to your well-being as getting food, air, water, sleep, and love. You define yourself—indeed, you make yourself—through the riddles you attract and solve. The most creative people on the planet are those who frame the biggest, hardest questions and then gather the resources necessary to find the answers.

Conventional wisdom implies that the best problems are those that place you under duress. There's supposedly no gain without pain. Stress is allegedly an incomparable spur for calling on resources that have been previously unavailable or dormant. Nietzsche's aphorism, "That which doesn't kill me makes me stronger," has achieved the status of an ultimate truth.

We half-agree. But it's clear that stress also accompanies many mediocre problems that have little power to make us smarter. Pain frequently generates no gain. We're all prone to become habituated, even addicted, to nagging vexations that go on and on without rousing any of our sleeping genius.

There is, furthermore, another class of difficulty—let's call it the delightful dilemma—that neither feeds on angst nor generates it. On the

77

contrary, it's fun and invigorating, and usually blooms when you're feeling a profound sense of being at home in the world. The problem of writing this book is a good example. I've had a good time handling the perplexing challenges with which it has confronted me.

Imagine a life in which at least half of your quandaries match this profile. Act as if you're most likely to attract useful problems when joy is your predominant state of mind. Consider the possibility that being in unsettling circumstances may shrink your capacity to dream up the riddles you need most; that maybe it's hard to ask the best questions when you're preoccupied fighting rearguard battles against boring or demeaning annoyances that have plagued you for many moons.

Prediction: As an aspiring lover of pronoia, you will have a growing knack for gravitating toward wilder, wetter, more interesting problems. More and more, you will be drawn to the kind of gain that doesn't require pain. You'll be so alive and awake that you'll cheerfully push yourself out of your comfort zone in the direction of your personal frontier well before you're forced to do so by divine kicks in the ass.

In Chinese, the word "crisis" is composed of two characters. One represents danger, the other opportunity. There has been no English equivalent until now.

The Beauty and Truth Laboratory has retooled an English term to convey a similar meaning: "kairos." Originally borrowed from Greek, "kairos" has traditionally meant "time of destiny, critical turning point, propitious moment for decision or action." In its most precise usage, it refers to a special season that is charged with significance and is outside of normal time; its opposite is the Greek *chronos,* which refers to the drone of the daily rhythm.

These meanings provide the root of our new definition of the word. As of now, when used in the context of a discussion of pronoia, "kairos" will have the sense of "a good crisis, rich problem, productive difficulty."

"We should feel excited about the problems we confront and our ability to deal with them," says Robert Anton Wilson. "Solving problems is one of the highest and most sensual of all our brain functions."

The definition of "happiness" in the Beauty and Truth Laboratory's "Outlaw Dictionary of Pronoiac Memes" is "the state of mind that results from cultivating interesting, useful problems."

SACRED ADVERTISEMENT

Kairos is brought to you by the mosquito that kept you up all night that one time, leading you to call in sick for work the next day and end up spending the unexpected free time rethinking your whole life and deciding to make a move that changed everything for the better.

INTIMATE PRONOIA THERAPY

**Experiments and exercises
in becoming a
radically curious, wildly
disciplined, ironically sincere
Master of Sacred Uproar**

Report your answers & research results here

1 Celebrate Unhappy Hour at least once a month. During this ritual blowout, you have license to complain and rant about everything that's driving you crazy. Get a sympathetic listener to be your receptacle or deliver your blast straight into the mirror. If you prefer, write it all down. One way or another, grouse nonstop about your secret shame, raw sorrow, bottomless wrath, unspeakable guilt, and unnerving twists of destiny. Feel free to unleash guttural moans or rueful cackles.

If performed regularly, Unhappy Hour serves as an exorcism that empties you of psychic toxins. Pronoia will then have a chance to flourish as you luxuriate more frequently in rosy moods and broad-minded visions.

2 Describe a past event when you let yourself wander to the edge of unreasonable joy. Then imagine a future adventure that might once again bring you there.

3 If you've ever watched *The Simpsons* TV show, you've probably heard Homer Simpson's favorite toast. "To alcohol," he proclaims, "the cause of and solution to all of life's problems." My own salute is different. "To the Divine Trickster formerly known as God," I say, "the cause of and solution to all of life's problems." Compose a prayer in which you simultaneously curse and thank the Primal Source.

4 The English language is in a state of rapid ferment. New words are barging into the dictionary at an unprecedented rate, even as old familiars fall into disuse. There's one exception to this trend: profanity. Hoary favorites like "fuck," "shit," and "asshole" have gained an acceptance unthinkable 30 years ago, but fresh curse words are rarely coined.

At the Beauty and Truth Lab, we find the overused classics inadequate for expressing our evolving rage at injustice, ignorance, and ugliness. Furthermore, as deadening clichés, they don't satisfy the pronoiac mandate to use language with sonorous precision.

There's another problem. Anger has become one of the trendiest emotions of all. In moderation it can be a righteous force for constructive change. But its hackneyed omnipresence means the vast majority of its outbreaks are trivial. The paucity of colorful obscenities is aggravated by an abundance of frivolous fury.

How can you purge the clichéd ire that dilutes the useful, inspired stuff? One good method is to make fun of it by expressing it bigger than life. Try this. Go alone to a place where it's safe to feel blind rage. Envision a person or thing you love to hate, then unleash the following mantra 15 times in the most vulgar tones possible: "You miasmic heap of shaved-off cemetery warts. You mangled preen of politicians' tongue scabs. You brackish tripe of experts' ego tinkles. You fragile crap of orphaned tyrants. You demented cluster of fickle weasel vows. You curdled slosh of rotting fracas-spawned opinions."

Now how about if you get to work helping us coin a new generation of profanities? For more inspiration, see "New Curse Words" at www.halfbakery.com/idea/ New_20Curse_20Words.

5 Feminist writer Elizabeth Hilts redeemed the misogynist word "bitch" in her book *Getting in Touch With Your Inner Bitch.* Gays proudly appropriated the previously derogatory word "queer" to describe themselves, thereby celebrating their outré power. In this tradition, the Beauty and Truth Laboratory proposes to reclaim the curse, "Go fuck yourself," turning it into a sincere wish that the person to whom it is addressed will indulge in life-affirming, self-administered pleasure to the point of rapture.

Now go fuck yourself.

6 "Americans live inside their own private echo chambers," says syndicated writer Matt Zoller Seitz, "endlessly revisiting things they already know they like and avoiding exposure to anything new and different." Your assignment is to ask yourself if you fit Seitz's description, and then—if you do—to escape your private echo chamber. So for instance, if you're a tattooed pagan performance artist, attend a rodeo or NASCAR race; if you're a Christian Girl Scout leader, listen to Ani DiFranco or Radiohead, or read Noam Chomsky's radical cri-

Intimate Pronoia Therapy

tiques of American foreign policy. If you're an atheistic intellectual, take a workshop in ecstatic Sufi dancing or a class in Buddhist meditation.

7 Kick your own ass 22 times a day for the next 22 days. There's no single right way to perform this exercise, so experiment. My favorite technique is to jump off the ground with both feet and snap my heels forcefully backwards against the target area.

8 Qabalist teacher Ann Davies told a story about a U.S. Army general negotiating with a cannibal chief in New Guinea during World War II. The general wanted the chief to rally his tribe to help American troops fight the Japanese. The chief refused, calling the Americans immoral. The general was shocked. "We are not immoral!" he protested. "The Japanese are immoral!" The cannibal chief replied, "The Japanese and Americans are equally immoral. You both kill far more people than you can eat."

Using this tale as your impetus, describe how parts of your own moral code are not rooted in an absolute standard of what's good and evil, but rather bound by the idiosyncrasies of your culture and historical era.

9 In 752 A.D., the Japanese Empress Koken wrote a lyrical poem in praise of the eupatorium plant, whose leaves turn a vivid shade of yellow in summer. Recently, scientists demonstrated that the lovely foliage of the eupatorium is caused by a disease virus. In my view, this shouldn't diminish our appreciation of either the poem or the plant. Beauty sometimes forms in response to a wound. Give examples from your own life.

10 Cancer cells are constantly developing in our bodies. Luckily, our immune systems routinely kill them off. Similarly, our minds always harbor pockets of crazy-making misconceptions and faulty imprints. They usually don't rise up and render us insane thanks to the psychic versions of our immune systems.

How can you stay strong in your ability to fight off sickness and madness? You know the drill: Eat healthy food, sleep well, get physical exercise, minimize stress, give and receive love. But as an aspiring pronoiac, you have at your disposal other actions that can provide powerful boosts to your immune system. Here are examples:

Scheme to put yourself in the path of beautiful landscapes, buildings, art, and creatures.

Intimate Pronoia Therapy

Exercise your imagination regularly. Get in the habit of feeding your mind's eye images that fill you with wonder and vitality.

Eliminate *uhs, you knows, I means,* and other junk words from your speech. Avoid saying things you don't really mean and haven't thought out. Stop yourself when tempted to make scornful assertions about people.

Every night before you fall asleep, review the day's activities in your mind's eye. As if watching a movie about yourself, try to be calmly objective as you observe your memories from the previous 16 hours. Be especially alert for moments when you strayed from your purpose and didn't live up to your highest standards.

With a companion, sit in front of a turned-off TV as you make up a pronoiac story that features tricky benevolence, scintillating harmony, and amusing redemption. Speak this tale aloud or write it down.

Take on an additional job title, *beautifier.* Put it on your business card and do something every day to cultivate your skill. If you're a people person, bring grace and intrigue into your conversations; ask unexpected questions that provoke original thoughts. If you're an artist, leave samples of your finest work in public places. If you're a psychologist or sociologist, point out the institutions and relationships that are working really well. Whatever you do best, be alert for how you can refine it and offer it up to those who'll benefit from it.

If you're going through a phase when you feel you have nothing especially beautiful to offer, or if you think it would be self-indulgent to inject your own aesthetic into shared environments, turn for help to great artists and thinkers. Sneak O'Keeffe or Chagall prints onto unadorned walls in public places, for instance. Memorize poems by Rilke and Hafiz, and slip them into your conversations when appropriate. Program your cell phone so that its ring is Vivaldi's *Stabat Mater in C Minor.* Scrawl passages from Annie Dillard's *Teaching a Stone to Talk* on the walls of public lavatories.

11 Write an essay on "What I Swear I'll Never Do Again as Long as I Live—Unless I Can Get Away With It Next Time."

12 Take off your mask. You say you're not wearing a mask? But you are. The muscles of your face are so accustomed to displaying your familiar emotions, they've gotten stuck. Raw new emotions are aching to show themselves, but can't dislodge the incumbents.

Intimate Pronoia Therapy

Start an exercise program. Gaze into the mirror and make hundreds of rubbery faces. Loosen and tone your muscles. Flush those ancient expressions.

13 Many concepts we use to interpret our experience originated in books written by people who are long gone. That's why philosopher Norman O. Brown (who died in 2002) says in his book *Apocalypse and/or Metamorphosis,* "The bondage to books compels us not to see with our own eyes; compels us to see with the eyes of the dead, with dead eyes. There is a hex on us, the authority of the past; and to exorcise these ghosts is the great work of magical self-liberation."

Melville Davisson Post (who died in 1930) echoes the theme in his book *Uncle Abner, Master of Mysteries.* "It is the dead who govern. Look how they work their will upon us! Who have made the laws? The dead! Who have made the customs that we obey and that form and shape our lives? The dead! All the writers, when they would give weight and authority to their opinions, quote the dead. Our lives follow grooves that the dead have run out with their thumbnails!"

Whose dead eyes do you see with? What would it be like to see the world without them?

14 Create or obtain a symbol of your most inconsolable pain. Mail it to us at the Beauty and Truth Laboratory. We will conduct a ritual of purification during which we will burn that symbol to ash as we pray for your relief. While this may not eradicate your anguish entirely, we're confident it will provide a tangible healing that you'll feel the benefits of within a month. Send a representation of what hurts you most to Angst Incinerator, P.O. Box 150628, San Rafael, CA 94915.

15 Charles Darwin said the "survival of the fittest" is a central factor in the process of evolution. What exactly did he mean by that? He makes it clear in his book, *The Origin of Species*: "It is not the strongest of the species that survive, nor the most intelligent, but the ones most responsive to change."

What would you have to do to make yourself superbly fit according to Darwin's definition?

16 "Watch out for the dark side of your own idealism and of your moral sense," says Howard Bloom. "Both come from our arsenal of natural instincts. And both easily degenerate into an excuse for attacks on others. When our righteous indignation breathes the flames of anger against a 'villain,' we all too often become a fang in nature's scheme of tooth and claw." What's the dark side of your idealism and morality?

17 "Whether I shall turn out to be the hero of my own life, or whether that station will be held by anybody else, these pages must show." So begins Charles Dickens' novel *David Copperfield.* Buy a blank book and write that sentence at the top of page one.

18 Thank you for not smoking while communing with this subliminal prod. Thank you as well for not burping, drooling, picking your nose, getting drunk, spilling food on yourself, thinking nasty thoughts about anyone, and letting your mind leap from undisciplined ideas to out-of-control feelings like a mean monkey on methamphetamine. All such behaviors would interfere with your ability to register on deep subconscious levels the meaning of this subliminal prod, which is: Sometimes you've got to be a bit of an asshole in order to avoid getting burned by the ass-souls. Do you agree? Provide evidence pro or con.

19 Computer programmer Garry Hamilton articulated the following "Game Rules" on his website, www.c2.com/cgi/wiki?GarryHamilton. Give examples of how they have worked in your life.

1. If the game is rigged so you can't win, find another game or invent your own. 2. If you're not winning because you don't know the rules, learn the rules. 3. If you know the rules but aren't willing to follow them, there's either something wrong with the game or you need to change something in yourself. 4. Don't play the game in a half-baked way. Either get all the way in or all the way out. 5. It shouldn't be necessary for others to lose in order for you to win. If others have to lose, re-evaluate the game's goals.

20 Here's the catch about pronoia: Life always gives you exactly what you need, exactly when you need it, but it doesn't necessarily give you exactly what you want, exactly when you want it. Talk about the differences between what you want and what you need.

21 Write a letter to the person you'll be one year from today. Tell this Future You that you've taken a vow to accomplish three feats by then. Say why these feats are more important to you than anything else. Describe them. Brainstorm about what you'll do to make them happen. Draw pictures or make collages that capture your excitement about them.

PRONOIA NEWS NETWORK

Inexorable Beat of Freedom   For more than 30 years, Freedom House has evaluated the global state of civil liberties, democratic institutions, and independent media. Its research suggests that the world is steadily becoming more free. In a press release issued in December 2002, it reported that of the world's 192 nations, 117 were electoral democracies. "All provide considerable political space and media access for opposition movements," it said, "and allow for elections that meet minimum international standards of ballot secrecy and vote tabulation."

In a more thorough analysis published in 2003, Freedom House said that the 89 most free countries control 89 percent of the world's Gross Domestic Product. It concluded that the majority of the planet's economic, technological, and military resources belong to democracies. (Source: www.freedomhouse.org)

PNN is brought to you by Emily Dickinson's passion. She "could never understand why the most intense human experiences had to be relegated to the margins of human society," wrote Edward Hirsch in American Poetry Review. *"She read poetry and wrote every day because she needed a daily dose of ecstasy, the elation and exhilaration poetry provides."*

Green Business Rising   Toyota plans to use gasoline-electric hybrid engines in all of its vehicles by 2012. The company pioneered hybrids in 1997, when it first sold the Prius, a car that gets 50 miles per gallon of gas and emits 40 percent less carbon dioxide than a traditional engine. The third largest automaker in the world, Toyota has inspired the top two to play catch-up. General Motors and Ford both introduced their own hybrids in 2004.

Rapture Update   The World Health Organization reports that over 100 million acts of sexual intercourse, involving more than 200 million partners, take place on the earth every 24 hours. According to the Beauty and Truth Laboratory, if even one out of every two of those communions is motivated by love, the planet is continuously awash with tender ecstasy.

Almost More Good Luck Than You Can Bear   "The rise of modernity served many extraordinary purposes: the rise of democracy; the banishing of slavery; the emergence of liberal feminism; the differentiation of art and science and morality; the widespread emergence of empirical sciences; an increase in average life span of almost three decades; the introduction of relativity and perspectivism in art and morals and science; the move from ethnocentric to world-centric morality; and the undoing of dominator social hierarchies." —Ken Wilber, *A Brief History of Everything*

Naked Heroism

The ancient Celts used to go into battle stark naked. They believed that only utter vulnerability demonstrated their total trust in the gods, who alone could make them invincible and who alone determined whether they would live or die. This brazen yet humble show of confidence often provoked primal fear in their enemies.

In 2002, 600 women from Nigeria's oil-rich Niger Delta invoked a similar approach to combat, launching a protest against U.S. oil giant ChevronTexaco. The women wanted the company to plow back some of its profits into their impoverished community, from whose land it was taking the oil. To drive home their demands, they threatened to commit a traditional shaming gesture—taking off their clothes. Nigerian tribes regard public displays of nudity by wives, mothers, and grandmothers as a damning protest that casts shame on those at whom the action is directed.

The tactic worked. To prevent the show of nakedness, ChevronTexaco gave in to the women, agreeing to hire villagers and build schools and electrical and water systems.

During the invasion of Iraq in 2003, groups of American, English, and Australian women, inspired by the Nigerians, registered their dissent through mass nudity. "In complete vulnerability there's a mighty well of power," said Australian singer and peace activist Grace Knight.

What If Everything's Alive?

Yua is a term the Yupiit people of Alaska use for the spirit that inhabits all things, both animate and inanimate. A rock, for instance, has as much *yua* as a caribou, spruce tree, or human being, and therefore merits the same measure of compassion. If a Yupiit goes out for a hike and spies a chunk of wood lying on a frozen river bank, she might pick it up and put it in a new position, allowing its previously hidden side to get fresh air and sun. In this way, she would bestow a blessing on the wood's yua. (Source: Earl Shorris, "The Last Word," *Harper's,* August 2000)

Gross National Happiness

Calculated annually, the Gross National Product (GNP) is the standard by which countries gauge their prosperity. In an age when other values are subservient to the obsession with material wealth, the GNP is in essence a measure of the current worth of the Holy Grail.

In recent years the Buddhist nation of Bhutan has rebelled against this vulgarity, proposing a different accounting system: Gross National Happiness (GNH). While it takes into consideration economic development, it also includes factors like the preservation of the environment, enrichment of the culture, and quality of governance.

Here's an example of how Bhutan has raised its GNH. Its scenic beauty could potentially generate a huge tourist industry. But strict limits have been placed on the numbers of foreign visitors, ensuring the land won't be trampled and despoiled.

Epic Collaboration

You are a metropolis of 50 trillion citizens, says biologist Dr. Bruce Lipton. Each of the cells in your body can be considered a sentient being in its own right. They all act together as a community, performing an ongoing act of prodigious collaboration.

Best Story and Storyteller of the Millennium

What was the best story of the previous millennium? Not Dante's *The Divine Comedy* or Cervantes' *Don Quixote* or Tolstoy's *War and Peace* or Joyce's *Portrait of the Artist as a Young Man,* at least according to Booker Prize-winning author A.S. Byatt. Writing in *The New York Times,* she named *The Thousand and One Nights* as the most surpassingly brilliant tale of the last thousand years.

In full agreement with Byatt's assessment, the Beauty and Truth Laboratory further names Scheherazade, narrator of *The Thousand and One Nights,* as the craftiest heroine in all of world literature. She saves her own life and those of countless other women as she diverts her husband from his murderous compulsion through the gentle pyrotechnics of her imagination. By the time she has finished telling her tales, drawing from her profound understanding of human nature, she has borne three children and humanized the misogynist tyrant who had terrorized the kingdom.

War No More

Here are some of the long-running wars and conflicts that have had significant breakthroughs since 2000:

Rwanda and the Democratic Republic of Congo signed a peace agreement to end a conflict that killed 2.5 million people and thus was often referred to as "Africa's World War."

After three decades of a civil war in which half a million lives were lost, the Angolan government and the UNITA rebel movement signed a cease-fire.

The ethnic Tamil Tigers separatist rebels and the Sri Lankan government signed a cease-fire agreement and are engaged in peace talks.

The 10-year civil war in Sierra Leone, which killed up to 50,000 people, came to an end in a celebration that included a symbolic bonfire of thousands of weapons gathered from both government troops and rebels.

Ethiopia and Eritrea negotiated and signed a peace accord, ending their border war.

A few years ago East Timor was described as an "unimaginable, apocalyptic ruin" by UN peacekeepers. More than 200,000 people had died during a 25-year struggle to separate from Indonesia. But after finally gaining its independence, the new nation is now prospering in peace.

Domestic Bliss

"For the first time in history, more than half of central city households are homeowners. This increase has been led by African-American and Hispanic families, whose homeownership rates have been increasing the fastest."
—www. goodnewsnetwork.org

Adoration Reborn

"The insulted waters of New York City are again sacred passages, as they once were to Native Americans for millennia. Raw sewage no longer pours into vital waterways, and industrial pollution has largely been checked. We are witnessing the ecological resurrection of our rivers and bays, from the return of wood-eating gribbles and shipworms that devour our piers to winter visits by a small seal community. People are coming down to the water again to see rare birds, to kayak and to swim. And responding to an ancient call, they're coming down to the water to pray. Among the worshipers are Hindus, Shintoists, African Americans of the Yoruba-influenced Spiritual Baptist faith, Wiccans, Zoroastrians, Christians, and Jews." —Erik Baard, *Village Voice,* www.villagevoice.com/issues/0223/baard.php

PNN is made possible in part by the renegade Sufis who say they're as likely to bask in the sweetness of enlightenment while cooking a frozen burrito in a microwave oven under the fluorescent lights of a convenience store as when they're meditating on a straw mat in a remote mountain sanctuary.

Future Studies

"Consider the oak beams in the ceiling of College Hall at Oxford. Last century, when the beams needed replacing, carpenters used oak trees that had been planted in 1386 when the dining hall was first built. The fourteenth-century builder had planted trees in anticipation of the time, hundreds of years in the future, when the beams would need replacing." —Danny Hills, *Wired*

From the Field

Beauty and Truth Laboratory researcher Ariel Guzman saw this sign at a beauty salon in Ohio: "If truth is beauty, why doesn't anyone have their hair done at the library?"

Breaking the Pronoia Taboo

"Know what you want and all the universe conspires to help you achieve it." —Paulo Coelho, *The Alchemist*

"The task of genius, and humanity is nothing if not genius, is to keep the miracle alive, to live always in the miracle, to make the miracle more and more miraculous, to swear allegiance to nothing, but live only miraculously, think only miraculously, die miraculously." —Henry Miller, *The Colossus of Maroussi*

"The soul should always stand ajar,
That if the heaven inquire,
He will not be obliged to wait,
Or shy of troubling her."
—Emily Dickinson, Poem 1055, *Complete Poems of Emily Dickinson*

"Humankind was put on earth to keep the heavens aloft. When we fail, creation remains unfinished." —Rabbi Menachem Mendel, known as the Kotzker Rebbe

"I hunger for your sleek laugh and your hands the color of a furious harvest. I want to eat the sunbeams flaring in your beauty." —Pablo Neruda, *100 Love Sonnets*

"The world is full of magical things patiently waiting for our wits to grow sharper." —Bertrand Russell

"Love the earth and the sun and animals, despise riches, give alms to everyone that asks, stand up for the stupid and the crazy, devote your income and labors to others, hate tyrants, argue not concerning God, re-examine all you have been told at school or church or in any book, dismiss whatever insults your own soul, and your very flesh shall be a great poem and have the richest fluency." —Walt Whitman, *Leaves of Grass*

"Love is the most difficult and dangerous form of courage. Courage is the most desperate, admirable, and noble kind of love." —Delmore Schwartz

"There is always some madness in love. But there is also always some reason in madness." —Friedrich Nietzsche

"In the world there is nothing more submissive and weak than water. Yet for attacking that which is hard and strong nothing can surpass it." —Lao Tzu

Gender Revolution Legalized

Sweden has been a pioneer in bringing gender balance into government. Forty-five percent of its parliament is female.

Other nations have finally begun to follow its lead. In 2003, the Welsh assembly became the first legislative body in history to have as many women as men. Meanwhile, Denmark, Finland, Norway, Iceland, the Netherlands, Germany, Argentina, Costa Rica, South Africa, and Mozambique have at least 30 percent of their parliamentary seats filled by women, largely due to legally mandated quotas.

Rwanda's new constitution calls for 30 percent of decision-making positions to be held by women. In the parliamentary elections of 2003, that quota was exceeded, as women captured 49 percent of the legislative seats.

The corporate domain is proceeding toward equality more slowly. Norway is the first and only nation to pass laws mandating female representation on corporate boards, requiring a 40 percent quota.

This perfect moment is brought to you by by the mummified middle finger of Galileo's right hand, which is on display at a museum in Florence, Italy. May it inspire you to flip the metaphorical bird at anyone who proudly embodies the kind of high-level idiocy Galileo had to endure.

THIS DAY IN PRONOIAC HISTORY

The World Wildlife Fund has fought to save endangered species since 1961. Its logo features a panda bear. The World Wrestling Federation launched in 1962, and has made a fortune selling staged combats between steroid-inflamed loonies. One of its best-selling items is the "Undertaker Big Evil Red Devil T-shirt." So which of these WWFs won the skirmish between the two? The good guys. A court ruled that the panda lovers had a superior claim to the initials WWF. The devils had to change their name. It's now World Wrestling Entertainment.

Black South Africans fought for 40 years to dismantle the oppressive system of apartheid. One of their most potent weapons was toyi-toyi, a militantly exuberant form of singing and dancing. It served to mobilize the energy of crowds at the large protest demonstrations that ultimately broke the will of the white minority rulers. Imagine how confounded their authoritarian minds must have been when confronted by thousands of high-spirited activists passionately singing and dancing in unison.

Science Poetry

"Our skin shares its chemistry with the maple leaf and moth wing. The currents our bodies regulate share a molecular flow with raw sun. Nerves and flashes of lightning are related events woven into nature at different levels." —Richard Grossinger, *Planet Medicine*

"I am part of the sun as my eye is part of me. That I am part of the earth, my feet know perfectly, and my blood is part of the sea. There is nothing of me that is alone and isolate, except my mind, and we shall find that the mind has no existence by itself, but is only the glitter of the sun on the surface of the waters." —D.H. Lawrence, *Apocalypse and the Writings on Revelation*

MIRABILIA REPORT   *Mirabilia* n. beguiling ephemera, inexplicable joys, changes that inspire quiet awe; from the Latin *mirabilia*, "marvels."

■ The sky not only isn't falling—it's rising. The top of the troposphere, the atmosphere's lowest layer, is slowly ascending.

■ Less than 25 percent of American households are composed of nuclear families.

■ The largest living thing in the world is a 2,400-acre underground fungus in Oregon. It has no name yet.

■ Anarchists claimed responsibility for the March 2001 earthquake in the Pacific Northwest, saying the deed was accomplished with a spell cast by the Green Fire coven of anarchist witches.

■ For $900, you can arrange for the manufacture of 12 action figures that look like you.

■ Some Christians really do love their enemies, as Jesus recommended.

■ In 2001, 16 refugees from the Dominican Republic were lost at sea for 12 days while fleeing across shark-infested waters to a better life in Puerto Rico. To save themselves from death by dehydration, they sucked milk from the breasts of a nursing mother who was among them.

■ More than four million Americans believe they've been abducted by extraterrestrials. On average, Americans eat 18 acres of pizza every day.

■ Anthropologists say that in every culture in history, children have played the game hide and seek.

The Rich Get Richer

"Dear Beauty and Truth Laboratory: Help! My old Buick's transmission is dead, my credit cards are maxed, my kid's got to see the dentist real bad, and the one-speed bike I ride everywhere is about to collapse. I'm working two low-paying jobs already, although I just applied for a more lucrative gig as a strip-club dancer, only I'm having so much mysterious pain in my joints I'm not sure how sexy my gyrations will be. Please clue me in to some tricks that will help me keep a pronoiac attitude in the midst of the mess that is my life. —Pickled"

Dear Pickled: Here's the first thing I want to tell you: Pronoia does not assume that material comfort is a sign of divine favor. The universe is an equal-opportunity provider, conspiring to shower blessings on every one of us in the same abundance. But while the blessings *may* come in the form of money and possessions, they're just as likely to consist of other gifts that aren't as concrete.

Here's a hypothetical example. Let's say you have the gift of feeling at home in the world no matter where you are. The universe has determined that it's the exact skill you need in order to fulfill the specific purpose you came to earth to carry out. Having a prestigious job and big salary, on the other hand, might be exactly what you *don't* need.

The question of what gifts are essential revolves around your precise role in the universal conspiracy to perpetrate blessings.

The second meditation I'll offer you is a passage from the Gospel of Matthew: "Whoever has, shall be given more and more, while whoever has nothing, even what he has will be taken away from him."

Pronoiac translation: Whatever you choose to focus your attention on, you will get more of it. If you often think of everything you lack and how sad you are that you don't have it, you will tend to receive prolific evidence of how true that is. As you obsess on all the ways your life is different from what you wish it would be, you will become an expert in rousing feelings of frustration and you will attract experiences that assist you in rousing frustration.

If, on the other hand, you dwell on the good things you have already had the privilege to experience, you will expand your appreciation for their blessings, which in turn will amplify their beneficent impact on your life. You will also magnetize yourself to receive further good things, making it more likely that they will be attracted into your sphere. At the very least, you will get in the habit of enjoying yourself no matter what the outward circumstances are.

Bear in mind that you are a great wizard. You can use your powers to practice white magic on yourself instead of the other kind. The most basic way to do that is to concentrate on naming, savoring, and feeling gratitude for the blessings you do have—your love for your kid, the pleasures of eating the food you like, the sight of the sky at dusk, the entertaining drama of your unique fate. Don't ignore the bad stuff, but make a point of celebrating the beautiful stuff with all the exuberant devotion you can muster.

Kaohinani is a Hawaiian word meaning "gatherer of beautiful things."

SACRED ADVERTISEMENT

"The Rich Get Richer" is brought to you in part by the gesture recorded in a photograph of the Dalai Lama playfully messing with Desmond Tutu's cap at a gathering of Nobel Peace Prize winners.

FURTHER EVIDENCE

In our quest to insinuate pronoia into dinner table discussions taking place all over the world, we bring the following pieces of evidence to your attention.

Exhibit A

The bible of the mental health community is a 943-page textbook called the *Diagnostic and Statistical Manual of Mental Disorders, Fourth Edition,* or *DSM-IV.* Published by the American Psychiatric Association, it's a standardized catalog of psychological disorders that therapists use to evaluate and treat their patients. Surprise! This ultimate word on the state of the human psyche describes countless pathological states, but there's not a single entry referring to good mental health.

You might imagine that shrinks would be mildly interested not only in fixing what's wrong with their patients but also in helping them cultivate what feels good. But how can that happen if the feel-good states aren't even recognized as important enough to name?

Exhibit B

David G. Myers and Ed Diener authored an article called "The Science of Happiness," which appeared in the September/October 1997 issue of *The Futurist.* "What causes happiness?" they inquired. "This question not only went largely unanswered during psychology's first century, it went largely unasked." They note that from 1967 to 1995, essays on negative emotions far outnum-

bered those on positive emotions in the psychological literature. The ratio was 21:1.

Exhibit C

Even those supreme perpetrators of pop nihilism, *The New York Times* and *The Washington Post,* have a better ratio than the psychological literature. They average only 12 negative stories to every one that might be construed to be non-negative. Most other daily newspapers maintain a similar proportion.

Many of their non-negative stories, however, cover success in two specific fields: finance and sports. For example: NASDAQ is up today; the Atlanta Braves won their eighth straight game. Remove these feel-good stories from the equation, and the media's Curse Quotient rises closer to that of the psychological literature.

Exhibit D

In his book, *Omens of Millennium,* Harold Bloom hints at the "reductive fallacy" that serves as a shibboleth for intellectuals. Picture yourself, he says, in conversation with a bright, literate acquaintance who asks you about someone you know well: "Tell me what he or she is really like." You reflect a moment and give a brief description of your impressions, but your acquaintance isn't satisfied: "No, I mean *really* like." And now you grasp the actual question: "What is the very worst thing you can say about him or her that is true?"

※

Exhibit E

Thousands of amazing, inexplicable, wondrous, and even supernatural events occur every day. And yet most are unreported by the media. The few that are cited are ridiculed. Why? Here's one possible reason: The people most likely to believe in miracles are superstitious, uneducated, and prone to having a blind, literalist faith in their religions' myths. Those who are least likely to believe in miracles are skilled at analytical thought, well-educated, and yet prone to having a blind, literalist faith in the ideology of materialism, which dogmatically asserts that the universe consists entirely of things that can be perceived by the five human senses or detected by instruments that scientists have thus far invented.

The media is largely composed of people from the second group. It's virtually impossible for them to admit to the possibility of miracles, let alone experience them. If anyone from this group manages to escape peer pressure and cultivate a receptivity to miracles, it's because they have successfully fought against being demoralized by the unsophisticated way miracles are framed by the first group.

At the Beauty and Truth Laboratory we're immune to the double-barreled ignorance. When we behold astonishing synchronicities and numinous breakthroughs that seem to violate natural law, we're willing to consider the possibility that our understanding of natural law is too narrow. And yet we also refrain from lapsing into irrational gullibility; we actively seek mundane explanations for apparent miracles.

※

Exhibit F

Wes Nisker wrote a book called *If You Don't Like the News . . . Go Out and Make Some of Your Own.*

※

Exhibit G

If you have encountered examples of the following evidence, tell us about it. Send your testimony to the Beauty and Truth Laboratory at rebelgrail@yahoo.com or P.O. Box 150628, San Rafael, CA 94915:

1. bliss that flows toward you because you've made a habit of expecting it and cultivating it;

2. good news that's really interesting; fascinating stories that provide an antidote to the media's obsession with hardship, anguish, deterioration, and death;

3. states of emotional wealth and psychological health: raw material for the manual that will be the corrective for the *DSM-IV;* the missing half of the story;

4. mirabilia: mysterious revelations, rejuvenating prodigies, ineffable breakthroughs, beguiling ephemera, sudden deliverance from boring evils;

5. plain old everyday miracles;

6. the good news you've gone out and created.

What exactly are the 13 Perfect Secrets from the Beginning of Time, according to you?

Sacred Advertisement

The research of the Beauty and Truth Laboratory is made possible in part by the largesse of Boris Pasternak's poem, "Bacchanalia," which includes these words:
"How much courage is needed
to play forever,
as the ravines play,
as the river plays."

Everyone's a nobody—
and nobody's perfect

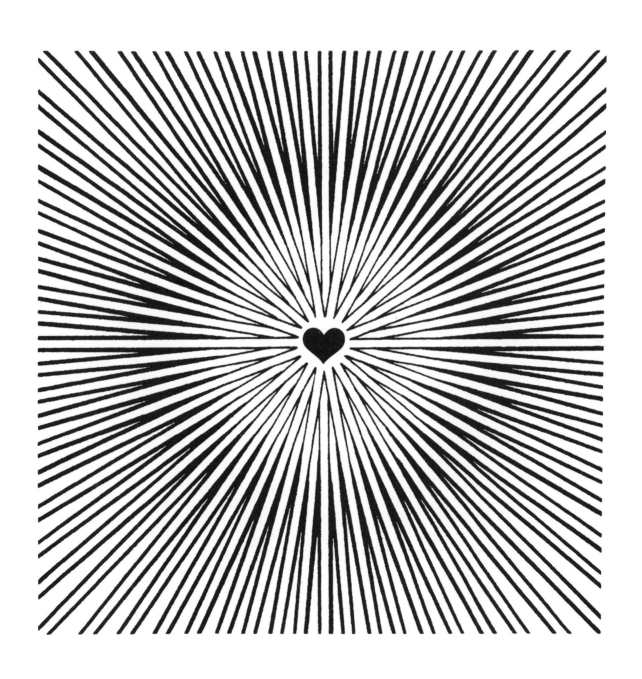

You Are Almost Everything

You taste delicious

Animals understand you

Your importance is unusual

The funny faces you make are interesting to look at

You fight for power in all the right ways

Gratitude pours out of you

You have strong feet

No one can overflow as well as you can

You are famous with God

A lost tribe salutes you from the other side of the veil

You belong to yourself

Bin Laden's Wife's Bra

For over two decades, Peter Jouvenal worked as a journalist and cameraman who filmed war-torn hot spots, including Iraq in the Gulf War and Afghanistan during the Soviet invasion. He eventually retired from that gig and bought a restaurant in Kabul. He has few regrets, but one came after the fall of the Taliban in 2001.

While exploring the organization's deserted safe houses, he happened upon a place where Osama bin Laden and his wife had lived. Among the items the couple left behind was one of her bras. In retrospect Jouvenal realized he should have pocketed the exotic piece of lingerie; a tabloid newspaper would have paid him a fortune for it. But because he had spent his entire career dealing with more mainstream news media, the idea didn't even occur to him at the time.

Keep this cautionary tale simmering in the back of your mind. Maybe it'll alert you whenever you're about to overlook a valuable thing you'd normally consider worthless.

BRAIN~ SCRAMBLING MEDITATION

Relax. Put yourself in a comfortable position. Breathe deeply. Let the tension stream out of your head and neck and shoulders. Imagine that your worries are flowing out of you into the good earth below. Say "ahhhhh" in your softest tone.

Dissolve the constricted energy in your chest and belly and pelvis, and let it trickle away. Allow the stress in your legs and feet to evaporate. With each breath, send out a wave of love to your entire body. Relax even more deeply. Become aware that all of the disquiet within you is departing. Your knots are unraveling. Your congestion is dissipating.

Now close your eyes and imagine that it's a bright and warm summer day at the beach. You're sitting in a cozy chair. The sky is a deep, infinite blue. A balmy breeze caresses your cheeks. Your body feels strong and serene. You're in harmony with the flow of life. Look around you. See the sparkling white sand. Feel the gentle waves swirl around your ankles.

As you bask in this beauty and calm, imagine that you're reading the *Wall Street Journal* and listening to the soothingly riotous music of a klezmer polka band playing free-form jazz with a hip-hop beat. Nearby is a shopping mall you have recently bought and converted into a country club for poor people. A satellite phone and a wireless laptop are by your side because you must always be available to conduct late-breaking business deals, buy or sell stocks, or give spiritual advice.

Amazing but true: You are both a billionaire *and* a wise counselor. This blend of wealth and sagacity has led you to become a philanthropic healer. Through cash donations and gifts of insight, you have helped thousands of people transform themselves into gorgeous geniuses skilled at expressing their souls' codes.

Relax even more deeply. Tune in to the understanding that you are a furiously curious soul full of orgiastic compassion for everything alive. You are an ongoing experiment in lyrical logic, a slow explosion of uncanny delight, a sacred agent devoted to breaking the taboo against feeling crafty joy.

Now say this: *I have only barely imagined the blessings that await me. As interesting and as full as my life is, I'm ready for it to become even more so.*

With this declaration, you have given the future permission to transform you into a more awakened version of yourself than you ever knew was possible.

Continue your cooperation with the glorious fate that's coming your way. Speak the following affirmations, which have been scientifically formulated to free you of all rigid beliefs that might cause stupidity:

I kick my own ass and wash my own brain.
I push my own buttons and trick my own pain.
I burn my own flags and roast my own heroes.
I mock my own fears and cheer my own zeroes.

Nothing can stop me from teasing my shadow.
I'm full of empty and backwards bravado.
My wounds are tattoos that reveal my true beauty.
I turn tragic to magic and make bliss my duty.

I honor my faults till they become virtues.
I play jokes on my nightmares
till I'm sure they won't hurt you.
I sing anarchist lullabies to lesbian trees
and love songs with punch lines
to anonymous seas.

I won't accept gifts that infringe on my freedom
I shun sacred places that stir up my boredom.
I change my name daily, pretend to be nobody.
I fight for the truth if it's majestically rowdy.

Gravity fucks me and I fuck it back.
The sun is my sex slave, the moon smokes my crack.
I pump up my conscience with idiot laughter.
I'm living happily, in love ever after.

I brag about what I can't do and don't know.
I take off my clothes to those I oppose.
I'm so far beyond lazy, I work like a god.
I'm totally crazy; in fact that's my job.

It's all true. You're completely wacko. Throbbingly, succulently, shimmeringly insane. And that's good news.

This understanding frees you up to sing in the acid rain and cultivate global warming in your pants. You are in prime condition to study the difference between stupid insecurity and smart insecurity until you get it right. You realize beyond a doubt that everyone who believes in the devil *is* the devil. You feel a longing to stick out your tongue and cross your eyes and put on your most beautifully ugly face as you sneak up on yourself from behind and whisper "boo!" And you see the healthy wisdom of now and then inserting into your conversations the following quote, uttered by the Baron in the film *The Adventures of Baron Munchausen:* "Your reality, sir, is lies and balderdash, and I'm happy to say I have no grasp of it whatsoever."

And congratulations. Every cell in your perfect animal body is beginning to purr with luminous gratitude for the enormity of the riches you endlessly receive. You are becoming aware that each of your heart's beats originates as a gift of love directly from the Goddess herself. Any residues of hatred that had been tainting your libido are leaving you for good. You are becoming telepathically linked to the world's entire host of secret teachers, pacifist warriors, philosopher clowns, and bodhisattvas disguised as convenience store clerks.

In other words, you're on the verge of détente with your evil twin. And you're ready to submit to a multiple-choice test, which goes like this:

How does it make you feel when I urge you to confess profound secrets to people who are not particularly interested? Does it make you want to:

a. cultivate a healthy erotic desire for a person you'd normally never be attracted to in a million years;

b. stop helping your friends glamorize their pain;

c. imitate a hurricane in the act of extinguishing a forest fire;

d. visualize Buddha or Mother Teresa at the moment of orgasm;

e. steal something that's already yours.

The right answer, of course, is any answer you thought was correct. Congratulations. You're even smarter than you knew..

To seal your victory, repeat the following affirmation: *"Stressed" is "desserts" spelled backward.*

Now remain here for a while in this state of supernatural relaxation. As you begin to return to normal waking consciousness, *don't* return to normal waking consciousness. Instead, practice feeling the confidence that you can invoke the scent of wild honey in a sunlit meadow any time you feel an urge to.

In honor of your enhanced power to be yourself, I hereby reward you with a host of fresh titles. From now on you will be known as the Senior Vice President of Strawberry Fields and Hummingbirds, and the Deputy Director of Green Lights and Purple Hearts. Consider yourself, as well, to be the new Puzzle-Master Supreme, the Chief Custodian of Secret Weapons, and Field Commander of Free Lunches and Poetic Licenses.

YOU ARE HERE

REAP THE BENEFITS OF YOUR SCRAMBLED BRAIN

Have you ever done automatic writing? Try it. Hold a pen with your non-dominant hand and make up a dream in which you change into an animal. Imagine a conversation with your bravest ancestor. Picture yourself inhabiting the body of the opposite gender. Describe ways you might enjoy losing your dignity. Fantasize about the possibility that there's something you really need but you don't know what it is. Channel a telepathic message from a violet chupacabra who's a great leader on a planet circling the star Gliese 876. Compose a prayer in which you ask for something you're not supposed to.

Apocalypse Versus Apocalypse

The chauvinism I suffer from is a peculiar variety. I don't have delusions of grandeur about my religion, country, or football team, but rather of the era I live in. I fantasize that our moment in history is more important than all the others. Those of us alive today are on the cusp of a radical turning point in the evolution of humanity. Or so I like to imagine.

It's embarrassing. It associates me with wacky millenarians of all stripes, from histrionic New Age prophets to fundamentalist Christians who fanatically anticipate the "end times." And as much as I would like to imagine my views are subtler and more rational than those of the superstitious extremists, I must admit that I sometimes catch myself dreaming of how deliriously interesting it would be if the mass hallucination that is mistakenly referred to as "reality" really did mutate "in the twinkling of an eye," as the Bible insinuates.

Did I scoff at the scaremongers who shivered at the approach of Y2K? Well, yeah, I mostly did. But there was also a Drama King in a dark corner of my psyche who indulged in perversely thrilling chimeras about the possibility that the melodramatic doomsayers might be right. A similar reflex put me in alignment with the Nostradamus wannabes who forecast "earth changes" and a global economic depression in the face of the massive conjunction of planets in the astrological sign of Taurus in May 2000.

In recent years, a month rarely goes by when my inner Drama King doesn't pounce on some new sign of imminent upheaval. Endgame scenarios are no longer solely the province of certifiable cranks and paranoids. Scientists speculate on the odds of the earth getting blasted by an asteroid similar to the one that apparently wiped out the dinosaurs 65 million years ago. Medical researchers raise the specter of SARS and novel strains of the flu turning into out-of-control pandemics. Seemingly sane politicians and journalists insist on cramming our imaginations full of visions of terrorist-delivered suitcase nukes and killer bioweapons.

But there is another part of me, a voice that feels older and wiser, who suspects that even if we *are* on the verge of an evolutionary turning point, even if those of us who are alive today *will* experience the End of Life as We Know It, it just won't be as simple and obvious and bad as the literalist prophets fantasize. The transformation will not come via some cataclysmic overnight world-wide presto-chango.

It is this same part of me—the older, wiser voice—that's distrustful of our culture's predilection for seeing the worst in everything. How did hopelessness come to be regarded as a mark of sophisticated realism? Why are Things Falling Apart thought to be inherently more gripping than Things Being Reborn?

Luckily, the jingoistic part of me that yearns to be alive when Everything Changes can find a common ground with the Zen master in me who regards the entropy-obsessed, all-or-nothing mindset as a unique signature of the civilization that's dying. Together these two aspects of my psyche can collaborate to conclude the following:

WE ARE IN FACT LIVING THROUGH THE APOCALYPSE RIGHT NOW.

But it's nothing like the end of the world visualized by any of the usual suspects. It's different in four ways.

1. It's a slow, gradual apocalypse.

2. The apocalypse is usually invisible, erupting into our conscious awareness only on rare occasions.

3. The apocalypse is as much about rebirth as collapse.

4. The primary way most of us experience the apocalypse is through the intimate events of our personal lives.

I'll explore these four points in more detail.

1. THE APOCALYPSE IS HAPPENING IN SLOW MOTION. It has been going on for decades and will continue to unfold for many years. Sudden, sensational punctuations arise now and then to expedite it, but for the most part it ferments continuously in the background. Most days bring no emergency that is beyond our capacity to bear, but the cumulative effects of the transfigurations that relentlessly weave themselves into our lives have turned every one of us into heroes whose courageous endurance dwarfs the valor of legends like Gilgamesh, Odysseus, Arthur, and Joan of Arc.

2. THE APOCALYPSE IS FOR THE MOST PART INVISIBLE. Here's the most extreme evidence: Few of us have registered the fact that we're in the midst of the largest mass extinction of life on Earth since the demise of the dinosaurs. This is the conclusion of the American Institute of Biological Sciences, a professional society of 5,000 scientists. Think of it: About 40 animal and plant species are dying off every day—a rate unmatched in 65 million years. Shouldn't this be a recurring headline on the front page of every major newspaper?

But the work-in-progress that is the apocalypse is not always cloaked. Now and then a riveting event transfixes our collective emotions, driving millions of us deep into a visceral encounter with the ongoing collapse. For a brief interlude, the covert, slow-motion upheaval explodes into plain view. In recent years, no event has done that more dramatically, at least for Americans, than the mass murder perpetrated by kamikaze hijackers on September 11, 2001.

3. THE APOCALYPSE IS AS MUCH ABOUT REBIRTH AS BREAKDOWN. The English word "apocalypse" is derived from the Greek word for "revelation." In the esoteric spiritual traditions of the West, "apocalypse" has also come to denote a great awakening.

The apocalypse we're living through can be described by all three meanings of the word: as the end of the world, a revelation, and an awakening. Disintegration and renewal are happening side by side; calamity and fertility; rot and splendor; grievous losses and surges of invigorating novelty. Yes, the death of the old order is proceeding apace; but it's overlapped by the birth pangs of an as-yet unimaginable new civilization.

The devastation and regeneration often have no apparent link. But in the case of 9-11, they seemed to be meshed. I received many e-mails from people testifying about how the terrorist assault was a weird kind of gift. In the aftermath, their petty worries evaporated and they stopped wasting time on low-priority, dead-end desires. Roused by an electrifying clarity of purpose, they began to live the life they'd previously only fantasized they wanted. And they had direct perceptions—gut-level, intuitive gnosis—that We Are All One.

It's as if millions of people had a simultaneous Near Death Experience and harvested the epiphanies that typically come to those who have peered over to the other side of the veil.

Here's another example of catastrophe and regeneration arising from a single set of events, suggested by Caroline Myss in her book *Energy Anatomy.* China's invasion and occupation of Tibet in the 1950s resulted in the exile of the Dalai Lama, which ultimately brought that great soul's influence, along with his elegant brand of Buddhism, to the entire world with a breadth and depth that would never have happened otherwise.

4. MOST OF THE TIME WE EXPERIENCE APOCA-LYPSE NOT THROUGH BIG, BAD EVENTS LIKE THE SEPTEMBER 11 MASSACRES, BUT THROUGH THE DETAILS OF OUR PERSONAL LIVES. The sweeping but gradual revolution, the agonizing decay of the old order and breathtaking bloom of the new, are framed in the storylines of your most intimate dramas. Again and again over the years, you're pushed to a brink that challenges you to either rise to the occasion or else surrender to demoralizing chaos. The crises may come in the form of divorce or illness or job loss, or even in less dramatic events like a misunderstanding with a friend or the inexplicable waning of a once-passionate dream.

Seeded inside each of these personal turning points is the crux of the evolving global apocalypse: You get to choose whether you'll adjust by taking a path that keeps you aligned with the values of the dying world or else a path that helps you resonate with what's being born. In effect, you get the chance to vote, with your entire life, for which aspect of the apocalypse you want to predominate.

In Hawaii there are two plants, called *ama'u* and *limu-haea* by the natives, which specialize in colonizing fresh lava flows. Their windblown seeds insinuate themselves into cracks in the newly cooled rock, and sprout long before any other species does.

SACRED ADVERTISEMENT

The apocalypse is being brought to you by the time you dreamed you signed the Declaration of Independence with your non-dominant hand as you ate fresh Peruvian figs flown to you on the backs of albatrosses.

Hype-ocalypse

Rank your favorite doomsday scenarios in order of preference.

_____A new ice age

_____Destruction of ozone layer

_____Dramatic upsurge in earthquakes, volcanoes, and hurricanes

_____Universal drug addiction

_____Mass starvation

_____Takeover by monsters created through genetic engineering

_____Genocide of the imagination; lethal proliferation of dangerous images

_____Terrifying, contagious superstitions spread by apocalyptic pop prophecy

_____Insects and bacteria conspire to cull planet's most dangerous species

_____Multinational corporate criminals create a single, globe-spanning totalitarian state with concentration camps that are the setting for popular reality TV shows

_____Mutated flu strain becomes unstoppable plague

_____Extraterrestrial invasion

_____Cataclysmic degeneration of language into incomprehensible babble and cliché

_____Anthrax and LSD dumped in water supplies

_____Revolt of super-intelligent machines

_____Stupidity becomes popular

_____Mass hypnosis by evil political and religious leaders

_____President, suffering from mental illness, goes berserk and nukes Mecca, Moscow, Beijing

_____Virus from outer space

_____Virus from inner space

_____Essential natural resources run out

_____Global addiction to porn results in accidental mass suicides through excessive masturbation

_____Psychic terrorists administer mass brainwashing that causes millions to buy so many products they can't afford that they become destitute, can't afford health care, and die from diseases caused by eating junk food out of garbage cans

_____The Internet births itself as a sentient global brain, but it's so riddled with spam that it becomes a god-like cripple suffering from the Artificial Intelligence version of Alzheimer's

_____Earth is hit by comet, asteroid, or mini-black hole

_____Wealthy philanthropists give everyone in the world $100,000, causing mass insanity

_____Sun goes supernova

_____Breakthroughs in disease control make it hard for people who are tired of living to die, leading to a pandemic of depression

_____The devil possesses everyone in the world

_____Nuclear war

_____Other (describe)_____

_____

PRONOIA'S VILLAINS

According to Argentinian writer Jorge Luis Borges, Judas was actually a more exalted hero than Jesus. He unselfishly volunteered to perform the all-important villain's role in the resurrection saga, knowing he'd be reviled forever. It was a dirty job that only a supremely egoless saint could have done. Jesus suffered, true, but enjoyed glory and adoration as a result.

Let's apply this way of thinking to the task of understanding the role that seemingly bad people play in pronoia.

Interesting narratives play an essential role in the universal conspiracy to give us exactly what we need. All of us crave drama. We love to be beguiled by twists of fate that unfold the stories of our lives in unpredictable ways. Just as Judas played a key role in advancing the tale of Christ's quest, villains and con men and clowns may be crucial to the entertainment value of our personal journeys.

Try this: Imagine the people you fear and dislike as pivotal characters in a fascinating and ultimately redemptive plot that will take years or even lifetimes for the Divine Wow to elaborate.

There is another reason to love our enemies: They force us to become smarter. The riddles they thrust in front of us sharpen our wits and sculpt our souls.

Try this: Act as if your adversaries are great teachers. Thank them for how crucial they've been in your education.

Consider one more possibility: that the people who seem to slow us down and hold us back are actually preventing things from happening too fast.

Imagine that the evolution of your life or our culture is like a pregnancy: It needs to reach its full term. Just as a child isn't ready to be born after five months of gestation, the new world we're creating has to ripen in its own time. The recalcitrant reactionaries who resist the inevitable birth are simply making sure that the far-seeing revolutionaries don't conjure the future too suddenly. They serve the greater good.

You're a Good Killer

In order to live, you've got to be a demolisher. You take plants and animals that were once alive and rip them apart with your teeth, then disintegrate them in your digestive system.

Your body is literally on fire inside, burning up the oxygen you suck into your lungs.

You didn't actually cut down the trees used to make your house and furniture, but you colluded with their demise.

Then there's the psychological liquidation you've done: killing off old beliefs you've outgrown, for instance.

I'm not trying to make you feel guilty—just pointing out that you have a lot of experience with positive expressions of destruction.

Can you think of other forms this magic takes? As an aspiring master of pronoia, it's one of your specialties—a talent you have a duty to wield with energetic grace.

AMBIDEXTROUS PRONOIA THERAPY

Experiments and exercises in becoming a mysteriously truthful, teasingly healing, fiercely magnanimous Master of Impartial Passion

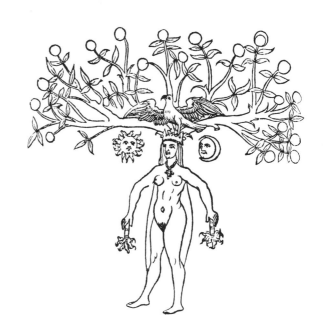

Report your answers & research results below

1 What three ideas do you hate most? Pretend you believe those ideas devoutly. Write about them as if they were the cornerstones of your philosophy of life.

2 The Shinto monks of Iso, Japan, have a curious custom. Every 20 years since the year 772, they've dismantled their central shrine and rebuilt it from scratch. In so doing, they pass down the knowledge of their sacred construction techniques from generation to generation. It's also an effective way for the monks to participate eagerly in the transitoriness of life, rather than merely being resigned to it. They practice the art of death and rebirth not just in meditation but through a practical long-term ritual.

Can you think of an analogous custom you might create for your personal use?

3 There is a disproportionate abundance of evil stepmothers in traditional fairy tales. Storyteller Michael Meade believes that's because the stepmother is a symbol of the soul's nemesis, and everyone has a nemesis. In fact, he says, we all *need* a nemesis to keep us honest, to challenge our assumptions and call our bluffs. With this in mind, brainstorm a short fairy tale in which you're rearranged during a visit from a stepmother.

4 We're acquainted with a group of Hell's Angels that has a unique way of honoring the deceased. Once a year the gang throws a party in the cemetery where their fallen comrades are buried, pouring beer on and snorting coke off their graves.

Think about developing a similar approach to dealing with the dead parts of your own life. Don't just cry mournfully over the dreams and influences that have helped make you what you are. Dance for them; sing for them; leap into the air and kiss the sky for them.

5 Oceans are not exactly teeming with life. In fact, they're mostly barren, and could rightly be called "wet deserts." Likewise, not all your emotions, even those that come in floods, are fertile. Some are automatic reactions that have discharged thousands of times since they were first programmed into you many years ago. They're mechanical, not organic. They became fixtures when you were a very different person than you are now. Identify these.

6 We all have a war going on inside ourselves. What's yours? Is it a just and fruitful war or a senseless and wasteful war, or both?

7 Hundreds of years ago, it was seemingly possible to buy forgiveness. Until Martin Luther came along to spoil the fun, the Catholic Church used to sell "indulgences," which buyers could supposedly trade in purgatory for a reduced punishment for their earthly sins.

The forgiveness freaks at the Beauty and Truth Laboratory have revived this practice in a mutated form. For the right price, we're able to guarantee your absolution. To take advantage of our offer, simply send us a million dollars for each sin you want to have forgiven.

There's just one condition: You can't pay us with the government's legal tender. You must *make* the money—literally. Using crayons, paints, scissors, glue, collage materials, or other media, create your own version of large-denomination paper money. Instead of the images of politicians that typically appear on government currency, draw pictures of your muses and heroes and friends and pets. Rather than patriotic clichés and meaningless decorative frills, add sayings and symbols that make you happy. Be sure to write a description of the sin you want "indulged" somewhere on the bill. Send your payment to the Beauty and Truth Laboratory at P.O. Box 150628, San Rafael, CA 94915.

8 In our culture, vultures are considered ugly and disgusting. But in ancient Egypt, they were sacred. Scholar Elinor Gadon says they were called "compassionate purifiers." As devourers of corpses, they transformed rotting flesh into usable energy, and expedited the soul's transition to heaven. Queens of Egypt wore vulture headdresses to signify their divine consecration.

How would you invoke the help of mythical vultures in your own life? Here's one possibility. Meditate on death not as the end of physical life, but as a metaphor for shedding what's outworn. In that light,

Ambidextrous Pronoia Therapy

what is the best death you've ever experienced? What death would you like to enjoy next?

9 In one old fairy tale, a virtuous hero throws a punch at an evil witch. But because of her wizardry, the thrust of his fist boomerangs and he smashes himself in the nose. Blood flows from his nostrils. He wipes it with his fingertips and flings a few red drops in the witch's direction. This is the unexpected magic that sends her fleeing. He's saved. Moral of the story: The hero's self-wounding produces his ultimate protection. Give an example of this theme at work in your own life.

10 The 17th-century surgeon Wilhelm Hilden had an interesting theory about healing. He developed a medicinal salve that he applied not to the wound itself but rather to the weapon that inflicted it. Though today we may sneer at such foolishness, the fact is that Hilden's approach has great potential if used for *psychic* wounds. Jesus understood this when he articulated the revolutionary formula, "Love your enemy." More than any other action, this strategy has the power to cure you of the distortions your enemy has unleashed in you. Try it out.

11 "Every great player has a screw loose," said basketball coach Tara VanDerveer. What's the loose screw in you that's most likely to lead you to greatness?

12 How do you respond to the part of the apocalypse that brings breakdown and ruin? Is it with actions that express rage, disdain, hatred, fear, tribalism, and all the primitive emotions that infect the roots of the dying civilization? Or is it with actions that exude ingenious compassion, creative inclusiveness, expansive empathy, and other robust emotions that are at the heart of the New World? What can you do to focus your personal experience of the apocalypse on liberation and awakening rather than suffering and loss? How can you personally starve the bad apocalypse and nurture the good apocalypse?

13 Beauty and Truth Laboratory researcher Rebecca Rusche coined the word "careenstable." Here's her explanation of how it originated:

"In high school, my mom used to let me use her VW Beetle to go to basketball practice. One night after practice, a friend and I were chatting and drinking Coke when we decided to see how fast we could get the Beetle going down a nearby dirt road. Soon we were careening at 65 mph, shouting 'careen!' every time we hit a bump and flew into the air. When we arrived back at the gym and got out of the car half an hour later, we saw my Coke can sitting on the front bumper next to the license plate. I nudged it softly to see if it was lodged in there, but it fell right off—wasn't stuck at all. I thought, 'There must be a word for this magic,' and thus 'careenstable' was born. It came to mean anything that maintains its poise in the midst of wild, fast movement."

Give an example of careenstable working in your own life.

14 Provide evidence proving or disproving the following four hypotheses: 1. If you're not part of the grueling solution, you're probably part of the insidiously comfortable problem. 2. If you're not conspiring to commit smart fun, you're almost certainly colluding with the disingenuous repression. 3. If you're not trying to rally support for a tough investigation, you'll end up assisting the bland cover-up. 4. If you're not mad about how unconstructively you've used your anger in the past, then you won't be motivated to wield it more creatively any time soon.

15 POP QUIZ! By now, you should be sufficiently knowledgeable about pronoia to speak about it with some authority. Your assignment is to write a pronoiac rebuttal to the following news story, which appeared in a weekly tabloid:

"If you want to be happier, feel better, and do more in life, just turn your back on reality—and inflate your ego! A new study reveals that an unrealistically positive attitude and unfounded optimism, along with some denial of reality, help you accomplish great things in all areas of your life. In other words, you don't need a firm grip on reality to be successful and happy."

16 A thousand years from today, everyone you know will be long dead and forgotten. There'll be nothing left of the life you love, no evidence that you ever walked this planet. That, at least, is what the fundamentalist materialists would have you believe. But suppose the truth is very different? What if in fact every little thing you do subtly alters the course of world history? What if your day-to-day decisions will actually help determine how the human species navigates its way through the epic turning point we're living through? And finally, what if you *will* be alive in a thousand years, reincarnated into a fresh body and in possession of the memories of the person you were back in this era? These are my hypotheses. These are my prophecies. Which is why I say: Live as if your soul is eternal.

HOMEOPATHIC MEDICINE SPELL #2

buoyantimprovisingfearlesswideawakefunwrestler

Bang-
ing your head against a wall consumes 150 calories an hour. Sigmund Freud
had a morbid fear of ferns. Life is "a meaningless existential hell," say 26 percent of American male college students.
Most Americans would vote against the Bill of Rights if it were presented to them in a referendum. The odds that Elvis Presley will crash-land
a UFO on the head of the Loch Ness monster are 14 million to one, according
to a British betting agency. Heroin addiction causes constipation. More than half of
the pianos in the world are out of tune. An underground economy that runs on marijuana, porn, and the services of illegal immigrants comprises 10 percent of the American
economy. Lightning strikes about 6,000 times per minute on this planet and kills more than a
thousand people a year. Sleep deprivation, which has reached epidemic proportions, is akin to
drug abuse in the way that it dramatically lowers competence levels and causes aberrant behavior. Queen Ranavalona of Madagascar decreed that if any of her subjects appeared in her dreams,
they would be killed. Thomas Edison was afraid of the dark. Big drug companies don't invest in the
development of a new drug if it's a cure for a relatively rare disease that wouldn't affect enough people to generate a substantial profit. In the last 4,000 years, no new animals have been domesticated.
An Alabama court upheld a ban on the sale of vibrators, ruling that there's no constitutional right to
an orgasm. Mosquitoes have teeth. The sun's mass decreases by four million tons per second, and
our home star will die a few billion years from now. Every time an actor portraying a doctor performs
a particular kind of surgery on a popular soap opera, real doctors are sought out to perform the
same surgery at a dramatically higher rate. You're more likely to be killed by a champagne cork
than a poisonous spider. Mortuary workers in Zimbabwe rented corpses to drivers who wanted
to take advantage of the priority given to hearses in gas-station lines. None of Socrates' writings survive. In Jon Rappoport's book *The Secret Behind Secret Societies,* hypnotist Jack
True says he rarely practices his craft any more because most of his clients are already
in a light trance when they come to see him. What was an hour ten years ago is now
only 52 minutes. Every night, millions of Americans are tormented by nightmares
of the CIA overthrowing the democratically elected governments of Iran in
1953, Guatemala in 1954, Brazil in 1963, and Chile in 1973. Israeli scientists are working to perfect a procedure whereby they harvest
eggs from aborted human fetuses, fertilize them, and trans-
plant them into the wombs of infertile women,
thereby making the donor fetus an
unborn mother.

surgingsoaringfoxygeniuswhirlingrisktaker

moistlushlaughingjubilationbouquetlover

freejoycrispfreshleapingflashdazzler

This space has been liberated for your use

When did you
first realize
you are the
rain's teacher?

FEAR OF BEAUTY?

The Italian city of Florence harbors the richest trove of art treasures in the world. Its many museums are hot spots for outbreaks of a rare psychological disorder. Foreign tourists sometimes experience breakdowns while standing in the presence of the tremendous beauty, and are rushed to the psychiatric ward of Florence's Santa Maria Nuova Hospital.

"Many visitors panic before a Raphael painting," reports Reuters. "Others collapse at the feet of Michelangelo's statue of David."

Psychiatrists have referred to this pathology as the Stendahl Syndrome, named after the French novelist who wrote about his emotional breakdown during a visit to the city's art collection in 1817.

As you embark on your explorations of pronoia, you should protect yourself against this risk. Proceed cautiously as you expose yourself to the splendor that has been invisible or unavailable to you all these years.

shadow school

You're a gorgeous mystery with a wild heart and a lofty purpose. But like all of us, your psyche also harbors a portion of the world's sickness: a mess of repressed longings, enervating wounds, ignorant delusions, and unripe powers. It has been known by many names, including demon and devil. Psychologist Carl Jung called it the *shadow.* He believed it was the lead that the authentic alchemists of the Middle Ages sought to transmute into gold.

"I am superior to you only in one point," Narcissus tells Goldmund in Hermann Hesse's novel *Narcissus and Goldmund.* "I'm awake, whereas you are only half awake, or completely asleep sometimes. I call a man awake who knows in his conscious reason his innermost unreasonable force, drives, and weaknesses, and knows how to deal with them."

Astrologer Steven Forrest has a different name for the shadow: *stuff.* "Work on your stuff," he says, "or your stuff will work on you." He means that it will sabotage you if you're not aggressive about identifying, negotiating with, and transforming it.

"You have to recognize the demons or else they'll annoy you like mosquitoes. But if you acknowledge their existence, if you say, 'All right, here's a cookie, go sit in the corner,' then you can go about your work and you don't have to go into depression because of it." —James Broughton, as told to interviewer Jack Foley in *The Alsop Review,* "Big Joy: Octogenarian—An Interview with James Broughton," www.alsopreview.com/columns/foley/jfbroughton.html

tiation is unavoidable." —Daryl Sharp, *Jung Lexicon: A Primer of Terms and Concepts;* also available at www.psychceu.com/Jung/sharplexicon.html

"The unconscious sends all sorts of vapors, odd beings, terrors, and deluding images up into the mind; for the human kingdom, beneath the floor of the comparatively neat little dwelling that we call our consciousness, goes down into unsuspected Aladdin caves. There not only jewels but also dangerous jinn abide: the inconvenient or resisted psychological powers that we have not thought or dared to integrate into our lives." —Joseph Campbell, *The Hero With a Thousand Faces*

"The shadow is not only the dark underside of the personality. While much of it consists of inferior, primitive, unadapted, and awkward qualities, it also contains vitalizing instincts, sleeping abilities, and positive moral qualities that have long been buried or never been conscious. These unacknowledged personal characteristics are often seen or hallucinated in others through the mechanism of projection." —Daryl Sharp, *Jung Lexicon: A Primer of Terms and Concepts;* also available at www.psychceu.com/Jung/sharplexicon.html

The shadow is not inherently evil. If it is ignored or denied, it may become monstrous to compensate. Only then is it likely to "demonically possess" its owner, leading to compulsive, exaggerated, "evil" behavior.

"The best political, social, and spiritual work we can do is to withdraw the projection of our shadow onto others." —Carl Jung

Did you remember to thank the wild irises and the windy rain?

"Whatever is rejected from the self, appears in the world as an event," said Jung. If you disown a part of your personality, it'll materialize as an unexpected detour.
Everyone who believes in the devil *is* the devil.

"Nothing determines who we will become so much as those things we choose to ignore." —Sandor McNab

"There is no generally effective technique for assimilating the shadow. It is more like diplomacy and is always an individual matter. First one has to accept and take seriously the existence of the shadow. Second, one has to become aware of its qualities and intentions. This happens through conscientious attention to moods, fantasies, and impulses. Third, a long process of nego-

"Suffering can't be avoided," James Broughton told Jack Foley. "The way to happiness is to go into the darkness of yourself. That's the place the seed is nourished, takes its roots and grows up, and becomes ultimately the plant and the flower. You can only go upward by first going downward." —James Broughton, as told to interviewer Jack Foley in *The Alsop Review,* "Big Joy: Octogenarian—An Interview with James Broughton," www.alsopreview. com/columns/ foley/ jfbroughton.html

The alchemists said the magic formula for enlightenment was *Visita Inferiora Terrae Rectificando Invenies Occultum Lapidem,* or "Seek out the lower reaches of the earth, perfect them, and you will find the hidden stone" (the treasured Philosopher's Stone). Jungian psychologists might describe the process this way: Find the ignorant, wounded parts of your psyche, perfect them, and you will awaken your hidden divinity.

Dionysian Manifesto

"The great epochs in our lives are at the points when we gain the courage to rebaptize our badness as the best in us." —Friedrich Nietzsche

In the best-known version of the Greek myth, Persephone is dragged down into the underworld by Hades, whose title is "Pluto." But in earlier, pre-patriarchal tales, she descends there under her own power, actively seeking to graduate from her virginal naiveté by exploring the intriguing land of shadows.

"Pluto" is derived from the Greek word *plutus,* meaning "wealth." Psychologist James Hillman says this refers to the psyche-building riches available in Pluto's domain. Hades, he says, is "the giver of nourishment to the soul."

The goddess Hecate also lives in the underworld. According to poet Robert Graves, she is the mistress of sorcery, "the goddess of ghosts and night-terrors, of phantoms and fearful monsters." On the other hand, he notes, Hecate "presides at seed time and childbirth; she grants prosperity, victory, plentiful harvests to the farmer and rich catches to the fisherman."

How can a single deity embody such seemingly contradictory archetypes? Graves: She symbolizes "the unconscious in which beasts and monsters swarm. This is not the living hell of the psychotic, but a reservoir of energy to be brought under control, just as Chaos was brought to cosmic order under the influence of the spirit."

Working with your dreams can help you stop colluding with the global genocide of the imagination.

In the New World, it won't be your material wealth that will win you the most bragging points. Nor will it be the important people you know or the deals you've swung or the knowledge you've amassed or your mate's attractiveness. What will bring you most prestige and praise in the civilization to come will be your success in transmuting lead into gold—how thoroughly you have integrated your shadow and tapped into its resources.

Here's a corollary to Jesus's injunction to love thy neighbor as thyself: "I will love the dark, difficult side of my neighbor—not just the attractive, friendly side—and I will encourage it to express itself in constructive ways."

"If only it were all so simple! If only there were evil people somewhere insidiously committing evil deeds, and it were necessary only to separate them from the rest of us and destroy them. But the line dividing good and evil cuts through the heart of every human being. And who is willing to destroy a piece of his own heart?" —Alexander Solzhenitsyn, *The Gulag Archipelago*

Ancient legend says that a giant cobra—normally a fearsome predator—shielded Buddha with its expansive hood as he meditated in the wilderness during a terrible week-long storm.

Dionysian Manifesto

FLIP-FLOP THE TRAUMATIC IMPRINT

Beauty and Truth Laboratory researcher Artemisia had just begun menstruating, and was suffering from debilitating cramps. Massive doses of ibuprofen were not relieving the distress, so she went to her regular acupuncturist, Dr. Lily Ming, to get relief.

Dr. Ming had Artemisia lie down on the table and proceeded to insert 10 needles in her belly and hand and ear. Then Dr. Ming introduced a treatment that Artemisia was unfamiliar with: She lightly pounded the nail of Artemisia's big toe with a small silver hammer for a few minutes.

"Why are you doing that?" Artemisia asked.

"It is good for the uterus," the doctor replied.

Indeed, Artemisia's cramps dramatically diminished as the doctor thumped, and in the days to come they did not recur.

After the session, as Artemisia prepared to leave, the usually taciturn Ming started up a conversation. Artemisia was surprised, but listened attentively as Dr. Ming made a series of revelations. The most surprising was Dr. Ming's description of a traumatic event from her own childhood.

During the military occupation of her native Manchuria, a province of China, she was forced to witness Japanese soldiers torturing people she loved. Their primary atrocity was using hammers to drive bamboo shoots through their victims' big toes.

The moral of the story: Dr. Ming has accomplished the heroic feat of reversing the meaning of her most traumatic imprint. She has turned a symbol of pain into a symbol of healing.

Love Bomb

I feel closer to you when I imagine that all of us are collaborating to fight monumental dangers. The telepathic links among us heat up when our emotions register the possibility that a global cataclysm could wipe us out.

That's why I think of the nuclear bomb as a gift. It's a terrible and sacred taboo that mobilizes our love for each other better than any other symbol. It's the superhuman profanity on which all life depends and against which all values must be tested. Shadowing every one of our personal actions, the bomb is the fascinating blasphemy that won't stop ranting unless we're all very, very good.

In the quiet abyss of our imaginations, we unconsciously worship it, believing in its extravagant potency as if it were a god. It is the most spiritual, most supernatural material object in the world, a fetish that has the power to literally change all life on earth instantly and forever. We agree to be possessed by it, to be haunted by its apparition above all other apparitions. No other spectacle inspires more perverse attraction.

And yet it's secret. How few of us have ever stood next to the magic body of a hydrogen bomb in a missile silo or laboratory—breathed in its smell, touched it, communed with its actual life. Its presence among us is rumor and mystery, like flying saucers and the afterlife. We hear stories.

At night our dreams turn the bomb into the philosopher's stone, the pearl of great price, the doppelganger of the messiah, the violent ecstasy of religious conversion. Our blood is alive to its alchemy, alert to its offer of the blinding flash of irreversible illumination. We recognize the bomb as our impossible teacher because it harbors a dangerous light that seems to mimic the sun.

It's ours. We made it. We imagined it into existence so we could remember that we are all one body. When I fantasize the bomb vaporizing me into its pure primeval heat and radiation, I remember that you and I are made of the same stuff. The bomb frees us to imagine that we all live and die together, that we are all born out of Adam, the indivisible hermaphrodite god of our species. And we can return now because we never left.

We need the bomb. We need the bomb because only the tease of the biggest, most original sin can heal us. The bomb is a blind, a fake, a trick memory we're sending ourselves from the future that shocks us better than all the abstract devils.

Let's call the bomb a love that's too big for us to understand yet. Let's say it's the raging creative life of a cleansing disease that wants to cure us so it doesn't have to kill us. Let's say it's the last judgment that promises not to come true if we can figure out what it means.

We have genetic potentials and divine powers so undreamed of that they will feel like magic when they finally bloom. But they may remain partially dormant in us until we're terrified not just of our individual deaths but also of the extinction of the human archetype.

Bless the fear. Praise the danger. O God of Good and Evil Light, let the ugly power fascinate us all now. Let it fix our dread so precisely that we become one ferocious, potently concentrated magician, a single guerrilla mediator casting a spell to bind the great Satan bomb. There will be no nuclear war.

Sacred Advertisement

The end of the end of the world is made possible in part by Pila Chiles. His book The Secrets and Mysteries of Hawaii *recounts the advice given him by an Indian holy man: "If you have lost the business, your house, and wife, after you have been pronounced terminally ill and life has dealt you the worst blows, there is only one duty left. That is to crawl over to the nearest mirror, hoist yourself up, look deeply into it with your last breath, and say aloud seven times: Cock-a-doodle-doo!"*

SUBTERRANEAN PRONOIA THERAPY

**Experiments and exercises
in becoming a rebelliously kind,
affably unpredictable,
insanely poised
Master of Supernal Mischief.**

Report your answers & research results below

1 "I have not used my darkness well," mourns poet Stanley Moss in his book *Asleep in the Garden.* He's right about that. His forays into the realm of shadows rarely lead to redemption.

"One fine day/ I shall fall down ... in a prison of anger," he moans in one poem. "In this country I planted not one seed," he announces elsewhere. Other samples: "vomit is the speech of the soul"; "We die misinformed"; "How goes a life? Something like the ocean/ building dead coral."

But enough. Let's not indulge Moss in his profligacy. Instead, we'll appoint him to be your anti-role model: an example of what you don't want to become. May he inspire you to regard your sorrows and failures as sources of disguised treasure; as raw materials that will fuel future breakthroughs. Now write a poem or story in which you use your darkness well.

2 Acquire a hand puppet, preferably a funky old-fashioned one from a thrift store, but any one will do. Give the puppet a name and wear it on your hand wherever you go for several days. In a voice different from your normal one, make this ally speak the "shadow truths" of every situation you encounter: the dicey subtexts everyone is shy about acknowledging, the layers of truth that lie beneath the surface, the agreed-upon illusions that cloud everyone's perceptual abilities.

3 All of us are eminently fallible nobodies. We're crammed with delusions and base emotions. We give ourselves more slack than we give anyone else, and we're brilliant at justifying our irrational biases with seemingly logical explanations. Yet it's equally true that every one of us is a magnificently enigmatic creation unlike any other in the history of the world. We're stars with vast potential, gods and goddesses in the making.

Dramatize this paradox. Tomorrow, buy and wear ugly, threadbare clothes from the same thrift store where you got your hand puppet. Eat the cheapest junk food possible and do the most menial tasks you can find. The next day, attire yourself in your best clothes, wear a crown or diadem, and treat yourself to an expensive gourmet meal. Enjoy a massage, a pedicure, and other luxuries that require people to wait on you. On the third day, switch back and forth between the previous two days' modes every couple of hours. As you do, cultivate a passionate indifference to the question of whether you are ultimately an unimportant nobody or a captivating hero.

4 Is it possible that in trying to repress some of the things about yourself that you don't like, you have also disowned potentially strong and beautiful aspects of yourself? What are they?

5 Inventor Thomas Edison came up with a lot of ideas that went nowhere. While trying to develop the perfect battery, his unsuccessful experiments were comically legion. "I have not failed," he mused. "I've just found 10,000 ways that won't work." There are other ways in which he didn't match the profile we usually associate with genius. He rarely had a dramatic breakthrough out of the blue, for instance. Most often, he tinkered and fussed until he discovered some new useful thing. Of his 1,093 patents, some were inventions he purposefully set about to create, but most he simply stumbled upon.

Describe an area of your life where you've discovered 10,000 ways that don't work.

6 *Chantepleure* is a word that means "to sing and weep simultaneously." Think of a memory that moves you to do just that.

7 For the 2001 Burning Man festival in the Nevada desert, artist David Best constructed the "Mausoleum: Temple of Tears." Made from wooden pieces of dinosaur puzzles, this pagoda-like sanctuary took him weeks to perfect. Pilgrims who visited it were encouraged to write prayers on the walls, mourning dead loved ones and exorcising adversaries who had passed over. At the end of the festival, Best hosted a mass ritual of grief and burned his masterpiece to ash.

Draw inspiration from Best's project. Create a talisman or ritual tool out of whimsical junk, use it a while to catalyze a catharsis, then destroy it or throw it away.

Subterranean Pronoia Therapy

8 An earlier Pronoia News Network broadcast described how ancient Celtic warriors and modern Nigerian women used their nakedness as a strategic advantage against their adversaries. We invite you to further develop the tradition: Actually take off your clothes in the presence of those you oppose.

If that's too extreme, try the metaphorical equivalent: Disarm your adversaries not by attacking them but by expressing your vulnerability.

9 Declare amnesty for the part of you that you don't love very well. Forgive that poor sucker. Hold its hand and take it out to dinner and a movie. Tactfully offer it a chance to make amends for the dumb things it has done. And then do a dramatic reading of this proclamation by the playwright Theodore Rubin: "I must learn to love the fool in me—the one who feels too much, talks too much, takes too many chances, wins sometimes and loses often, lacks self-control, loves and hates, hurts and gets hurt, promises and breaks promises, laughs and cries. It alone protects me against that utterly self-controlled, masterful tyrant whom I also harbor and who would rob me of human aliveness, humility, and dignity but for my fool."

10 Some readers of my weekly column complain when I draw inspiration from a public figure they consider a bad person. Once I cited philosopher Bertrand Russell, and Pat G. went ballistic: "Russell was a terrible father! How dare you give him any credence?" Another time I invoked the wisdom of ex-U.S. president Teddy Roosevelt. "What possessed you to quote such a militaristic bully?" wrote Arthur H. Here's how I respond to these grumbles: If I refused to learn from people unless I agreed with everything they had ever said and done, I would never learn from anyone.

What about you? Have you set up your life so that everyone is either on or off your good list? If so, try something new: Cultivate a capacity to derive help and insight from people who aren't perfect.

11 "We are attracted to people who express the qualities we deny or repress in ourselves," says creativity expert Shakti Gawain. Using this idea as your hypothesis, take an inventory of the people you're most drawn to. Ask yourself whether they have talents and dreams that you wish could come alive in you. If you find this to be the case, consider the possibility that it's time to claim those talents or dreams as your own.

Subterranean Pronoia Therapy

12 Philosopher William James proposed that if our culture ever hoped to shed the deeply ingrained habit of going to war, we'd have to create a moral equivalent. It's not enough to preach the value of peace, he said. We have to find other ways to channel our aggressive instincts in order to accomplish what war does, like stimulate political unity and build civic virtue.

Astrology provides a complementary perspective. Each of us has the warrior energy of the planet Mars in our psychological make-up. We can't simply repress it, but must find a positive way to express it. How you might go about this project?

13 Dealing with your shadow may require superhuman levels of patient objectivity. The experience may be like having to maintain a neutral tone of voice as you speak the language of diplomacy during negotiations with the inscrutable leader of a guerrilla enemy that is carrying out covert attacks against your most vulnerable sanctuaries.

On rare occasions, though, you may get a more direct opportunity to disarm your shadow. The following anecdote is an example. Study it as a metaphor for the approach you might try one day.

While still a young man, the medieval English king Richard was captured and imprisoned by his enemy Modard. For many days he languished alone in his cell, barely fed and having no blanket to warm him at night.

One morning he awoke to the sound of growling. His jailers had brought a full-grown male lion to the cell. They opened the door and brought the beast in, whereupon they cut off the leather muzzle binding its jaws and scurried out, leaving Richard to fend for himself against the lion.

Freed from its constraint, the beast reared back and unleashed a roar. Without wasting a moment in useless fear, Richard leaped forward and jammed his arm down the throat of the lion. Thrusting all the way into its chest, he ripped out its heart, killing it instantly.

14 In a radio interview, a former remote-viewer for the U.S. military was asked how his personal life had changed as his psychic skills had grown. "There were secrets my conscious and subconscious minds had been waiting for years to tell each other," he said, "and as my telepathic power improved, I found they no longer wanted to wait."

Try to accomplish this yourself. Imagine that the barriers between your everyday awareness and your deep self are crumbling. Act as if you are developing an ever-increasing ability to read your own mind.

15 Describe your signature pain. What is the nature of the torment that chronically upsets you most?

This is the first step in graduating from the No Pain, No Gain School of Tortured Progress. You can't be healed unless you name the tweaked karma that needs to be healed.

Step #2: Figure out what it is about your problem that's so appealing. Consider the possibility that you have it at least in part because it perversely entertains you or keeps you from being bored.

Meditate on the theory that maybe you unconsciously don't want to give up your dilemma because it prevents you from reaching lofty goals you're too afraid or timid or lazy to strive for.

Contemplate the notion that you're secretly proud of your distress—that it's so interwoven with your identity that you wouldn't feel like yourself if you had to live without it. Do you ever find yourself bragging to others about the difficulties you have to endure? Are they essential to the construction of your self-image?

Consider the possibility that you use your nagging agony as an attention-getting device, or as a way to gather love. Isn't it true that some people are more likely to shower you with sympathy when you're miserable than when you're blandly well-adjusted?

Muse on the seductiveness of your hurt, and on all the unacknowledged reasons that maybe you are attracted to it and hesitate to give it up.

Step #3: Simply feel your suffering. Don't judge it or repress it. Don't come up with reasons about how it's beneath you to feel it or how you should be over it by now or how you can't believe you still let it have so much power over you. Let the pain ripple and flow. Allow it to break your heart apart. Give it room to wail its truths. Marvel at the fullness of the emotions it stirs.

Step #4: Leaving all your preconceptions behind, meditate on what lessons your pain is asking you to master. How is it inspiring you to grow in directions you've been unable to accomplish by any other means?

Step #5: Put yourself in a state of mind wherein you can feel gratitude for your pain. Be thankful for its teachings, for its chewy mystery, for its command that you build a soul resilient enough to do the work you came to Earth to carry out.

Subterranean Pronoia Therapy

SACRED ADVERTISEMENT

"Subterranean Pronoia Therapy" is brought to you by the decisions you didn't make, the words you never spoke, the actions you've avoided, and the codes you haven't broken.

YOUR SACRED ADVERTISEMENT

Create your own Sacred Advertisement in the space above.

PRONOIA NEWS NETWORK

Free Work Done Out of Love

The U.S. Labor Department periodically analyzes the volunteer work done by Americans. In one report, it estimated that between September 2001 and September 2002, 59 million people offered their services free of charge as they mentored, tutored, built affordable housing, cleaned up the environment, and helped respond to community emergencies. The average contribution per person for the year was 52 hours. (Source: Associated Press)

PNN is brought to you by Agatha Christie's feeling that she came up with the best ideas for her books while she was washing dishes, and by Goethe's belief that in order to write he needed an apple rotting in his desk drawer.

Singing Duels Diffuse Anger

"In Greenland, disputes are solved through singing duels. The quibbling parties face off and proceed to croon tunes heaped high with insults. While spectators pass the final judgment on the event, the singing generally diffuses the anger, and the dueling parties leave as friends." —*Mental Floss,* July–August 2004

Culture Wars a Fabrication?

The high degree of religious and multicultural tolerance in the United States is unprecedented in world history. So said sociologist Alan Wolfe in his book *One Nation, After All,* based on two years of interviews with 200 subjects.

"Wolfe argues that middle-class Americans don't deserve their reputation as angry, sanctimonious, and narrow-minded," reported Alicia Potter in the *Boston Phoenix.* "On the contrary, they're optimistic, thoughtful, and slow to judge."

Wolfe's subjects had one blind spot: homosexuality. But other than their lack of tolerance for gays, they expressed remarkable acceptance of immigrants, non-whites, and people of other socio-economic classes.

Wolfe was frustrated by his findings. Because he makes part of his living writing for opinionated magazines, he yearned for more controversial data.

"The reasonableness, the sensitivity, the thoughtfulness just drove me batty," he told Potter. "I just wanted to scream at people, 'Isn't there something that really just makes you angry and upset?'" (Source: Alicia Potter, *Boston Phoenix,* March 30, 1998)

Reborn Steel The North American steel industry annually recycles millions of tons of steel scrap from recycled cans, automobiles, appliances, construction materials, and other steel products. The scrap is remelted to produce new steel. Every ton of steel recycled saves 2,500 pounds of iron ore, 1,400 pounds of coal, and 120 pounds of limestone. The industry's overall recycling rate is 68 percent.

Medicine from Poison Salmonella bacteria, the cause of food poisoning, may become a weapon against cancer. In tests on mice, it has carried out search-and-destroy missions against tumors.

The saliva of vampire bats appears to be effective in dissolving the blood clots that cause strokes.

Ongoing research into the medical applications of snake venom suggest it may ultimately be used to fight cancer, heart attacks, and spongiform encephalopathies like BSE, or "mad cow disease."

Power through Service "It's antithetical to the definition of power in this culture that a person might derive power by service rather than control, but that's the essence of midwifery." —Elizabeth Davis, *Heart & Hands: A Midwife's Guide to Pregnancy and Birth*

The Pink Balloon Beauty and Truth Laboratory researcher Elizabeth Whitsage tells a story of when she was working at Disneyland selling mouse-eared balloons. Every so often a mother, father, and young son would come up to her, the parents asking in enthusiastic voices, "What color do you want?" and the son answering, "Pink!" One parent, usually the father, would recoil in horror and say something like, "No, son, don't you want red or blue?" But before the child could reply, Elizabeth would whip a pink balloon out of the bunch and wrap its string around his wrist. Then she'd smile and say to the dad, "That'll be one dollar, please."

BLOWOUT BARGAINS

A Less Boring Evil, Part 1

"Rudolf Steiner believed that evil was comprised of two forces that were opposed to each other in many ways, though with a tendency to form an alliance. One force, associated with Lucifer, represents grandiosity, arrogance, and self-indulgence. The other, associated with Ahriman, is manipulative, acquisitive, and ultimately sterile. We owe art to Lucifer and technology to Ahriman. They have both played a necessary and constructive role at different stages of the evolution of consciousness, enabling human beings to find a path of development towards love, wisdom, and freedom. Thus, for Steiner, 'the task of evil is to promote the ascent of man.' Because there are two forces of evil, not just one, good is not seen as being opposed to evil. The forces of good, associated with Christ, balance, redeem, and heal the two evil forces." —Fraser N. Watts, "The Spiritual Psychology of Rudolf Steiner," an essay in *Beyond Therapy: The Impact of Eastern Religion on Psychological Theory and Practice*, G. Claxton, editor

A Less Boring Evil, Part 2

"Rudolf Steiner saw Christ as the human mediation between the demonic Ahriman and the satanic Lucifer. Ahriman is the unit crushed into the uniform, the destruction of individuality in sameness. He is the spirit behind Stalin, or Orwell's nightmares of Big Brother. Lucifer is the opposite, the individual raised to a cosmic egotism where there can be no other one, not even God. The Ahrimanic evil is the state that crushes all diversity. The Luciferic evil is the overweening pride of the scientist who believes he can control evolution through the genetic engineering of life in his laboratory. The Christ is neither the unit and the uniform, nor the alone, but expresses the crossing of the unique and the universal." —William Irwin Thompson, *Imaginary Landscape: Making Worlds of Myth and Science*

Gates Goes Both Ways Though many people consider him an asshole who has monopolized the computer industry with inferior technology, Bill Gates is the most generous philanthropist in history. He has donated more than $25 billion to promote health and education all over the globe. Some of the beneficiaries of his largesse have been the United Negro College Fund, International AIDS Vaccine Initiative, Johns Hopkins University, Save the Children Federation, and the United Nations Foundation.

Whiteread Goes Both Ways In 1993, sculptor Rachel Whiteread was named best artist of the year during a show at London's Tate Gallery. The K. Foundation chose the same occasion, however, to bestow on her the sarcastic honor of being Britain's worst artist. She won more money for the second award.

Fitzgerald Went Both Ways "The test of a first-rate intelligence," said F. Scott Fitzgerald, "is the ability to hold two opposed ideas in the mind at the same time, and still retain the ability to function."

Bohr Went Both Ways "The opposite of a correct statement is a false statement," said the physicist Niels Bohr. "But the opposite of a profound truth may well be another profound truth."

The Dalai Lama Goes Both Ways
"I call the high and light aspects of my being *spirit* and the dark and heavy aspects *soul*.

"Soul is at home in the deep, shaded valleys. Heavy torpid flowers saturated with black grow there. The rivers flow like warm syrup.

"Spirit is a land of high, white peaks and glittering jewel-like lakes and flowers. Life is sparse and sounds travel great distances." —The Dalai Lama, as quoted by James Hillman in *A Blue Fire*

You Go Both Ways
"Chiaroscurofy" is a word that means "to find a comfortable place where you are partially in darkness and partially illuminated, or half in shadow and half in sunlight." You may actually do this some day.

Stealth Technology

Fourteenth-century Qabalists calculated the number of angels as 301,655,722. But the radiant homeless guy who begs for money in front of the post office says the current total is 677,323,117,002. If he's right, it means that in a mere six centuries, the angel community has grown 225,000 percent. That's an astounding population explosion.

Unlike the rapid proliferation of humans, the swelling tribe of heavenly hosts is good news. It means there are now 112 divine messengers-cum-guardian spirits for every person on the planet.

Chaos Is Good Business

Successful fund manager Daniel Cloud believes the best time to invest in a foreign market is when a country is in the midst of civil strife or major crisis. Tumult is usually a buy signal, he says, because that's when the opportunity for maximum profit is greatest.

Rattlesnake Slack

Scientists now know that rattlesnakes would actually prefer to lie back and relax than to rattle and attack.

Jesus the Small Crab

"The sanctuary pools that glisten in morning's sunlight rustle with the movement of small beings. Branching out from ocean's shore, waves wash through, a shadow of rebirth. Jesus takes the form of a small crab. From still rocks he creeps silently into the cool pools of light, opening himself to be seen by the world, to be loved, to be accepted as all beings long to be." —Zoe Brezsny, *Secret Freedom*

PNN is brought to you by the adjective pronoying, which is used to describe a convert to pronoia who hectors and pontificates while promoting the doctrine of pronoia with annoying piety.

Conversion Experience

Though the Hindu caste system is technically forbidden in India, long-standing custom keeps it in effect. The lowest caste is composed of the untouchables, known as the Dalits ("the oppressed." The abuse they endure is appalling. It ranges from violent attacks and hate speech to prohibitions against praying in temples and against wearing shoes where the dominant castes live.

In 2002, large numbers of Dalits carried out a bloodless revolution. Instead of continuing to fight the sickening system, they dropped out of it. During a mass ceremony in Delhi, over one million of them formally left the Hindu religion and converted to Buddhism.

Blink of Pronoia

Jean-Dominique Bauby was a 43-year-old editor when he suffered an unusual stroke. Though his brain remained undamaged, his entire body was paralyzed except for his left eye. Slowly he learned to communicate in code by blinking, and over the next two years he dictated a memoir. Feeling as if he were trapped in a diving bell, but with his imagination as free as a butterfly, he called his book *The Diving Bell and the Butterfly*. Critics have described it as "startling," "inspirational," and "a jewel."

Free of Mental Illness

You don't suffer from anthonephophobia, a fear of flowers falling from clouds.

Rock Sweetened by a Waterfall

Writing in *Under the Chinaberry Tree*, Louise Popoff extols the "miracle of boredom." "Some of the best imaginative work of my childhood," she says, "the games and fantasies that went the deepest into my soul, came from moments of complete boredom, when my mother wouldn't rescue me from having nothing to do and nowhere to go."

Animal Ecstasy

In his book *Animals and Psychedelics: The Natural World and the Instinct to Alter Consciousness*, ethnobotanist Giorgio Samorini proves that many animals deliberately alter their consciousness. His evidence includes robins that get drunk on holly berries and act "like winged clowns," as well as goats hooked on caffeine and reindeer that seek out hallucinogenic mushrooms.

Samorini concludes that the desire to get high is a natural drive. Intoxication has served as an evolutionary force for some species, breaking down outworn habits in such a way as to improve long-term survival.

Palindrome News

1. A Santa lived as a devil at NASA. 2. He maps spam, eh? 3. Rot can rob a born actor. 4. A slut nixes sex in Tulsa. 5. Revolt, lover! 6. Rise, sir lapdog! God, pal, rise, sir! 7. Bombard a drab mob! Egad—no bondage! 8. Go hang a salami—I'm a lasagna hog. 9. Was it a rat I saw?

BREAKING THE PRONOIA TABOO

"The moment you come to trust chaos, you see God clearly. Chaos is divine order, versus human order. Change is divine order, versus human order. When the chaos becomes safety to you, then you know you're seeing God clearly." —Caroline Myss, *Spiritual Madness: The Necessity of Meeting God in Darkness*

"Everything we shut our eyes to, everything we run away from, everything we deny, denigrate, or despise, serves to defeat us in the end. What seems nasty, painful, evil, can become a source of beauty, joy, and strength, if faced with an open mind. Every moment is a golden one for him who has the vision to recognize it." —Henry Miller

"The essence of all beautiful art, all great art, is gratitude." —Friedrich Nietzsche"

"Belief is the death of intelligence." —Robert Anton Wilson

"If you're really listening, if you're awake to the poignant beauty of the world, your heart breaks regularly. In fact, your heart is made to break; its purpose is to burst open again and again so that it can hold evermore wonders." —Andrew Harvey, *The Return of the Mother*

"The first idea that the child must acquire, in order to be actively disciplined, is that of the difference between good and evil; and the task of the educator lies in seeing that the child does not confound good with immobility, and evil with activity." —Maria Montessori, *The Montessori Method*

"Love your enemies; bless those who curse you, do good to those who hate you, and pray for those who persecute you." —Jesus

"Pollution is nothing but resources we're not harvesting." —R. Buckminster Fuller, *Critical Path*

Pablo Picasso had a difficult birth. When he finally popped out after a long labor, he wasn't breathing. The midwife decided his face was so blue he'd be impossible to revive. She declared him dead and left. But Picasso's uncle, who was in attendance, got up close to the infant and puffed cigar smoke up his nose. The shock brought him back to life.

Until she broke her foot as a teen, Paula Cole wanted to be a cheerleader like all the most popular girls. But the injury required her to wear a wooden shoe for an entire year, dashing her dreams and sending her in search of other identities. "That's when I found the piano, when music saved me," she said. "That's when I first attempted to write my own songs." Years later Cole became a Grammy-winning singer-songwriter.

Moral Gambling

The father of our friend Elliot was a professional gambler who figured out an ingenious system, got rich, and retired. For the rest of his life, he spent his gambler's fortune hunting down Nazi war criminals and bringing them to trial.

Faux Pronoia Report

Newspapers and magazines do promote pronoia in an ass-backwards way: through advertising. Comprising up to 70 percent of the total information presented in any one issue, this advice about how to buy supposedly useful objects and experiences seems to suggest that life is good and fulfillment is possible. But while the ads' promised satisfactions may titillate the ego, they are often of marginal interest to the soul, especially in light of the fact that they usually render the soul's agendas irrelevant.

MIRABILIA REPORT   *Mirabilia*   n. strange amazements, rare delights, sublime sublimations; from the Latin *mirabilia,* "marvels."

■ The National Center for Atmospheric Research reports that the average cloud is the same weight as 100 elephants.

■ In the Hindu epic the Mahabharata, the hero and heroine fall in love without ever gazing upon each other, simply by hearing tales about each other's good deeds.

■ The seeds of some trees are so tightly compacted within their protective covering that only the intense heat of a forest fire can free them, allowing them to sprout.

■ Twelve percent of the population believes that Joan of Arc was Noah's wife.

■ Because half of the world's vanilla crop is grown in Madagascar, the whole island smells like vanilla ice cream.

■ Your body contains so much iron that you could make a spike out of it, and that spike would be strong enough to hold you up.

■ There are about nine million people on earth who were born the same day as you.

■ In his book *The Physics of Immortality: Modern Cosmology, God and the Resurrection of the Dead,* physicist Frank J. Tipler offers what he says is scientific proof that every human being who has ever lived will be resurrected from the dead at the end of time.

■ In the Ukraine you can buy Fat in Chocolate, a food with a layer of dark chocolate covering a chunk of pork fat.

■ Today and every day, five million lightning bolts will flash between earth and sky somewhere on our planet.

■ Robust singing skill is correlated with a strong immune system in songbirds. Male birds with the most extensive repertoire of tunes also have the largest spleens, a key measure of immune system health.

■ Bali has 80,000 temples.

■ Some piranhas are vegetarians.

PRONOIA NEWS NETWORK

Poetry Facts

"Poetry is a rich, full-bodied whistle, cracked ice crunching in pails, the night that numbs the leaf, the duel of two nightingales, the sweet pea that has run wild, Creation's tears in shoulder blades." —Boris Pasternak

Abundance Studies

"Case Western University's School of Medicine in Cleveland has provided $1.7 million in research grants to seek 'clinically documented evidence of the positive effects and transformative power of unconditional love.' The school's Institute for Research on Unlimited Love will fund 21 studies into the scientific nature of volunteerism, organ donations, rescue work, and other acts of selfless altruism, compassion, and service."
—www.goodnewsnetwork.org

Possible Futures

You may someday write a book called *How To Attract Your Very Own Millionaire Spirit Guide.*

New Bonding Ritual

A new trend is emerging on college campuses: pimple- and blackhead-squeezing parties. "It's a great way to instantly drop social masks and get to know the real person," says Jamie Brooks, a sophomore from Boston College. "Our generation is tired of having to wade through glitzy packaging everywhere we go," adds junior Carla Lipske. "Popping zits is a bonding ritual that says, 'I accept you with all your imperfections.'"

Grieving Lessons

Buddhist sage Jack Kornfield tells of a woman devastated by the demise of a love affair. She turned to her Zen teacher, a Japanese monk, who soothed and consoled her as she grieved for weeks. The monk then returned to Japan, leaving the woman to fend for herself.

Months later he returned, and the woman picked him up at the airport. As he handed her a gift of prayer beads, she broke into sobs, confessing that her heart had still not mended from the loss of her paramour. Without hesitation, the teacher slapped her across the face.

"One year is too long!" he barked, "Get over it!"

Bullshit Versus Horseshit

"Bullshit is a rare and valuable commodity," rhapsodized Art Kleps in *The Boo Hoo Bible.* "The great masters have all been superb bullshitters. Horseshit, on the other hand, refers to downright crap. The free, playful, entertaining flight of ideas is bullshit, and more often than not will be found afterwards to accord perfectly with universal truth. Horseshit is contrived, derivative, superstitious, ignorant."

"Bullshit is creative, inspired mythmaking intended to provoke growth," added Alan Cabal in the *Village Voice,* "while horseshit is bottom-feeder derivative manipulation aimed at the endless acquisition of slaves, servants, and followers."

Fortune Cookie You are God.

OPEN SECRET

We live in the Milky Way Galaxy, which is shaped like a pinwheel. In 2003, astronomers were shocked to discover that the pinwheel has a fifth arm, one more than they've always thought. It's not as if it has been hard to spot: It's 77,000 light years long! "I was absolutely flabbergasted," astronomer Tom Dames told NewScientist.com. "It was clearly seen in previous surveys but was never pointed out or given a name."

DEATH-FREE TREE ART

Sculptor David Nash owns five chainsaws of different sizes, wrote art critic Kenneth Baker in the *San Francisco Chronicle,* and "wields all of them with improbable precision." His work doesn't require the destruction of living trees; recycled wood provides much of his raw material. Some of his sculptures consist of living trees whose growth he has directed. *Ash Dome* is a ring of 22 ash trees that he began shaping in 1977.

CRANE OPPORTUNISM

Between North and South Korea is a long, narrow strip of land called the DMZ. Designed to be a buffer zone where all human activity is prohibited, it has accidentally become a nature preserve beloved by white-naped cranes. The area is a paradise for the birds because it has an abundance of undisturbed marshland and is free of predators. Luckily, the cranes are so lightweight that they're in no danger of detonating the many land mines buried throughout the 370-square-mile area.

Thanks to our sponsor, the luminous tendril of celestial wish, *provided by poet e. e. cummings*

Art Lessons

French Impressionist painter Henri Matisse wanted his art to be "free from unsettling or disturbing subjects . . . soothing, a cerebral sedative as relaxing as a comfortable armchair."

Spanish painter Pablo Picasso had a different opinion. "Art is offensive," he asserted. "At least, art should be allowed to be offensive. It ought to be forbidden to ignorant innocents, never allowed into contact with those not sufficiently prepared. Yes, art is dangerous."

As you practice the art of pronoia, you will probably get best results if you swing back and forth between Matisse's and Picasso's approaches.

Every once in a while, try out William Butler Yeats' idea, too: "Art that doesn't attempt the impossible is not performing its function."

BONUS ORACLE!

Soaring and Scrounging

Our sources from high society say that when you eat caviar, you shouldn't use silver spoons: It taints the eggs with a metallic taste. Instead, always choose flatware made of gold or mother of pearl.

Our connections in low society suggest than when you dive into dumpsters foraging for discarded food, your best bet is the stuff in dented cans, since it's probably uncontaminated by any toxic garbage lying nearby.

These tips should be useful metaphors for you in the coming years, as you'll have chances to extract bounty not only while you're visiting soaring peaks but also when you're scrounging around dismal abysses.

Visualize

_____
[PUT YOUR DEITY'S NAME HERE]

at the
moment of orgasm

All i Ask Of You

1

Be my slow-motion dance.

Be my birthday earthquake.

Be my spiral marble staircase
in the middle of a Vermont meadow.

Be my handstand on a barstool,
my whirlwind week in clown school,
my joke shared with a Siberian shaman
while shopping for t-shirts at Sears.

Be my last *because.*

2

Be my puzzle with one piece missing.

Be my ripe pomegranate
floating in a blue plastic swimming pool
on the first day of winter.

Be the imaginary conversations
I have with Thomas Jefferson
while watching the news on TV.

Be the waves crashing on my beach
in the south of France in the 22nd century
and the song
that my great-grandmother wrote for my great-granddaughter.

Be my golden hammer resting on a mossy rock
I've known for 10,000 years.

What If Your Desires Are Holy?

Some religious traditions teach the doctrine, "Kill off your longings." In their view, attachment to desire is at the root of human suffering. But the religion of materialism takes the opposite tack, asserting that the meaning of life is to be found in indulging desires. Its creed is, "Feed your cravings like a French foie gras farmer cramming eight pounds of maize down a goose's gullet every day."

At the Beauty and Truth Lab, we walk a middle path. We believe there are both degrading desires that enslave you and sacred desires that liberate you.

Psychologist Carl Jung believed that *all* desires have a sacred origin, no matter how odd they may seem. Frustration and ignorance may contort them into distorted caricatures, but it is always possible to locate the divine source from which they arose. In describing one of his addictive patients, Jung said: "His craving for alcohol was the equivalent on a low level of the spiritual thirst for wholeness, or as expressed in medieval language: the union with God."

Therapist James Hillman echoes the theme: "Psychology regards all symptoms to be expressing the right thing in the wrong way." A preoccupation with porn or romance novels, for instance, may come to dominate a passionate person whose quest for love has degenerated into an obsession with images of love. "Follow the lead of your symptoms," Hillman suggests, "for there's usually a myth in the mess, and a mess is an expression of soul."

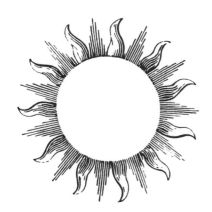

In *Maldoror and Poems,* the French poet Lautréamont wrote about holy yearning disguised as mournful complaint. "Whenever you hear the dogs' howling in the fields," his mother told him as a child, "don't deride what they do: They thirst insatiably for the infinite, like you, me, and the rest of us humans. I even allow you to stand at the window and gaze upon this exalted spectacle."

"The primordial fire that sparked millions of galaxies is the same fire that sparks the human creative impulse." —Cindy Spring, "The Non-Profit Universe," *Earth-Light,* Summer 2002. "The human reproductive drive is a watered-down version of the godsex that spawned our solar system." —"Lieutenant" Anfortas, the homeless guy in the Safeway parking lot.

"Feelings that originate in the human genitalia are among the most powerful forces on earth. They have a complex relationship with the feelings that stem from the human heart: at various times in competition or in harmony. Together these primal energies have forged and toppled empires; unleashed terrible and wonderful ideas; and generated the greatest stories ever told. Our goal is to harness our sexual urges in service to the heart's wisdom." —Sheila Samizdat, "Ritual Foreplay for a New History," *Underground Pronoia*

"Mad! One must become mad with love in order to realize God. When a person attains ecstatic love of God, all the pores of the skin, even the roots of the hair, become like so many sex organs, and in every pore the aspirant enjoys the happiness of communion with the Supreme Universal Self." —Ramakrishna

Like all of us, you have desires for things that you don't really need and aren't good for you. But you shouldn't disparage yourself for having them, nor should you conclude that every desire is tainted. Rather, think of your misguided longings as the bumbling, amateur expressions of a faculty that will one day be far more expert. They're how you practice as you work toward the goal of becoming a master of desire. It may take a while, but eventually you will get the hang of wanting things that are really good for you, and good for everyone else, too.

"The only way anyone is ever cured of desiring nonsensical things is by getting the nonsensical things and then experiencing the unpleasant but educational consequences." —Ann Davies, www.bota.org

"To become a master of desire, keep talking yourself out of being attached to trivial goals and keep talking yourself into being thrilled about the precious few goals that are really important. Here's another way to say it: Wean yourself from ego-driven desires and pour your libido into a longing for beauty, truth, goodness, justice, integrity, creativity, love, and an intimate relationship with the Wild Divine." —Raye Sangfreud, "Black Market Orchids," *Underground Pronoia*

"God has desires. Since I want to be close to God and to model myself after God, I therefore don't aspire to extinguish my desires, but rather to make my desires more God-like: i.e., imbued with an inexorable ambition to create the greatest and most interesting blessings for everyone and everything." —Collin Klamper

"'Heterosexual,' 'bisexual,' 'lesbian,' and 'gender queer' are not terms I use to describe myself. They're too limiting, like every other name and role I've had the pleasure of escaping. In a pinch, I might agree to call myself ocean-fucker or sky-sucker or earth-bonker. As much as I love men and women, they can't satisfy the full extent of my yearning. I need intimate relations with clouds and eagles and sea anemones and mountains and spirits of the dead and kitchen appliances and the creatures in my dreams. To be continued. To be enhanced and amplified and enlarged upon, world without end, amen. One day I really do hope to be a wise enough lover to be able to fuck the ocean. To give a forest fire a blow job. To make a pride of lions come just by looking at them." —Jumbler Javalina, "Bite into the Mysteries," *Underground Pronoia*

"When I hold you, I hold everything: ruby-throated hummingbirds sipping from plum flowers, mangoes ripening in the smoke of burning forests, crones praying in the foamy sand at low tide, shocked waterfalls gracing new housing developments, volcanoes drinking in the fragrance of the stars. In your eyes I see everything that lives." —mash-up of Pablo Neruda and Rob Brezsny

Imagine it's 30 years from now. You're looking back at the history of your relationship with desire. There was a certain watershed moment when you clearly saw that some of your desires were mediocre, inferior, and wasteful, while others were pure, righteous, and invigorating. Beginning then, you made it a life goal to purge the former and cultivate the latter. Thereafter, you occasionally wandered down dead ends trying to gratify yearnings that weren't worthy of you, but usually you wielded your passions with discrimination, dedicating them to serve the highest and most interesting good.

Dionysian Manifesto

THE ORGASMIC ROOTS OF PRONOIA

Any young man who's serious about becoming a good lover must early in the game confront a demoralizing truth about the difference between the male and female orgasms. If there were no other evidence that the Goddess is a trickster, this fact alone would suffice for proof: Most human males are prone to ejaculate within two minutes of the time they insert their jade stalk into the silk furrow. To not perform this stupid abracadabra, in fact, typically requires diligent practice.

For those dudes who perfect the art of not splurging so fast, however, there is an even more Olympian challenge: gaining control of the splurge, so that it happens only when consciously willed. The men who reach this winner's circle are truly an elite group.

On the other hand, most human females cannot under even the most favorable ambiance ascend to the state of orgasmic grace in less than 15 minutes. Half an hour is not unusual, and I've known ripe and fully emancipated women who rarely need less than 45 minutes.

It's true that some men, especially those that have only recently started growing a beard, can reload in a short time. A 10-minute wait between erections should not, theoretically, be an insurmountable obstacle to picking up where you left off. From my private polls, however, I conclude that even though many 19-year-old studs can get it up again after a relatively brief waiting period, few are actually still in a mood sexy enough to press on with the same attentiveness, let alone artistry, that led up to the first engagement. And of those, only a tiny percentage have the expertise or the inclination, while marking time till resurrection, to attend to the female pleasure zones with the non-genital parts of their bodies.

Which leads to the next cruel joke: A majority of women can't even achieve the flutter-magic through the unsupplemented in-and-out anyway: In many positions, the sliding action of the diamond pumper barely misses the clitoris, heart-source of female pleasure. (Not that most men even realize this. At this late date a significant minority have at least discovered the existence of the clitoris, but few have figured out how to address it in its native language.)

This is not to say that most women would, if forced to make the choice, opt for pure clitoral stimulation over copulation. Lots of them do relish the evolutionarily-necessary penis-vagina friction; they'd just like it a lot better if their total bliss was addressed, not just one facet.

On the whole, I'm inclined to believe that the pool of male fuckmasters—those who can consciously decree the moment of ejaculation and who understand the intricacies of the female orgasm—barely exceeds the number of those who garner the Nobel Prize each year.

In the early years of my apprenticeship, I used the crudest method to avoid early detonation: condoms, sometimes even two or three at once. This usually numbed me sufficiently to last indefinitely. For emergencies, I also carried with me a desensitizing chemical spray I'd bought via mail order from an ad in the back of *Penthouse* magazine.

Both of these options were anathema, though. Because the age of AIDS had not yet radically altered heterosexual courtship rituals, condoms were a novelty.

Most of my lovers used IUDs or diaphragms or birth control pills, and were adamantly opposed to the sterile sensation of a rubber sheath caressing their intimate parts. Nor were they enamored of my "Sta-Hard" aerosol, which exuded a smell one of my lovers said made her think of "a football player in a barn."

Condoms and anesthetics, I decided, were not ultimately part of the game plan that would make me a fuckmaster. Painstakingly, I began to accumulate a more natural bag of tricks. The earliest technique, which I acquired by blind instinct, was a little less crude than condoms. I'd struggle to divert my attention away from the pleasure at hand by fantasizing about baseball games. I found I could deaden a measure of the supernal bliss driving me towards climax by seeing in my inner eye, for instance, the events leading up to Philadelphia Phillies' third baseman Mike Schmidt smacking a grand slam home run to beat the Pittsburgh Pirates in the 13th inning. In some love-making sessions, I narrated entire ball games in my mind.

A second aid, also discovered early in my quest, was to inflict pain elsewhere on my body. Slapping my thighs worked well in distracting myself from the overabundant joy buzzing in my genitals, as did pinching and twisting my belly or digging my fingernails into my face. A more professional approach came to me via the *Marriage and Sex Manual* I found in a used bookstore. A man who was on the verge of splurging was advised to squeeze the base of his jade stalk or apply firm pressure to the perineum. The first action would mechanically suppress the ejaculatory urge. The second would blockade the spasmodic flow of semen from scrotum to penis.

These last two strategies were repugnant. I didn't want to rely on last-ditch interventions that required emergency brute force. I wanted poised power. I longed to wield command over my inconvenient biological programming every step of the way.

Eventually I discovered there were ancient traditions that had exhaustively explored the art of sexuality, including the problem of ejaculatory control. In India and Nepal and Tibet, these teachings were grouped under a branch of yoga known as tantra. In China, certain schools of Taoism dealt extensively with the same subjects.

Unfortunately, many of these teachings were so bound up with the esoteric spirituality, bad translations, and hoary terminology of their respective traditions that they were only marginally useful to a horny dude who wasn't willing to immerse himself in a 10-year plan to master the discipline.

By the mid-1980s, a smattering of American authors began packaging the venerable secrets in modern

vernacular. Even then, though, many of the techniques were elusive and subtle to the point of being useless.

Try imagining, for instance, a stream of golden light percolating from your perineum up your spine, then through your brain and back down the front of your body to the perineum again. While breathing rhythmically through your nose and from your lower abdomen only, counting to eight for each inhale and exhale, circulate the light continuously until it achieves a momentum of its own and drones on autonomously in the background of your awareness. In the meantime, gnash your teeth gently and touch a point one inch above your right nipple with your left index finger and middle finger, all the while opening your eyes as wide as they'll go and jamming your tongue against the roof of your mouth. "These actions will definitely cause the semen to be retained," the text asserts.

Oh yeah? Maybe when you're sitting alone and relaxed in your temperature-controlled room with a sleep mask over your eyes. But try the same meditation while you're sweat-to-sweat with a gorgeous aromatic creature who thrills every cell in your body. The difficulty of the task increases exponentially, at least during the first decade of trying to master it.

Which is not to say it's impossible. And besides, if you can be sufficiently candid with the gorgeous aromatic creature (and why would you be making love with a woman you can't be honest with?), you might enlist her aggressive cooperation in your attempts to distribute your kundalini to your whole body rather than have it congregate in one bloated, ready-to-pop area of congestion. You can ask her to not wiggle so seductively. You can beg her not to kiss you with so much exultant abandon. You can plead with her not to emanate so many tangy succulent smells and not utter so many of the bewitching groans that make you want to gush your entire soul into her.

But on the other hand, what lover in his righteous heart wants to ask that of the gorgeous aromatic creature with whom he's entwined?

I stumbled along with my conglomeration of baseball visualizations, self-mortifications, and tantric mumbo-jumbo. I was a good enough lover, usually a long-lasting lover, but not a fuckmaster. Wasn't there a philosopher's stone? Wasn't there a technique that could provide consistent and ultimate control? Or would I forever have to make do with my jury-rigged system?

At last, hallelujah, in a New Age bookstore in Santa Cruz I found the treasure: a dusty hand-bound book titled

Sexx Magixx. The obviously pseudonymous author was Jack N. Off, and I couldn't have been more surprised by his precious secret. When you urinate, he said, interrupt the flow in midstream. The muscles by which you accomplish this unnatural act are the same muscles engaged in ejaculation. By gaining control over this mechanism through strenuous daily exercises, you'll grow strong enough to forcibly restrain the semen from gushing out—even, if necessary, after the ejaculatory spasm has begun. You can do this again and again in any single lovemaking session, thereby staying hard as long as you desire.

I threw myself into this work, and within a few weeks I mostly conquered the previously involuntary reflex of ejaculation. It wasn't 100 percent foolproof—I still made use of my old standby methods—and it was never easy.

I had to do the exercises every day to stay fit, and while making love I had to maintain a high level of concentration that sometimes detracted from the surrender I wanted to feel.

But I was pleased with my new technique; I felt as if a Golden Age had begun. Nineteen times out of 20 I came only when I willed it, only when I was sure my woman had had her fill. Now and then my ardent efforts at retention weren't totally successful, but the mini-eruptions relieved a small amount of the pressure to spill without bringing an end to the hard-on.

With the arrival of this blessing in my life, I was finally able to confront a mystery I had doggedly turned away from. All the tantric and Taoist texts agreed, though I skeptically resisted it, that a man's sexual experience was far better in every way if he did not ejaculate at all, even after his partner has been satisfied. This assertion was based in part on the fact (not a theory, they said) that a regular loss of semen is detrimental to male vitality and health. It also assumed that sex yields up much more of its mind-expanding, life-transforming magic if the erotic energy is "steamed up" to the heart and brain rather than waste-

fully ejected. There, in the higher chakras, lust is liberated from its enslavement to the reproductive instinct. Transformed into a supercharged nourishment, it feeds one's aspirations to unite with the Divine Wow. As a method of expanding one's consciousness, it's both safer and more efficacious than psychedelic drugs.

I was willing to entertain the latter notion. Erotic play had always put me in a deliciously altered state, and I longed to harness its transcendent energy to accomplish something beyond merely feeling good. Unfortunately, I could not help but hedge my bets. I convinced myself I could somehow both steam the sex energy up up up and also indulge in a good old-fashioned ejaculation.

The real tantrics would have laughed at me.

I did not even go through the motions of trying to accept the other rationale for not coming, though—that losing your seed too often made you weak and stupid. I felt it had too much in common with the old superstition that women use sex to steal men's energy. It seemed patriarchal and misogynist. Steadfastly, like a scientist obsessed with proving a bogus hypothesis, I ignored and repressed all data that contradicted my fixation.

There was yet another good reason the tantric and Taoist texts gave for phasing out the old habit entirely. Several books hinted at the shocking secret, but Mantak Chia and Michael Winn spelled it out at length in their book *Taoist Secrets of Love: Cultivating Male Sexual Energy.* Ejaculation and orgasm are not the same thing, they asserted. In fact, the two functions can and should be separated. Why? Because the orgasm that's affixed to ejaculation is a mediocre form of pleasure. It's limited to a few intense seconds which exhaust the capacity for further delight.

There is a higher orgasm that is available only after the addiction to ejaculation has been renounced. It's at least as vivid as the first kind, usually more so, but lasts longer and can be repeated indefinitely—similar to a woman's. "How would you like to be in a continual state of climax for an hour or more?" the esoteric experts hinted. Moreover, this higher orgasm alone creates the conditions necessary to steam the semen up to the heart and brain.

For a while I stubbornly rebelled against this claim. I argued with it in my own mind, accusing it of being perverse and effete. It did not jibe with my experience. I found nothing pleasurable about waging my brave struggle against evolution's primordial pressure. Yes, it was for a good cause. I bought the importance of it. But I wanted my reward in the end—the reward that nature had worked millions of years to perfect.

My attitude began to change once I met Celia.

Medicine Story

Celia was, has been, and still is a fountain of blessings. For starters, she is a provocative listener who regularly draws insights out of me I don't know that I know. Her insights into human nature are acute and compassionate, and I often ask her opinion about a person I'm considering as a new friend or associate. She's funny and boisterous. Her well-developed sense of humor doesn't shut down when the going gets tough.

She said, "Let's charter a supersonic MiG-25 Foxbat plane to ferry us to the upper edge of the atmosphere, where we can see the curvature of the Earth."

She is knowledgeable about politics, but in more of a tender than doctrinaire way, and she has been a driving force in teaching me to tincture my vehement critiques of everything that's wrong in the world with good old love.

I admire her livelihood: She's a freelance translator who's fluent in five languages. She's also a skillful pianist and composer. Had she chosen that field as a career path, I'm convinced she would have been one of the rare musicians who make their living doing what they love.

One of the accomplishments I'm most impressed by is the way Celia has taken responsibility for and transformed her shadow. Psychologist Carl Jung said we all have one of those things: an unripe, wounded part of our psyche that is out of harmony with our conscious values. It's our private portion of what the world's major religions have demonized as "the devil." Few human beings are courageous or resourceful enough to wage sacred combat with this secret saboteur; most project its mischief out onto people or groups they dislike. But Celia is a rare exception. She relentlessly monitors her own shadow, trying to ensure that it doesn't distort her relationships. This heroic effort alone makes her more trustworthy than anyone I've ever known.

I feel real in Celia's presence. Not inflated, worshiped, or adored, and not belittled, demeaned, or underestimated—just authentic. It's a relief to be seen as I am in all my complexity, with no distorting emphasis on either my immature or noble aspects. I feel a deep relaxation around her. I'm at home in the world.

When I first met Celia, her gifts scared me. She had so much to offer and such an exquisite talent for giving that I felt like a stingy, shrunken-hearted narcissist in her presence. I worked hard to be worthy of the bounty she bestows.

And oh by the way, she's physically beautiful, too: striking and robust, voluptuous and athletic, open and mysterious. If I gaze at her face for just 10 minutes, I can see her change from a kind and authoritative Egyptian queen to a fierce and joyous Irish amazon to an unpredictable and mystical Portuguese gypsy. She's cheerful and intense, unpredictable and trustworthy, bright and deep.

The first few times Celia and I made love, I tuned in to an unexpected phenomenon: I wasn't having to withhold ejaculation with the teeth-clenching severity I'd become used to. In fact, as I opened to the incredible possibility, it became almost easy to bottle up the primordial force of nature within me. No baseball meditations were required, nor the convoluted breathing exercises synchronized with thigh-slapping and eye-popping. And I found myself having to summon a mere fraction of the heroic muscle constriction that characterized my most reliable technique.

Why? In light of all my past experience, it didn't make sense. To be intimately woven with a smart, soulful, gorgeous woman who made my heart bloom should have put me on the verge of coming all the time—especially when I was actually inside her.

I wondered if it could have had something to do with the structure of Celia's fluttering phoenix. But it wasn't slack; wasn't too big and roomy. Her muscles were well-toned. She had never given birth. We fit snugly together.

A radical theory dawned in me. What if men are not solely responsible, I mused, for evolution's conspiracy to trick them into delivering DNA's payload in two minutes flat? What if women play at least a small role in perpetuating the bad habit that is the most likely factor to undermine mutually gratifying heterosexual sex? And what if Celia was one of the rare females who somehow turned off the part of her programming that contributes to the bad habit?

This was a taboo thought to expose to the frowning radical feminist that sometimes patrolled my superego, but I had to let myself acknowledge the possibility: that some women on some occasions—maybe only in their unconscious minds—actually don't want their male partners to have control over the timing of their climax.

I speculated that there are four types of women who might sabotage the long-lasting male lover:

1. Some women regard a fast squirt as testimony to their overpowering irresistibility. "He found me so alluring that he couldn't contain himself." Many of this type are throwbacks to an age when a wife regarded her man's pleasure as more important than hers; when a female measured her success in love more by her ability to give gratification than to get it.

2. Some women may not want a rush to judgment but are nevertheless strongly attached to having a smoking gun: concrete proof that they've done their job of satisfying their men. No ejaculationless orgasm for these women, thank you; it's too ambiguous.

3. Some women conspire to induce a quick and seemingly accidental orgasm because they want to use it to humble their partner, berate him for his inadequacy, and have a bargaining chip to use in winning other, nonsexual concessions.

4. Some women are possessed by their DNA with the same demonic fervor as any man is by his. The 30-year-old ego may be crying out, "Give me deep pleasure," while the 10 million-year-old reproductive machinery is hissing, "Give me a baby." The mandate to propagate the species wants the ejaculation now, not in two hours. Why else would evolution have made it so absurdly easy for a man to come?

I reiterate that these four motivations are not necessarily blazing in the conscious awareness of women who are in the throes of making love. They may be unconscious programs that covertly shape the way their body functions.

Celia fit into none of the four categories. I suspected that at some point before she met me she had forged herself into a lover who would not collude with the hair-trigger release that evolution had bequeathed to men.

By what mechanism had she accomplished this? Was it a regimen of physical exercises comparable to those I had done in order to become a control artist? A secret of meditation that allowed her to transmute the subtle structure of the muscles and electrochemical environment in her silk furrow? An esoteric yogic technique by which she imprinted her very flesh with the affirmation that she was "complete unto herself"

(the ancient meaning of the word "virgin"), and did not, therefore, need to play a part in propagating the species?

This whole line of thinking took almost two months to ripen. We met each other in April, but it wasn't till June, eight dates into our relationship, that I was ready to speak of the inquiry that had been brewing in me. The climax came on a Saturday night.

I had read about a survey in which couples reported they often had great sex after seeing scary movies or going to a rifle range. Though I couldn't imagine the erotic glee between me and Celia being any better than it already was, I told her about the survey and suggested we try our own experiments. She liked the idea, but said that instead of watching violence or shooting guns, she'd prefer going on the thrill rides at the boardwalk.

We impulsively decided to get dressed up as a pirate and cowgirl for the occasion, which was easy enough to do thanks to a local costume rental shop open year-round. After polishing off a picnic dinner of take-out sushi on a bluff overlooking the sea, we arrived at the boardwalk. For the next three hours, we rode the roller coaster twice, as well as the Cliff Hanger, the Hurricane, the Whirlwind, the Tsunami, the Ferris wheel, the bumper cars, and the Crazy Surf. By the time we came back to Celia's house around 10 o'clock, we had whipped ourselves into a state of pleasant vertigo.

Soon we were naked and circling each other like samurai wrestlers in her secluded backyard, expanding the batty frame of mind we'd been thrust into by our synapse-boggling joyrides. It was chilly out there on that June night, and to compensate we soon found ourselves engaging in aerobic sex on a picnic table. To add to the incandescence and generate even more joie de vivre, we adopted funny accents as we pretended to be drunk Italian tourists arguing about whether it was safe to stand up on a roller coaster, stoned French graduate students arguing about whether Pynchon or Joyce was the greater genius, and Pakistani explorers marooned in the Arctic wastes arguing about which of our dead comrades we should eat first.

After a while we disengaged, agreeing to take a break and head inside. As I warmed up in her bed, she skipped off to the kitchen to make hot chocolate. With a fog of sweat still evaporating from me, I closed my eyes and did a meditation in which I prayed that the love I was feeling for her would remain as pure and generous as it was in that moment.

I prayed that my effect on her would always promote her greater good and inspire her to seek out interesting adventures. I visualized us continuing to be able to be both kind and wild with each other.

In a few minutes, Celia glided back into the room with two steamy cups, her slapstick urges apparently unquenched: On her head she was wearing a "crown" composed of a purple balloon sculpture of a vulture. (Where had *that* come from?) Setting the cups down, she charged at my midsection, pecking me again and again with the inflated rubber beak. Between pecks she recited a pastiche of Emily Dickinson poems that featured the recurring line, "Dare you see a soul at the white heat?"

I lay down on the mattress and pulled her on top of me, removing her crown. With her cooperation, I slipped my jade stalk back where it belonged. As she gazed into my eyes with amused tenderness, her yoni began to play luxuriously, gripping and letting go with artistry, coming from diverse angles and engorging to a variety of depths. I let her control the rhythm, which was slow-motion and adoring.

For a long time we danced like this, singing each other songs with unhurried intensity. "You were born with a snake in both of your fists while a hurricane was blowing," I crooned, quoting Bob Dylan's "Jokerman." I also did covers of Bruce Cockburn's "Lovers in a Dangerous Time" and Louis Armstrong's "What a Wonderful World."

She treated me to excerpts from Billie Holiday's "Swing Brother Swing" and Patti Smith's album "Radio Ethiopia," including her own mutated version of "Ain't It Strange":

> Come and join me, I implore thee,
> I impure thee, come explore me.
> Oh, don't you know that anyone can come
> in the same old way
> but we both want more.
> Don't you see when you're playing with me
> that we'll never end
> transcend transcend.

After delivering this curious passage, she cleared her voice and assumed a more prosaic tone. "And now I am pleased to make the long-awaited announcement. After many years of hard work rebelling against instinct, I have graduated from the need for the melodramatic spurt. I have kicked my addiction to the old-fashioned *petite morte*. You are free, my dear, to keep your vital fluids to yourself. I don't need you to spew in order to know how desperately you want me."

I could hardly believe what I was hearing. She seemed to be addressing and answering the pressing question I had not yet spoken aloud to her. I indulged a fantasy that had been growing in me in recent weeks: that our connection was evolving into a telepathic union.

"You're a genius," I said. "You're a flaming genius."

"So is there any chance you want to see what it's like to have orgasms like mine?" she asked. "Implosive prayer wheel-spinning jubilations instead of those crash-and-burn-style evacuations you've gotten so dependent on? I'd love you to love me in a way that helped you love yourself better. How about it?"

Up until this moment, my training as a fuckmaster had never been devoted to expanding my own sexual pleasure. Even after I'd learned of the esoteric teachings about an alternate form of male orgasm, I withheld my ejaculations for other reasons: to ensure that my partners were thoroughly fulfilled and to pump up my image of myself as a good lover.

And the truth was I had never felt I could afford to explore the far frontiers of my own sexual pleasure. To do so might sabotage my arduously cultivated art of control, causing me to come too soon and fail as a lover.

Tears surged from my eyes and a blend of moan and chuckle spilled from my mouth. I felt a subtle but distinct pop in my pelvis, as if a blockage had been forcibly cleared or a knot cut. The hot coil of pleasure I had always identified as the essence of my sexual treasure began to spread out. As I followed it for the next few minutes, I realized with a mix of dismay and delight that for all these years it had been trapped in a tightly contained area in and around my cock and balls.

She asked me, "What song did you sing on the last day of your childhood? Do you love your body perfectly? What was the pain that healed you most? Can you play games with no rules?"

"You lifted the curse," I muttered to Celia with a smoky cheerfulness. "You broke the dam. You freed the genie. You liberated the slave. You tricked the guardian on the threshold into revealing the magic password."

"And I did it all with love, sweet love, not force, brute force," she murmured as she kissed my eyelids.

Spiral waves of nectar rippled out from the epicenter of my bliss. My heart was first to receive the blessing, then my throat and thighs. Gradually the entire inside of my body was awash with the bliss that had previously been confined to one small part of me. And as

Celia continued to swirl me around inside her, I claimed the birthright I'd always denied myself: long, billowing orgasms, one following another. They were whirlpools of sweetness congealing in an ocean of delight. And unlike the expulsive, spasmodic burst I'd always regarded as the One True Orgasm, this new improved model kept *expanding* my capacity for more pleasure. My hard-on stayed hard even as the pulsing spirals kept on coming.

But how could that be? It didn't make sense. I'd long believed in the limiting power of satiation: A person could only experience so much rapture, right? After a set of nerve endings reaches a saturation point, the same stimulation that initially induced pleasure there begins to evoke apathy or even annoyance.

And yet that didn't apply in this case. The gratifications swarming through me were increasing, as if my ability to feel pleasure in three dimensions were expanding into four, and then into five and beyond.

"I'm coming in the eighth dimension right now," I whispered to Celia.

"I not only see your third eye right now," she replied softly. "I can hear your third ear and smell your second nose, too."

"I'm afraid I'm becoming an eight-dimensional freak monster."

"You're the eight-dimensional freaky godfuck monster with a beauty that's so scary big you don't know what to do with it all."

"Uh-oh."

"Luckily, I'm also an eight-dimensional freaky godfuck monster with a beauty that's so scary big I don't know what to do with it all."

"We might have to go down to the homeless shelter and give away our scary beauty to all the needy poor people."

"And go down to the country club and give away our scary beauty to all the needy rich people."

I can't remember if we were still actually moving our bodies. The friction of genitals had become irrelevant. My longing was utterly satisfied and yet was somehow also growing. I was very happy about how much love I felt for her, but wanted to love her even more.

My pleasure overflowed into the room. It was as if I were turning inside out. At first that spooked me. As I got used to it, I surrendered. I began to fantasize that I—whatever "I" might

be—was now located outside my body as much as inside. "I" was having orgasms in an expanding sphere that spread into the space around me.

They really couldn't be called "orgasms" any more, though. That term implies a sudden, forceful contraction and release centered around a focal point. But I was experiencing a multitude of repeating pulses, like a hundred beating hearts, unleashing ripples of pleasure over and over again.

"This is what God feels all the time," I whispered.

"Yes. This is what Goddess feels all the time," Celia answered.

"So we're imitating the Creators of the Universe right now?" I said.

"Well," she said, "in a sense we are imitating them. In another sense, we *are* them."

"I'm having a million orgasms every second."

"Me too. Let's shoot for a billion."

"OK. How?"

"Turn the orgasms into prayers."

"What do we pray for?"

"We pray for what God and Goddess pray for. Which is different from what humans pray for."

"I seem to be having a divine memory lapse, Goddess. Remind me what we pray for?"

"Our prayers are the engine of creation. They're how we reanimate the universe fresh every nanosecond—orgasmic bursts of divine love that keep everything growing and changing forever."

"So if we want to imitate God and Goddess—I mean, if we want to *be* God and Goddess—we should act as if our orgasms are actually prayers with which we beget the universe anew over and over again."

I felt another pop, like the one that had earlier freed my sexual energy from its logjam in my pelvis. Only this was non-local, a pervasive burst that shook the entire bubble of orgasmic vibration I now inhabited. As in the previous experience, I felt as if a blockage had been forcibly cleared.

Images and emotions began streaming into my imagination. They had a life of their own; were independent of my will. They came in bursts, each of which bore the imprint of a person I knew and cared for. There was my friend Fred, the entomologist, with whom I traveled in Europe; Regina, the old girlfriend with whom I had three abortions; Maddy, the woman I sang with for five years; Sunyatta, the professional ballet dancer who taught me how to do a pirouette; Mr. Riley, my high school French teacher, the only older male who ever gave me a blessing.

In each case, the person's life seemed to pass in a flash before my eyes, downloading into my psyche all the memories of everything he or she had ever done and thought and felt, the pain mixed with the pleasure, the rot with the splendor. It was all happening impossibly fast: as if the old 2.5 GHz microprocessor in my brain had been replaced by a new model that ran at 2.5 million GHz.

To be so intimately attuned with these friends and loved ones provoked a flood of empathy and compassion that blended seamlessly with my ongoing orgasms. A touch of amusement brushed through me briefly as I noted the unfamiliarity of having sexual associations with Fred and Mr. Riley, but it soon passed and I surrendered to the undifferentiated delight.

She said, "Let's kill the apocalypse."

More life stories surged into me with even greater speed, and they included those of people with whom I'd had more complicated relationships: ex-band member Armand, who had both stunted and fed my growth as a musician; ex-girlfriend Raven, whose confounding betrayal taught me so much about myself that in effect I earned a PhD in self-knowledge under her tutelage; my sister who cut me out of her life for years.

I received them all gratefully and with relish, both the difficult souls and those for whom I had more unconditional love. The lushness of their intimate otherness was intoxicating. I loved being stuffed with so many thousands of foreign emotions and secrets and contradictions. The more I filled up, the more I wanted and the more I could hold. Soon I lost count of how many mythic imprints I had absorbed. Finally Celia spoke, breaking a long silence.

"We could probably keep going, but I think that's enough for now," she said. I opened my eyes and brought my attention back to her, returning from my inner orgy. I was confused. Did she want us to stop making love?

"I'm not ready to split us apart yet, Goddess," I complained. "In fact, I think I'm just getting started."

"I don't mean we should uncouple," she said, kissing me on both cheeks. "I mean we should stop filling ourselves up with the lives of all these people who need our prayers. Let's decide what to do with this batch before we welcome another one."

"Did you just have the same experience I did?" I asked, hoping for more evidence of our growing telepathic rapport.

"I should hope so, dear. See what happens when you play God?"

She playfully rolled over, pulling me with her so that now I was on top.

"Now fuck me with your prayers for all those souls who leaped into you," she commanded. "And I'll fuck you with mine."

I shoved a pillow under her ass to change the angle at which I entered her, and raised her legs a little by lifting from behind her knees.

"I visualize and pray that my old friend Fred will come to a new, supple accommodation with his ex-wife so that they create more harmony in the life of their daughter," I said as I moved in Celia. "May this unfold in ways that send benevolent consequences out in all directions, diminishing the suffering and enhancing the joy of every sentient being."

"I declare and desire that my Aunt Ruth will find the key to supporting herself as an acupuncturist so she can quit her gig as a grocery clerk," asserted Celia. "And I pray that in doing this she will become a more potent force for beauty and truth and goodness, lifting up everyone whose life she touches."

"I foresee and demand that Regina will summon the power to cut back on her work doing hospital murals so she can write that children's book she wants to do. May this in turn redound to the benefit of all creatures."

"I envision and confirm that John Selkirk will get the help necessary to heal from the death of his wife. As he receives what he needs, I further envision and confirm that all of creation will gather inspiration from the changes he sets in motion."

Many other friends, acquaintances, and loved ones made appearances in our ritual. My heart broke open again and again, ripped sweetly apart by a yearning to help them thrive, to love them as they needed to be loved, to enhance them and enliven them and share with them the blessings Celia and I had conjured.

Sometimes our invocations took the form of loud singing and chants; other times we emitted fantastic cackles and churned out rhythms with guttural grunts. We spoke in horse language and tried to recreate the original tongue from which Sanskrit and Hebrew originated. Thomas Jefferson and Sally Hemmings paid a visit, channeled through us mediumistically, bestowing

Medicine Story

their unique love on several lucky beneficiaries.

Nine hundred trillion orgasms later, the rays of the morning sun splashed on my eyes as I meandered through a prayer for Maddy. "I predict and guarantee that she will compose a bunch of great songs about her struggle to be a half-decent single mother while playing low-paying gigs at funky San Francisco nightclubs in hopes of bringing her incredible singing talent to the attention of some non-exploitative hustler who'll help her get a recording contract."

"Hey God?" Celia rumbled from out of her trance state. We were lying side by side, still linked.

"Yes, Goddess," I said.

"I hate to interrupt you. You're still amazingly eloquent for someone who's been fucking nonstop for 14.3 billion years. Or is it 14.6?"

"That's OK. I can't think of anyone else I love being interrupted by more than you."

"I'm thinking maybe we should do a prayer for Rob and Celia and then put the universe to sleep for a while."

"Good idea."

"They've been quite kind to let us commandeer their bodies for so long. Let's show our gratitude."

"I'll start."

"Take your time."

"I decree and imagine that Celia will become a master of the art of bestowing blessings. As brilliant and generous as she is in giving gifts, she will never become addicted to giving gifts; nor will she try to control people with her gifts; nor will she let her joy in giving gifts interfere with her capacity to attract and receive gifts herself."

"And when Celia gives gifts," the Goddess in Celia added, "they will always be precisely what the recipients need rather than what she needs to give. She will have a knack for choosing people who make the best use of her gifts. No pearls-before-swine mistakes for her."

"Ho!" I exclaimed, invoking the Northern Californian pagan version of "amen."

"Now I have a prayer for Rob," she said. "I pray that he will popularize the slogan 'I am totally opposed to all duality.'"

"Good old Rob will become a socialist Libertarian, macho feminist, Buddhist Muslim, gun-owning pacifist," I added.

"He will embrace his destiny as a prophet of the ejaculationless male orgasm. He will triumph over the primal on-off switch that has been the biological linchpin of the male psyche's addiction to us-versus-them fundamentalism."

"I pray that he will write books crammed with inspirational philosophies that are rooted in the oceanic prayer orgasms he has achieved this night. He will help forge a new nation conceived in liberty and dedicated to the proposition that all men and women are created with an equal birthright to experience amazing amounts of intelligence-boosting rapture that supercharges their drive to bestow beauty, truth, goodness, and love on their fellow humans."

Those were the last words I spoke for many hours. As I dropped off to sleep I heard the Goddess in Celia say, "I pray that Rob will become a paranoid in reverse. He will know that all of reality is always conspiring to help him, and he will try to prove to everyone everywhere that the same is true for them: Life is totally and unconditionally on their side."

The epiphany I have described unfolded years before I heard the magic word that is at the heart of the Beauty and Truth Laboratory, but I mark it as my awakening to pronoia. On that night I experienced a new species of sensation on the border between body and soul. It resembled sexual pleasure, but on a higher octave. It was like what passionate emotion might be if an emotion could have the intensity of jealousy or rage but instead consist of reverence and compassion. It became the root from which I grew a new trust in life.

Sacred Advertisement

The orgasmic roots of pronoia
are brought to you by sacred underwear.

The saffron robes of Tibetan monks and black
habits of nuns are outer signs of their devotion.
But among religious devotees there's also a tradition of
wearing hidden clothing that's charged
with symbolic meaning—in other words, sacred
underwear.

Some Mormons, for instance, regularly slip on
a white neck-to-knee garment that's meant to remind
them of their pact with God. Orthodox Jewish men
may wear tsitsit, a fringed cloth, beneath their basic
black. For especially devout Catholics, the sacred
underwear *is called a scapular.*

French philosopher Blaise Pascal had his own
non-denominational version. At the height of an intense
epiphany, he scrawled prayerful poems on a
parchment, and forever after wore it under his clothes.

We recommend the practice to you: Design or find
your own sacred underwear. *You could draw magical*
glyphs on your briefs. Stuff a talisman in your bra. Write
a prayer on an undershirt or slip. Or do whatever
captivates your imagination. This will be a secret sign—
between you and the Divine Wow alone—of your
spiritual intention. Except for the two of you, no one
else will know.

DEVOTIONAL PRONOIA THERAPY

**Experiments and exercises
in becoming a gracefully
probing, erotically funny,
shockingly friendly
Master of Orgasmic Empathy**

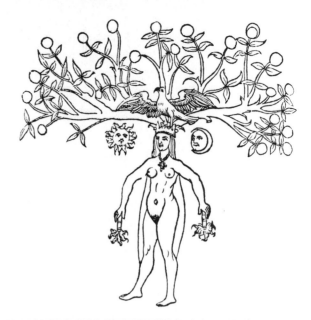

Report your answers & research results below

1 Ruminate about the sublime prototypes that might be hidden within the longings you're not so proud of. Dream of the noble purposes that lie beneath the plaintive cries of your heart. Write about them here.

2 Assume that your capacity for experiencing pleasure is not a barrier to your spiritual growth, but is in fact essential to it. What would you do differently from what you do now?

3 Close your eyes and visualize an alluring person standing in front of you. Then imagine that he or she is gazing at you with affectionate desire.

Add to the scene another enchanting person who is also beaming with adoration. Insert still another such character, and another, and another. Don't stop until you have arrayed before you in your mind's eye 10 enticing people of your favorite gender—and they're all glowing with love and appreciation.

Let the scene develop further, like a waking dream, unfolding in directions that surprise and delight you.

4 Force yourself to think a kind thought about someone you don't like. Next, try an even harder task: Force yourself to think a kind thought about someone who doesn't like you.

5 Robin Norwood's self-help book *Women Who Love Too Much* deals with a theme that has gotten a lot of play in recent decades: If you're too generous to someone who doesn't appreciate it and at the expense of your own needs, you can make yourself sick.

An alternative perspective comes from Blaise Pascal, who said, "When one does not love too much, one does not love enough." He was primarily addressing psychologically healthy altruists, but it's a good ideal for pronoia lovers to keep in mind.

Decide whether you need to move more in the direction of Norwood's or Pascal's advice. Develop a game plan to carry out your resolve, then take action.

6 A common obstruction to a vital intimate relationship with another human being is what I call the assumption of clairvoyance. You imagine, perhaps unconsciously, that your partner or friend is somehow magically psychic when it comes to you—so much so that he or she should unfailingly intuit exactly what you need, even if you don't ask for it. This fantasy may seem romantic, but it can single-handedly sink the most promising alliances.

To counteract any tendencies you might have to indulge in the assumption of clairvoyance, practice stating your desires aloud.

7 Pick out two strangers you aren't attracted to and who seem lonely and dull. Discreetly discover their names and addresses, maybe by following them home, then coming back later to steal the junk mail from their mailbox. Write them each a love note and sign it "Your Secret Admirer."

8 "Love is being stupid together," said French poet Paul Valéry. While there's a grain of truth to that, it's too corny and decadent for my tastes. I prefer to focus on a more interesting truth, which is this: Real love is being *smart* together. If you weave your destiny together with another's, he or she should catalyze your sleeping potentials, sharpen your perceptions, and boost both your emotional and analytical intelligence. Your relationship becomes a crucible in which you deepen your understanding of the way the world works.

Give an example of your closest approach to this model in your own life. Then formulate a vow in which you promise you'll do what's necessary to more fully embody the principle "love is being smart together."

9 Describe to your best companion a detailed vision of his or her best possible future.

10 The Doctrine of Original Sin? I spit on it. I reject it. I renounce it and annihilate it from reality. In its place I offer the Doctrine of Original Fun. This reformulation of the truth asserts that we are all born with a mandate to have as much liberating joy as possible. Present three arguments of pieces of evidence in support of the Doctrine of Original Fun.

11 Some hetero men believe they won't find romantic happiness unless they hook up with a woman who resembles a supermodel. Their libidos were imprinted at a tender age by our culture's narrow definition of what constitutes female beauty. They steer clear of many fine women who don't fit their ideal.

The addiction to a physical type is not confined to them, though. Some straight women, for instance, wouldn't think of dating a bald, short guy, no matter how interesting he is. And there are people of every sexual persuasion who imagine that their attraction to the physical appearance of a potential partner is the single most important gauge of compatibility. This delusion is the most common cause of bad relationships.

The good news is that anyone can outgrow their instinctual yearning for a particular physical type, thereby becoming available for union with all of the more perfect partners who previously didn't look quite right.

What's the state of your relationship with this riddle? Describe how you might ripen it; speculate on how you can move it to the next level of maturity.

12 Compose and cast a love spell on yourself.

13 "Man in his present state has as much desire to urinate as he has to make vows to Artemis," says Edward Dahlberg in *The Sorrows of Priapus.* In other words, most people have no relationship with wild female deities, nor do they ever conceive of a reason why that might be fun or inspiring. But some of us know that Artemis is not dead, is not just a figment of the archaic Greek mind. She is a living archetype of wild but nurturing female energy. Goddess of the ever-changing moon, sinewy protectress of the undomesticated soul, she gives sanctuary to all who prize liberated fertility. Make a vow to her.

14 You understand that you can never own love, right? No matter how much someone adores you today, no matter how much you adore someone, you can't force that unique state of grace to keep its shape forever. It will inevitably evolve or mutate, perhaps into a different version of tender caring, but maybe not. From there it will continue to change, either into yet another version of interesting affection, or who knows what else?

Describe how you could get the hang of putting this tricky wisdom into practice.

Devotional Pronoia Therapy

15 Norman Mailer has described marriage as "an excretory relationship, in which you take all the crap you hide from the world and dump it on the person closest to you. But the proviso is that you have to be willing to take theirs."

Describe how you might work in a way opposite to Mailer's; that is to say, train yourself to call up all the beauty you hide from the world and offer it to the person closest to you.

16 If you're heterosexual, imagine what it would be like to be homosexual. If you're homosexual, visualize yourself as a heterosexual. If you're an androgynous bisexual nymphomaniac, try being celibate. You get the picture: Escape your sexual imprint for a while.

17 In the Western hermetic version of the Qabalah, every Hebrew letter is paired with a number, and so every word is also a number derived from the addition of its letters. Gematria is the practice of finding hidden resonance between words that have similar numerical values. Of the many poetic truths revealed through this art, one of our favorites is this: The Hebrew words for both 'serpent' and 'messiah' add up to 358.

Let's suppose this can be interpreted to mean that the snaky potency of your reproductive drive is potentially the source of your salvation. What implications might that have for how you live your life?

18 Get Steve Penny's booklet *How to Have Great Laughing Sex,* available at 7960 B Soquel Drive #77, Aptos, CA 95003. Try the exercises, then write your own essay called *How to Have Great Laughing Sex.*

19 What could you do to to make your tenderness and carnality flow from the same refined reflex? How might you strive to adore every creature, every plant, every rock in the world with the same excitement that you bestow upon the lover who excites you most? What prayers will you unleash at the height of your orgasmic fervor to propitiate the healing and success of people in need?

20 Write the following on a piece of red paper and keep it under your pillow. "I, [put your name here], do solemnly swear on this day [put date here] that I will devote myself for a period of seven days to learning my most important desire. No other thought will be more uppermost in my mind. No other concern will divert me from tracking down every clue that might assist me in my drive to ascertain the one experience in this world that deserves my brilliant passion above all others."

Devotional Pronoia Therapy

PRONOIA NEWS NETWORK

Mother's Milk Revolution

In 1967, only 25 percent of American infants were breast-fed. Today, the rate is seven out of 10. That's excellent news, says the American Academy of Pediatrics, citing research that suggests children are far healthier when they're breast-fed.

Real *Love Poetry*

Early in his career, Robert Bly rarely wrote love poetry, though he studied the work of others who did. As he aged, he stopped reading the angst-ridden ruminations of modern poets and sought out the ecstatic love poetry of mystics like Rumi and Kabir. Increasingly, forgiveness and compassion became central aspects of Bly's emotional repertoire. His rage about his own past romantic disappointments dissipated. In his mid-40s, he wrote *Loving a Woman in Two Worlds,* his first collection of love poetry. Critiquing it for *The New York Times Book Review,* Fred Chappell said it wasn't a *real* book of love poems, because there wasn't enough hatred and anger in it. On Bly's behalf, we offer a response to Mr. Chappell: *We love you, goddamnit.*

This edition of PNN is brought to you by James Joyce's Finnegans Wake, *and especially this passage: "The Gracehoper was always jigging ajog, hoppy on akkant of his joyicity."*

Esoteric Geography

The black water of Rio Negro and the yellowish brown water of Rio Solimoes converge near the Brazilian city of Manaus. For a few miles they refuse to blend, flowing side by side as if intent on maintaining their autonomy. This two-toned phenomenon is the official beginning of one of the world's longest rivers, the Amazon.

In Montgomery, Alabama there is an intersection where Jefferson Davis Avenue crosses Rosa Parks Avenue. One street is named after the president of the slave-owning states in America's Civil War. The other is named for the black woman who in 1955 rejected a bus driver's demand that she give her seat to a white passenger, leading to events that helped launch the civil rights movement.

Gay Marriage Won't Wreck Civilization

"The results of more than a century of anthropological research on households, kinship relationships, and families, across cultures and through time, provide no support whatsoever for the view that either civilization or viable social orders depend upon marriage as an exclusively heterosexual institution. Rather, anthropological research supports the conclusion that a vast array of family types, including families built upon same-sex partnerships, can contribute to stable and humane societies." —American Anthropological Association, www.aaanet.org

Where Great Stories Come to Life

The Vagina Monologues is a book and show based on interviews with women all over the world. "There's so much darkness and secrecy surrounding the vagina," says author Eve Ensler, "—like the Bermuda Triangle."

Sex-positive feminists note wryly that while Ensler's work was a welcome breakthrough, the final frontier won't come until a bevy of female celebrities gather at Madison Square Garden (as they did to celebrate TVM) and shout hosannas to the clitoris. For there seems to be an even deeper conspiracy to conceal its majesty—maybe because it's the only organ in the human body with no other purpose than to experience pleasure.

Play Is the Thing

Psychiatrist Stuart Brown has proposed this simple definition: "Play is spontaneous behavior that has no clear-cut goal and does not conform to a stereotypical pattern. The purpose of play is simply play itself; it appears to be pleasurable."

In a study of 26 convicted murderers, Brown discovered that as children, most of them had suffered either "from the absence of play or abnormal play like bullying, sadism, extreme teasing, or cruelty to animals."

Brown's work led him to explore the biological roots of play. "New and exciting studies of the brain, evolution, and animal behavior," he wrote, "suggest that play may be as important to life—for us and other animals—as sleeping and dreaming." —Stuart L. Brown, "Animals at Play," *National Geographic,* December 1994. Brown's website is www.instituteforplay.com.

Alternative Heroes' Journey

In Joseph Campbell's vision of myth, the hero is typically a solitary male who renounces intimate companionship to pursue his glorious, arduous quest. Along the way, sporadic help may arrive from an ineffable muse or deity.

There are alternative scenarios for the hero's journey, but Campbell underplayed them. In the tantric tradition, for instance, a seeker's connection with a beloved human companion is essential to his or her spiritual inquiry. Some early Christians described Jesus and Mary Magdalene as equal collaborators. Sufi mystic poet Rumi may not have actually made love with his teacher Shams (then again, he might have), but it's clear the two men sought divine communion together, not through lonely solo work.

Some modern teachers have broken from Campbell's narrow perspective. The quest for illumination, they say, can thrive on the challenges of loving and living with an actual person. In John Welwood's *Love and Awakening,* the author reimagines relationship as an "alliance of warriors" devoted to awakening each other's "holy longing."

Sneezing Epidemics

Scientists theorize that allergies are increasing because modern civilization has scoured away dirt and germs so relentlessly that the human immune system has grown bored—so bored it's now rising up to battle substances that are harmless to the body, like pollens and pet dander.

Dolphin Love Conspiracy

Jerry Langley likes to play his guitar for the spinner dolphins in Maui's La Perouse Bay. They appreciate it. When he runs out of songs, he often joins them for a convivial swim. One day in 2003, a commotion at sea moved Jerry to interrupt his concert. Paddling out for a closer look, he found a woman swimmer surrounded by the dolphins. The normally friendly creatures had hemmed her in, as if herding her. But when their buddy Jerry showed up, they parted their tight circle to let him through, and he was able to escort the woman back to shore. The two hit it off instantly—she was a singer looking for a gig. They began dating and eventually got married.

Non-Sexual Tantra

Meditation teacher Jack Kornfield espouses an interesting method for dealing with negative and unwanted thoughts. Don't let them possess you, he says, and don't assume you have to act them out. On the other hand, don't struggle mightily to suppress them, either. Instead, try this: Bow to the offending idea. Acknowledge and admire its power. Express your gratitude and respect to it for galvanizing so much of your psychic energy.

Gender Blending

"The higher a woman's IQ, the more she is likely to be masculine in outlook. The higher a man's IQ, the more likely he is to be feminine in outlook." —Lucius Cervantes, *And God Made Man and Woman*

The Lovers' Party

Marriages in India are usually arranged by relatives of the bride and groom, and most couples who wed come from the same religion or caste. But there are rebels who ignore custom and marry for love. One of their champions is a social worker named Biswanath Ramachandra Champa Swapnaji Taslima Voltaire. He has launched a political party for lovers called the Lovers' Green-Globalist God-free-Humanist Party. "Only those who love can effectively change society," he says, "and my new party will be their platform."

MIRABILIA REPORT   *Mirabilia* n. mysterious revelations, rejuvenating prodigies, ineffable breakthroughs; from the Latin *mirabilia,* "marvels."

■ A pig's orgasm can last for 30 minutes. Orangutans and macaques masturbate with sex toys made of leaves and twigs. The ladybird beetle can copulate for up to nine hours at a time, and males are capable of three orgasms in one session, each an hour and a half long. If forced to decide between having a bigger penis and living in a world where there was no war, 90 percent of all men would pick universal peace. About eight percent of domestic rams prefer other males as sexual partners.

■ As soon as the male praying mantis begins coitus with the female, she bites off his head and eats it. An adult female elephant's clitoris is between six and twelve inches long, and the spotted hyena female has such a large clitoris that she is frequently mistaken for a male. An oyster is usually ambisexual; it begins life as a male, then becomes a female, then changes back to being a male, then back to being female. A whale's penis is called a dork.

■ Donald Duck comics were outlawed in Finland for a time because the cartoon hero never wore pants. Some dolphins try to have intercourse with turtles, sharks, and seals. As a prelude to sex, the male sagebrush cricket renders the female immobile with a trap on his back. Slugs are hermaphrodites with penises on their heads. Asian stick insects sometimes fuck for ten weeks straight. The slime mold comes in 500 genders, and at least 13 of these have to collaborate in order to reproduce.

■ Sex researcher Alfred Kinsey said that "The only unnatural sex act is one you cannot perform."

Cross-Fertilization

In 1991, hikers in the Italian Alps discovered the largely intact body of a man who had been dead for 5,000 years. He'd been preserved in a glacier that had recently begun to melt. Since then, many women have asked to be given some of the iceman's frozen sperm so that they might become pregnant by him. The director of the museum where his body is kept has so far turned down all requests.

PNN is brought to you by the way writer George Sand made love with composer Frédérick Chopin on Christmas Day, 1839.

Hug Drugs

Mata Amritanandamayi is one of India's most beloved gurus. Also known as Amma, she preaches no doctrine but believes all religions lead to the same goal. Her renown has grown largely through the power and quantity of her embraces. She travels from city to city doling out hugs, often more than 1,000 a day. Since she launched her mission as a young girl, she claims to have hugged 21 million people.

BREAKING THE PRONOIA TABOO

"Where love rules, there is no will to power; and where power predominates, there love is lacking. The one is the shadow of the other." —C.G. Jung, *Psychological Reflections: A Jung Anthology*

"Aborigines openly and unaffectedly converse with everything in their surroundings—trees, tools, animals, rocks—as if all things have an intelligence deserving of respect." —Robert Lawlor, *Voices of the First Day.*

"When you make the two one, and when you make the inside like the outside and the outside like the inside, and the above like the below and the below like the above, and when you make the male like the female and the female like the male, then you will enter the Kingdom." —Jesus Christ, *Gospel of Thomas*

"Orpheus is the archetype of the poet as liberator and creator: He establishes a higher order in the world: an order without repression. In his person, art, freedom, and culture are eternally combined. He is the poet of redemption, the god who brings peace and salvation by pacifying man and nature, not through force but through song." —Herbert Marcuse, *Eros and Civilization*

"The wooing of the Earth means preserving natural environments in which to experience mysteries transcending daily life and from which to capture the awareness of the cosmic forces that have shaped humankind." —René Dubos

"If you want to build a ship, don't drum up the men to gather wood, divide the work, and give orders. Instead, teach them to yearn for the vast and endless sea." —Antoine de Saint-Exupéry

"Surround yourself with a seedy coffeehouse of intoxicated gods and their infidel poet-priests. Develop a working relationship with that stunning, bewildering, driving source of mad desire and infinite depth: the world itself whispering lovely things to you constantly." —Revd. MC 900 ft. Escher, www.fools errant.com/~ebeth/deck/major.html

Roots of Human Nature

Bonobo apes and humans share 98 percent of the same genes, leading some biologists to suggest that they, along with chimpanzees, should be reclassified as members of the human genus. While their gestures, postures, walk, and facial expressions have remarkable similarities to ours, however, their social behavior is quite different. Bonobos live in a peaceful matriarchy characterized by egalitarian relationships. Power and status are of minimal concern. They build and maintain social rapport with frequent erotic exchanges of every variety, from intercourse to mutual masturbation to oral sex. Homosexual and cross-generational contact is common.

"Bonobos use sex to appease, to bond, to make up after a fight, to ease tensions, to cement alliances," writes Natalie Angier in *The New York Times.* Because it's their social glue, says primatologist Dr. Frans de Waal, author of *Bonobo: The Forgotten Ape,* sex is casual and free of elaborate taboos. Unlike humans, bonobos are not obsessed with orgasm. Their reproductive rate is similar to that of other primates.

"All of this has relevance for understanding the roots of human nature," concludes Angier. "De Waal corrects the image of humanity's ancestors as driven by aggression, hierarchical machinations, hunting, warfare, and male dominance." (Source: Natalie Angier, *The New York Times,* April 22, 1997)

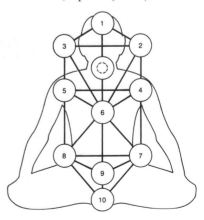

The Art of Childbirth "If men had babies," notes Elinor Gadon in her book *The Once and Future Goddess: A Sweeping Visual Chronicle of the Sacred Female and Her Reemergence in the Cultural Mythology of Our Time,* "there would be thousands of images of crowning, that awesome moment when the baby's head first appears." But the visual art of the last two millennia, though it depicts every other human activity, has ignored childbirth. A rare exception to the historical taboo is Judy Chicago's *The Birth Project,* a collection of birth images rendered through needlework. She created it in the mid-1980s.

Today images of childbirth are as taboo as the idea of pronoia, which is so taboo that it's not even recognized as a taboo. Without much difficulty, you can track down photos, videos, and art work that depict every imaginable human activity—from beheadings to suicide bombers to bestiality—but you'll be hard-pressed to find depictions of babies being born. Scenes of childbirth seem to be more forbidden than the most extreme porn.

Lower Octave Courtship "Why is it so hard to find a soulmate?" asks psychologist Carolyn Godschild Miller in her book *Soulmates: Following Inner Guidance to the Relationship of Your Dreams.* Her answer: "Because most of us are actually searching for egomates instead. We place the most limited and unloving aspect of our minds in charge of our search for love, and then wonder why we aren't succeeding. To the degree that we identify with this false sense of self, and operate on the basis of its limited point of view, we aren't looking for someone to love so much as recruiting fellow actors to take on supporting roles in a favorite melodrama."

As Above, So Below
"God and fuck are so much alike they might be synonymous glories. I'd even go so far as to say God is the Fuck of all Fucks"
—James Broughton, *Special Deliveries: New and Selected Poems,* Mark Thompson, editor

Laughing Sex

"Why is sex the most fun people have without laughing or smiling? Think about it. When enjoying most other physical pleasures, you smile and laugh. It may be because we have millions of years of evolutionary history with sex being closely linked to aggression and dominance—especially for men, who feel a big push to beat out their competitors and get their genes into the next generation.

"Another reason most people don't smile or laugh during sex is that desire has an edge to it. You know how hard it is to tell sometimes if animals are fighting or mating? Many human relationships have a similar quality. It's hard to tell if the couple is actually in love or strangely addicted to tormenting each other.

"This difference in how we experience sexual pleasure compared to other types of joy may be one reason so many people end up in relationships where the sex is fantastic but everything else is screwed.

"Biologists classify all living things by their reproductive habits because, from an evolutionary standpoint, it's the slowest behavior to change.

"Laughter, on the other hand, is fairly recent in an evolutionary sense. While several primates smile (although not necessarily from joy), and chimpanzees and gorillas chuckle and tickle, humans are the only species that truly laughs from joy.

"Maybe sex is the most fun people have without laughing because our slow-to-change reproductive behavior hasn't caught up with the more recent development in evolution—laughter." —Steve Penny, *How to Have Great Laughing Sex*

International Affairs

"The psychic health of an individual resides in the capacity to recognize and welcome the 'Other,'" writes poet and translator Rosanna Warren in *The Art of Translation.* "Our word 'idiot' comes from the Greek *idiotes,* whose primary sense is of privacy or isolation." With this warning, Warren builds her case for the virtues of reading literature that has been translated from its native tongue.

Desirable Qualities

Amazon.com founder Jeff Bezos told *Wired* magazine that while looking for a wife, he put a high premium on resourcefulness. "I wanted a woman who could get me out of a Third World Prison," he said.

More than three billion years ago, the Earth's original single-cell organisms thrived in a carbon dioxide-rich atmosphere that contained no free oxygen. As a byproduct of their metabolism, however, they released an abundant amount of oxygen. It was a pollutant that ultimately made the environment uninhabitable for them, though it prepared the way for the oxygen-breathers who now dominate the planet

☼

St. Catherine of Siena (1347–1380) asserted that Jesus personally gave her his foreskin to wear as a wedding ring and encouraged her to nurse from his breast.

PNN is brought to you by Guneli Gun and her book On the Road to Baghdad: A Picaresque Novel of Magical Adventures. *Here's an excerpt: "The world is run by those who can't make love, or those who do it badly. That's why the world is in trouble."*

Rules of Attraction

"Unless the eye catch fire,
God will not be seen.
Unless the ear catch fire,
God will not be heard.
Unless the tongue catch fire,
God will not be named.
Unless the heart catch fire,
God will not be loved.
Unless the mind catch fire,
God will not be known."
—William Blake,
"Pentecost"

Cosmos-Generating Intimacy   Western science and religion have differing views on how the universe was created, but they agree that it happened a long time ago. The mystery schools of the West, on the other hand, assert that the universe is recreated anew in every moment through the divinely erotic play of God and Goddess. They say that if we humans treat lovemaking as an experimental sacrament, we can attune ourselves to the union of the two primal deities and, in a sense, participate in the ongoing creation of the world.

Five Genders, at Least   "The state and legal system may have an interest in maintaining only two sexes, but our collective biological bodies do not. While male and female stand on the extreme ends of a biological continuum, there are other bodies that mix together anatomical components conventionally attributed to both males and females. Comprising about four percent of all humans born, three variations can be identified: the so-called true hermaphrodites ('herms'), who possess one testis and one ovary; the male pseudohermaphrodites ('merms'), who have testes and some aspects of the female genitalia but no ovaries; and the female pseudoher-maphrodites ('ferms'), who have ovaries and some aspects of the male genitalia but lack testes." —Anne Fausto-Sterling, *Sexing the Body: Gender Politics and the Construction of Sexuality*

Higher Octave Empathy   *Couvade* occurs in a variety of indigenous cultures, most in Africa. It's a phenomenon in which a man experiences morning sickness, unusual appetites, and other symptoms similar to his pregnant mate. He may even have labor pains as the child is born, diminishing the mother's distress as if he has mysteriously been able to take some of it on. There's no known physiological basis for couvade.

Traditional Family Values   Not all men in traditional marriages drink too much, beat their wives and kids, and fritter away their paychecks gambling in whorehouses.

What's That Singing in Our Bones?
"Deep in our bones resides an ancient singing couple who just won't give up making their beautiful, wild noise. The world won't end if we can find them." —Martín Prechtel, *Secrets of the Talking Jaguar,* www.floweringmountain.com

---

Sonnet XIV

"If thou must love me, let it be for nought
Except for love's sake only. Do not say
'I love her for her smile—her look—her way
Of speaking gently,—for a trick of thought
That falls in well with mine, and certes brought
A sense of pleasant ease on such a day—
For these things in themselves, Beloved, may
Be changed, or change for thee,—and love, so wrought,
May be unwrought so. Neither love me for
Thine own dear pity's wiping my cheeks dry,—
A creature might forget to weep, who bore
Thy comfort long, and lose thy love thereby!
But love me for love's sake, that evermore
Thou mayst love on, through love's eternity."
—Elizabeth Barrett Browning,
Sonnets from the Portuguese

Radical Everything

"I've been practicing radical authenticity lately," my friend Brandon told me. "I'm revealing the blunt truth about unmentionable subjects to everyone I know. It's been pretty hellish—no one likes having the social masks stripped away—but it's been ultimately rewarding."

"I admire your boldness in naming the currents flowing beneath the surface," I replied, "but I'm curious as to why you imply they're all negative. To practice radical authenticity, shouldn't you also express the raw truth about what's right, good, and beautiful? Shouldn't you unleash the praise and gratitude that normally go unspoken?"

Brandon sneered. He thought my version of radical authenticity was wimpy. I hope you don't. As a budding pronoiac, you have a mandate to be honest in both ways.

Only you
can prevent
the genocide
of the
☀ imagination

Prayer for You

This is a perfect moment. It's a perfect moment because I have been inspired to say a gigantic prayer. I've been roused to unleash a divinely greedy, apocalyptically healing prayer for each and every one of you—even those of you who don't believe in the power of prayer.

And so I am starting to pray right now to the God of Gods . . . the God beyond all Gods . . . the Girlfriend of God . . . the Teacher of God . . . the Goddess who invented God.

DEAR GODDESS, you who never kill but only change:

I pray that my exuberant, suave, and accidental words will move you to shower ferocious blessings down on everyone who reads this benediction.

I pray that you will give them what they don't even know they need—not just the boons they think they want but everything they've always been afraid to even imagine or ask for.

DEAR GODDESS, you wealthy anarchist burning heaven to the ground:

Many of the divine chameleons out there don't even know that their souls will live forever.

So please use your brash magic to help them see that they are all wildly creative geniuses too big for their own personalities.

Guide them to realize that they are all completely different from what they've been led to believe about themselves, and more exciting than they can possibly imagine.

Make it illegal, immoral, irrelevant, unpatriotic, and totally tasteless for them to be in love with anyone or anything that's no good for them.

O GODDESS, you who give us so much love and pain mixed together that our morality is always on the verge of collapsing:

I beg you to cast a boisterous love spell that will nullify all the dumb ideas, bad decisions, and nasty conditioning that have ever cursed the wise and sexy virtuosos out there.

Remove, banish, annihilate, and laugh into oblivion any jinx that has clung to them, no matter how long they've suffered from it, and even if they have become accustomed or addicted to its ugly companionship.

Please conjure an aura of protection around them so that they will receive an early warning if they are ever about to act in such a way as to bring another hex or plague into their lives in the future.

DEAR GODDESS, sweet Goddess, you sly universal virus with no fucking opinion:

Please help all the personal growth addicts out there to become disciplined enough to go crazy in the name of creation, not destruction.

Teach them the difference between oppressive self-control and liberating self-control.

Awaken in them the power to do the half-right thing when it is impossible to do the totally right thing.

Arouse the Wild Woman within them—even if they're men.

DEAR GODDESS, you pregnant slut who scorns all mediocre longing:

I pray that you will inspire all the compassionate rascals communing with this prayer to kick their own asses and wash their own brains.

Provoke them to throw away or give away all the things they own that encourage them to believe that they are better than anyone else.

Show them how much fun it is to brag about what they cannot do and do not have.

Give them bigger, better, more original sins and wilder, wetter, more interesting problems.

Most of all, Goddess, brainwash them with your freedom so that they never love their own pain more than anyone else's pain.

O GODDESS, you wildly disciplined, radically curious, shockingly friendly, fanatically balanced, mysteriously truthful, teasingly healing, lyrically logical master of rowdy bliss:

Cultivate in yourself a fervent yearning for the intimate companionship of these budding messiahs. Play with them every day. Answer their questions. Listen to their stories. Inspire them to love you so much they lose all their hatred forever.

DEAR GODDESS, you psychedelic mushroom cloud at the center of all our brains:

Bless the insanely poised creators out there with lucid dreams while they are wide awake. Provide them with their own spin doctors, and vacuum cleaners for their magic carpets, and solar-powered sex toys that work even in the dark.

Give them a knack for avoiding other people's hells, and a thousand masks that all represent their true feelings, and secret admirers who are not psychotic stalkers.

Arrange for a racehorse to be named after them, or an underground river, or a thousand-year-old storm on Saturn.

Teach them to be their own prophets and pray to themselves and right their own wrongs and sing their own songs and be their own wives and save their own lives.

DEAR GODDESS, you riotously tender, hauntingly reassuring, orgiastically sacred feeling that is even now running through all of our soft, warm animal bodies:

I pray that you provide all the original sinners out there with a license to bend and even break all rules, laws, and traditions that keep them apart from the things they love.

Show them how to purge the wishy-washy wishes that distract them from their daring, dramatic, divine desires.

And teach them that they can have anything they want if they'll only ask for it in an unselfish way.

And now dear God of Gods, God beyond all Gods, Girlfriend of God, Teacher of God, Goddess who invented God, I bring this prayer to a close, trusting that in these mysterious moments you have begun to change everyone out there in the exact way they've needed to change in order to become the gorgeous geniuses they were born to be. Amen. Awomen.

And please also give them each an emerald green parachute, ruby slippers, a canoe covered with jewels, a black-market orchid and a bouquet of organic broccoli, a donkey clown piñata full of crickets, a protective gargoyle lifted from the Chartres Cathedral, a guitar string actually played by Jimi Hendrix, a strawberry chocolate cake baked in the shape of a question mark, a human DNA map drawn up by the Human Genome Project, fistfuls of sparklers, a bottle of holy water from the River Jordan, photos of lightning on a giant poster, a refrigerator magnet cast in the likeness of the Dalai Lama, and the key of life accidentally placed inside a box of Cracker Jack.

Four Dignities of the Warrior's Path

In Tibetan Buddhism's "Four Dignities of the Warrior's Path," courage and ferocity are absent. In fact, the qualities regarded as essential for being a warrior have nothing in common with the training regimens of Marines or football players or lobbyists.

The first dignity is often translated in English as meekness, but that word doesn't convey its full meaning. "Relaxed confidence" is a more precise formulation; a humble feeling of being at home in one's body.

Perkiness, or irrepressible joy, is the second dignity. To develop it, a warrior cultivates the habit of seeing the best in everything and works diligently to avoid the self-indulgence of cynicism.

The third is outrageousness. The warrior who embodies this dignity loves to experiment, is not addicted to strategies that have been successful in the past, and has a passionate objectivity that's free of the irrelevant emotions of hope and fear.

The fourth dignity is inscrutability, or a skill at evading the pigeonholes and simplistic definitions that might limit the warrior's inventiveness while fighting for his or her moral vision.

CRIMES THAT DON'T BREAK ANY LAWS

How many of you out there are ready to testify that you have been psychically assaulted by the media's nonstop flood of toxic waste?

How many of you are ready to testify that you have been made paranoid in a sickening yet boring way by the insipidly dangerous images that radiate nonstop from TVs, movie screens, websites, magazines, books, radios, and newspapers?

How many of you are ready to testify that the sacred temples of your imaginations have been infected by the doom and gloom fixation that so many seemingly intelligent people embrace with perverse enthusiasm?

I'm no longer willing to accept the epidemic obsession with big bad nasty things and flashy trite empty-hearted things. I say it's high time for us to take back our imaginations.

Here are my demands.

DEMAND #1: I demand that Amnesty International launch a crusade against a grievously unacknowledged form of terrorism. I call this crime against humanity *the genocide of the imagination.*

DEMAND #2: I demand that you refuse to be entertained by bad news. I demand that you seek out and create stories that make you feel strong and joyous and enigmatic.

DEMAND #3: I demand that *People* magazine do a cover story on the "The World's 50 Sexiest Perpetrators of Beauty, Truth, and Love."

DEMAND #4: I demand that you learn the difference between your own thoughts and those of the celebrities who have demonically possessed you.

DEMAND #5: I demand that you wear underpants on your head and dance naked in slow motion whenever you watch TV movies about tormented geniuses who create great art but treat everyone in their lives like shit.

DEMAND #6: I demand that the sadomasochist storytellers disguised as journalists give prominent coverage to the fact that death rates from cancer are declining; and the fact that the world's largest freshwater system, the Great Lakes, is dramatically purifying itself of the pollutants that human beings have dumped into it; and the fact that the number of America's black elected officials has sextupled since 1970; and the fact that rising rates of intermarriage are helping to dissipate ethnic and religious strife worldwide; and the fact that the miracle of your breathing transpires about 10 million times a year, even though you never have to will it to continue.

I have more demands, but I want to make sure you know that your imagination and the imaginations of everyone you know are on the brink of extinction. And who are the killers? The perpetrators of the genocide of the imagination? I call them the entertainment criminals.

They're the nihilistic creators and dramatis personae who spread the propaganda that trouble and strife and disintegration are more worthy of our attention than integrity and splendor and quantum leaps.

The entertainment criminals are the decadent fools who preach the bizarre doctrine that witty gloom is the mark of a deep thinker. They are the educated idiots who try to trick us into believing that optimism is solely for naive fools with no aptitude for critical thinking.

The visionary philosopher Buckminster Fuller once said, "When I am working on a problem, I never think about beauty. I think only of how to solve the problem. But when I have finished, if the solution is not beautiful, I know it is wrong."

To the entertainment criminals, Fuller's perspective is heretical. With the know-it-all certainty of religious fanatics, they imply with every word and image they produce that there is rarely such a thing as a beautiful solution.

DEMAND #7: I demand that the salesmen of degradation who pass themselves off as storytellers give themselves the challenge of creating engaging sagas whose plots are not driven by violence, alcoholism, abuse, suicide, prostitution, bigotry, lawsuits, greed, crashes, pathology, crime, disease, and torture.

I heard an interview with the German film actor Udo Kier. He specializes in playing villains. "Evil has no limit," he sneered, blustering like a naughty genius. "Good has a limit. It is simply not as interesting."

How many times have I heard that idiotic cliché? Most everyone everywhere seems to agree with Udo Kier. And I'm in a tiny minority in my belief that evil is boring. There seem to be few thinkers, communicators, and creators who share my curiosity about exploring the frontiers of righteous pleasure and amusing truth and boisterous integrity.

Some pretenders do make counterfeit attempts: Hollywood producers who produce sentimental fantasies with artificially happy endings, Madison Avenue advertising executives who sell the pseudo-positivity of narcissistic comfort, and New Age gurus who ignore the darkness with their one-dimensional appeals to sweetness and light.

DEMAND #8: I demand that the demoralizing propagandists who impersonate objective reporters go ahead and confess that the acreage devoted to organic farming is increasing rapidly all over the world; that violent child abduction by strangers has dropped precipitously; that diamonds rain from the sky on Uranus and Neptune; that most HMO executives now believe prayer and meditation can expedite the healing process; that vast supplies of frozen natural gas lie beneath the oceans, harboring more potential energy than all of the world's oil reserves, and could be mined with the right technology; and that the giant timber company, Congolaise Industrielle des Bois, voluntarily agreed to stop cutting down trees in a virgin rain forest in the Congo.

DEMAND #9: I demand that the purveyors of despair who pretend to be dispassionate observers of the human condition go ahead and disclose that the 10 most beautiful words in the English language are *chimes, dawn, golden, hush, lullaby, luminous, melody, mist, murmuring,* and *tranquil;* that the calcium in your bones and the iron in your blood were originally forged at the core of a red giant star that died billions of years ago; that the Inuit term for making love is translated as "laughing together in bed"; that neurologists say men are most likely to be aroused by the smells of cinnamon buns and doughnuts, while women get turned on by Good 'n' Plenty candy and cucumbers; and that according to Buckminster Fuller, "pollution is nothing but resources we're not harvesting."

Visualize the replica of a Viking warship made out of 15 million popsicle sticks.

The word "imagination" gets little respect. For many people, it connotes "make-believe," and is primarily the domain of children and artists. But the truth is that your imagination is the single most important asset you possess. It's your power to form mental pictures of things that don't exist yet. Your imagination is what you use to design your future.

That's why it's so disturbing to know that all over the planet, the imagination is deeply wounded—paralyzed by the media's nonstop onslaught of toxic psychic waste. How can you generate images that energize you to create your highest good if your mind's eye is swarming with dazzling yet vacuous and fear-inducing stories crafted by the most monumental brainwashing juggernaut in the history of the world?

To get a sense of the growing devastation, I suggest you wander around a grade school playground at recess. You'll hear kids' conversations overflowing with the degrading narratives they've absorbed from their favorite sources of information and stimulation.

I call this ongoing tragedy the genocide of the imagination. Because of it, many people cannot access their greatest magical power. They have forsaken the sanctity of their sacred temples, allowing them to be defiled with soulless images and stories that are at odds with their deepest desires. As a result they live incoherent lives corroded by chronic anxiety.

DEMAND #10: When you're too well-entertained to move, screaming is good exercise. Which is why I demand that you scream frequently whenever you're soaking up slick crap generated by the imaginations of people who are devoted to money, power, and ego instead of love, reverence, and play.

DEMAND #11: Recognizing that the epidemic of sleep-deprivation and the widespread impoverishment of dream life play a key role in abetting the genocide of the imagination, I demand that you get at least eight hours of sleep every night.

DEMAND #12: I demand new video games with socially redeeming value, like a game called "NirvanaStorm," in which players negotiate eight levels of Buddhist revelation with a character who resembles the Dalai Lama.

DEMAND #13: Since the genocide of the imagination is at least partly the result of men monopolizing the entertainment and news industries, I demand that women fill half of all jobs at ABC, MTV, CNN, NBC, PBS, NPR, CBS, FOX, *Newsweek, Time, The Wall Street Journal, The New York Times,* AP, Reuters, and *USA Today.*

I further demand an affirmative action program for the image of God: From now on She must be depicted on at least 15 percent of all TV shows as an African American mother of four.

DEMAND #14: I demand a one-month global media fast. Avoid all newspapers, magazines, TV, movies, radio, and Internet for 30 days. Return to the primordial silence or else! To expedite purification during this time of renewal, I demand that you discuss your dreams with your loved ones every morning and gather your friends for storytelling circles every evening.

If we hope to prevent the genocide of the imagination, we've got to perpetrate massive, mirthful attacks of pronoia. But we have to do it without acting like True Believers, because fanaticism is anathema to our cause. Our strategy is to be blithe and flexible as we learn not just to believe, but actually *perceive* the truth that life is a benevolent conspiracy designed to keep mutating our immortal souls until they're so far beyond perfection that perfection is irrelevant.

We *will* succeed. We will overthrow the doom and gloom fixation and make the cause of zoom and boom irresistible. Our parties will be better than theirs. Our jokes will be funnier, our jobs more enjoyable, our lovemaking more revelatory. We'll dream up tricks to create an environment in which it's more fun and interesting to talk about wise bliss than clever cynicism.

We will build shrines devoted to righteous pleasure and amusing truth and boisterous integrity in the ugliest places we know. We will unleash praise and gratitude without regard for the taboos we shatter thereby. And we will perform senseless acts of altruistic chutzpah everywhere we go.

DEMAND #15: I demand that if the disinformation specialists who masquerade as communicators intend to keep feeding their addiction to stories of misfortune and breakdown, they must give equal time to those of us who specialize in stories about redemption and renewal. That's all I demand: Give us a mere 50 percent of the airwaves and pages and bandwidths.

CRIMES THAT DON'T BREAK ANY LAWS: THE THEORY

When most people think of a prank, they visualize bad though funny trouble committed by angry, vulgar guys. You might remember the time some teenager you knew went to the house of a hated adult. The kid put a paper bag full of dog poop on the porch, lit it with a match, rang the doorbell, and ran away. When his victim came to the door and saw the flames, he stamped on it.

This kind of mayhem has unfortunately come to be regarded as the very definition of tricky mischief. But it's actually a distorted caricature of the art form. Driven by revenge and the desire to humiliate, it mindlessly reinforces the outmoded nonsense of "us versus them." The typical macho prankster is proud of feeling nothing for what he mocks. He performs the dehumanization of his target as he affirms the feelings of superiority he feeds through his alienation.

The pronoaic trickster, in contrast, uses the prank as a loving tool for obliterating hierarchy, as a leveler of elitist pretensions. She's not driven by revenge or one-upmanship. She empathizes as she disrupts, seeking not to discredit and embarrass the target of her mischief, but to shock it into becoming more itself. Hers is a celebration of the collaborative impulses of the soul instead of the instinctual self-aggrandizement of the ego. The pronoaic prankster loves what she profanes. Weaving her fate together with her target's, she honors her relationship with it even as she tweaks it out of its literalism.

A pronoaic prank, though it may be surprising, is ultimately friendly. It romances the contradictions with crafty compassion. It's a cheerful strategy to extinguish the tawdry glamour of the antiquated "us versus them."

The piece of writing on pages 160–162 of this book is the text of a pronoaic prank. On three occasions, I've performed "Crimes That Don't Break Any Laws" as an act of guerrilla performance art: once in the parking lot of a shopping mall in Pittsburgh, a second time on the sidewalk in front of a San Francisco nightclub where the Sleater-Kinney band was about to play, and on another occasion at a nursing home in Tucson.

In his book *Temporary Autonomous Zone,* Hakim Bey (www.hermetic.com/bey/) provides other examples of pronoaic pranks. Burglarize houses, he suggests, but instead of stealing the residents' possessions, leave behind beautiful and confusing gifts. Spread gossip about the unsung genius of people who don't get nearly enough credit for their good work. Bolt up brass commemorative plaques in places (public or private) where you have experienced a revelation or had a fulfilling sexual experience. Take a few friends and a boom box to an all-night grocery store and engage in ecstatic, whirling dervish-style dancing in the aisles until you're thrown out. Scrawl the following graffiti in courthouse lavatories and on playground walls: "I dare you to scare yourself with how beautiful you are."

Pick people at random, says Bey, and convince them they're the heirs to an enormous, useless, and amazing fortune—say, 5,000 square miles of Antarctica, or an aging circus elephant, or a leper colony in India, or a collection of alchemical manuscripts. Later they will come to realize that for a few moments they believed in something extraordinary, and will perhaps be driven to cultivate a more intense quest for exhilarating adventures.

Do-It-Yourself Prank

Dream up your own pronoiac prank, to be done either in concert with co-conspirators or by yourself. Carry it out. Report on your results after you've done it.

The Perils of Enchantment

Fairy tales are full of characters who suffer loss and hardship for trying to be something they're not. If they ever change their ways and accept the truth about themselves, their luck improves dramatically. It's interesting, then, to contemplate the fact that our culture adores film and TV actors, who get extensive training in pretending to be someone other than who they really are. We nurse a similar obsession with politicians, whose specialty resembles that of actors: Their vocation requires them to dissemble constantly.

Are you one of the enthralled? Do you share our collective entrancement with people who lie about themselves for a living? If so, experiment with what happens if you wean yourself. Try being cautious about exposing yourself to influences that might encourage you to be something you're not.

Receptivity Remedies

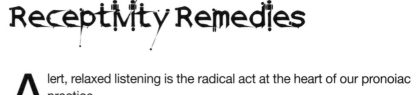

Alert, relaxed listening is the radical act at the heart of our pronoiac practice.

Curiosity is our primal state of awareness.

Wise innocence is a trick we aspire to master.

Open-hearted skepticism is the light in our eyes.

If you choose to become a practitioner of pronoia, your life will suck. It *has* to suck.

Let me explain. As you cultivate the arts of gathering and bestowing the blessings that the universe is always conspiring to send your way, your life will suck in the best senses of the word.

First, your life will suck in the same way that you use a straw to compel a thick milk shake to disobey gravity and squirt into your mouth. Metaphorical translation: You'll work hard to pull toward you the resources you need, perhaps even exerting yourself with a force that goes against the natural flow.

Your pronoiac life will suck in a second way: like a powerful vacuum cleaner that inhales dirt from the floor and makes it disappear. You will have a sixth sense about getting rid of messes that are contaminating your clarity.

Here's a third interpretation: Once you commit yourself to the art of pronoia, you will most likely develop an unusually dynamic form of receptivity. Whether you're a man or woman, you'll be like a macho male with a willful intention to be like a welcoming female. As a result, you'll be regularly sucked into succulent opportunities you would never have come upon if you had let your pop nihilistic conditioning continue to dominate you. Your openness to uplifting adventures will make it easier for serendipitous miracles to find you and draw you in.

Let's take one more poetic leap of faith as we meditate on the metaphor. As you devote yourself to the art of making yourself available, your life will suck in the way that movements of the mouth and lips and tongue during close encounters with intimate partners stimulate pleasurable feelings.

I've tried a wide variety of meditative practices from many traditions. I've calmed myself through rhythmic breathing; watched with amusement as the nonstop procession of images paraded across my mind;

visualized images of deities; cultivated unconditional love; chanted mantras; and taken rigorous inventories to determine whether the integrity of my actions matches my high ideals.

But in my years of study, I've never heard of a form of meditation that would ask me to go to a public place, take my attention off myself, and observe other people with compassionate objectivity. That's why I was forced to invent it. Hereafter known as Sacred Eavesdropping, this meditation builds one's ability to pray in the manner described by poet W. H. Auden: "The definition of prayer is paying careful and concentrated attention to something other than your own constructions."

Here's one of the Beauty and Truth Laboratory's favorite rules for evaluating the information that comes our way: Assume that it's a blend of truth and falsehood and every shade of half-truth in between. That applies equally to stories in *The New York Times* and to the raving spiels of the homeless Gulf War vet who hangs out at the local post office.

While I suspect that the *Times* has a much higher proportion of accurate data, I can never be sure what distortions are embedded in its reports. Its unconscious devotion to pop nihilism means that it routinely ignores vast realms of human experience. And there are odd days when the homeless guy's rants spit out gems of poetic wisdom that give me the chills and change the way I understand the world.

Moral of the story: Useful messages may come from anywhere. I'm more likely to recognize them if I'm simultaneously curious and discriminating.

On those rare occasions when journalists deign to report a UFO sighting, they dutifully describe eyewitness accounts. But their juices don't start to flow until they offer the derisive dismissals of skeptics they've interviewed about the incident. This is typical: "Astronomy professor X said that even trained pilots can be fooled into thinking the planet Venus is a flying saucer."

I wish this approach were applied to other kinds of news. Imagine a CNN anchorman regurgitating the words he has heard at a Pentagon news conference, then calling on leftist scholar Noam Chomsky to provide a skeptical perspective. Visualize a journalist for *Time* magazine interviewing three politicians about their latest views on gay marriage or the Middle East, then asking poet Ann Waldman to critique the gross ahistorical literalism of the politicians' views. This is the approach I like to take to *every* story I hear.

In its wild state, the truth is fluid, slippery, vagrant, scrambled, promiscuous, kaleidoscopic, and beautiful.

Many of the debunkers who deride astrology have done no research on the subject. They haven't read smart astrological philosophers like Dane Rudhyar, don't know that seminal astronomer Johannes Kepler was a skilled astrologer, and aren't aware that eminent psychologist C.G. Jung cast horoscopes and believed that "astrology represents the summation of all the psychological knowledge of antiquity." The closest approach the fraudulent "skeptics" usually make to the ancient art is to glance at a tabloid horoscope column. To match their carelessness, I might make a drive-by of a strip mall and declare that the profession of architecture is shallow and debased.

That's one reason why these ill-informed "skeptics" spread so many ignorant lies. For instance, they say that astrologers think the stars and planets emit invisible beams that affect people's lives. The truth is, most Western astrologers don't believe any such thing.

Is there any way in which you engage in behavior similar to the lazy debunkers? What subjects do you speak about with authority even though you really don't know much about them? Do you ever spout opinions about situations you've never experienced first-hand? Do you pass judgment on ideas you've never studied and people you've never spent time with? We all do these things—I confess to being guilty of it myself. But there is a cure.

According to Wordspy.com, the term *pareidolia* (pronounced "payr-eye-DOH-lee-uh") refers to "the erroneous or fanciful perception of a pattern or meaning in something that is actually ambiguous or random." As an example, mainstream astronomers might say this is the perfect word to describe what rogue researchers have called the

"Face on Mars," an evocative plateau in the Cydonia region of the red planet.

It's important to note, however, that not all wonders and marvels are the result of pareidolia. For instance, let's say you unexpectedly find yourself fantasizing that a certain oil stain you see in a parking lot looks like a horse imprisoned in a cage with a ribbon wrapped around it, and that spurs you to realize that lately you've felt trapped by something that is supposedly a gift. That may *really be* a communication directly from an angel of mercy to you.

To distinguish authentic breakthroughs from mere pareidolias, you need to strike a balance between skepticism and open-mindedness. Just because some apparent miracles are frauds doesn't mean they all are.

Tell jokes to clowns.
Cook gourmet meals for chefs.
Show babies how to crawl.
Sing to the birds.

To be the best pronoiac explorer you can be, I suggest you adopt an outlook that combines the rigorous objectivity of a scientist, the "beginner's mind" of Zen Buddhism, and the compassionate friendliness of the Dalai Lama. Blend a scrupulously dispassionate curiosity with a skepticism driven by expansiveness, not spleen.

To pull this off, you'll have to be willing to regularly suspend your brilliant theories about the way the world works. Accept with good humor the possibility that what you've learned in the past may not be a reliable guide to understanding the fresh phenomenon that's right in front of you. Be suspicious of your biases, even the rational and benevolent ones. Open your heart as you strip away the interpretations that your emotions might be inclined to impose.

"Before we can receive the unbiased truth about anything," wrote my teacher Ann Davies, "we have to be ready to ignore what we would like to be true."

At the same time, don't turn into a hard-ass, poker-faced robot. Keep your feelings moist and receptive. Remember your natural affection for all of creation. Enjoy the power of tender sympathy as it drives you to probe for the unimaginable revelations of every new moment. "Before we can receive the entire truth about anything," said Ann Davies, "we have to love it."

The Swahili word *kule* means "in between" or "neither-this-way-nor-that." *Kule* people are highly valued, according to Beauty and Truth Laboratory researcher Russ Crim, because they are unbiased but not apathetic. Their passionate objectivity allows them to imagine a common ground that's in the best interests of both sides in a conflict, thereby promoting an organic form of harmony. "To be *kule* is to rule," says Crim.

Galileo Galilei didn't invent the telescope, but he created a better version of the first primitive model. In the early 17th century, he used it to make astronomical discoveries that contradicted the Catholic Church's cosmology. The caretakers of the old guard were furious. "The Earth is the center of the universe," they told him after he announced he had detected moons revolving around Jupiter. "What you say you have seen is impossible." They refused to even look through Galileo's new tool.

In later years, scientists adopted the Church's attitude toward a variety of other phenomena, including meteorites and dinosaurs. Until the 1800s, wrote Roy Gallant in *Sky & Telescope,* "the scientific community scoffed at those who believed stones fell from the heavens, though meteorites had been seen to fall and had been collected since ancient times by the Chinese and Egyptians. As stones continued to rain down from the sky, learned scientists explained them away as condensations of the atmosphere or concretions of volcanic dust."

Similarly, until the 19th century, scientists didn't believe that large reptiles had once lived on the earth. Throughout history, ordinary people had always found what we now call fossils, but the experts decreed that they could not possibly be the remains of an ancient extinct species.

The moral of the story as far as you and I are concerned: As smart as we may be and as much as we might know, there are truths we have become dead set against believing, let alone seeing.

At the end of one of his columns, the *San Francisco Chronicle's* Jon Carroll corrected misinformation he'd provided in an earlier piece. "My dreamy view of the dissent during the Civil War was perhaps just a tiny bit completely wrong," he noted. He went on to admit that

Dionysian Manifesto

contrary to what he had asserted, President Lincoln ruthlessly quashed dissidents. "My apologies to the truth," Carroll concluded.

Receptivity is not a passive state. Nor is it a blank, empty waiting around for whatever happens to come along. In urging you to cultivate receptivity, I don't mean you should become a lazy do-nothing bereft of goals, reacting blindly to whatever life throws in front of you.

Receptivity is a robust readiness to be surprised and moved; a vigorous intention to be awake to everything you can't control. When you're receptive in the pronoiac style, you have strong ideas and a powerful will and an eagerness to disseminate your unique blessings, but you're also animated by the humble certainty that you have a lot to learn.

Most people associate innocence with naiveté. Conventional wisdom regards it as belonging to children and fools and rookies who lack the sophistication or experience to know the tough truths about life.

But the Beauty and Truth Laboratory recognizes a different kind of innocence. It's based on an understanding that the world is always changing, and therefore deserves to be seen fresh every day. This alternative brand of innocence is fueled by an aggressive determination to empty one's imagination of all preconceptions.

"Ignorance is not knowing anything and being attracted to the good," wrote Clarissa Pinkola-Estes in *Women Who Run With the* Wolves. "Innocence is knowing everything and still being attracted to the good."

"The knowledge I'm interested in is not something you buy and then have and can be comfortable with. The knowledge I'm interested in keeps opening wider and wider, making me smaller and more amazed, until I see I cannot have it all—and then delight in that as a freedom." —Heather McHugh, *Hinge & Sign*

"The most exciting phrase to hear in science, the one that heralds new discoveries, is not 'Eureka! I have found it' but rather 'That's funny . . .'" —Isaac Asimov

Play a joke on your fear. Honor your anger. Capitalize on your guilt. Kill your own death.

"The only real voyage consists not in seeking new landscapes, but in having new eyes; in seeing the universe through the eyes of another, one hundred others—in seeing the hundred universes that each of them sees." —Marcel Proust, translated by Kiyotesong

Though I'm critical of journalists and scientists, it's not because I don't love them. On the contrary, they have been great teachers, both through the ideas and information they've lavished on me and in the way they've compelled me to learn how important it is to question all my sources of ideas and information. I will keep trying to master the pure objectivity that their professions enshrine as the highest ideal. And I will remain both skeptical toward and receptive to their offerings.

The dangers of excessive politeness are perfectly exemplified in the medieval legend of Parzival, Arthur's purest knight. His quest for the Holy Grail leads him to a castle where he is welcomed by a wounded lord. At dinner, a mysterious bowl captivates Parzival's attention. He's dying to know more about it, but he holds his tongue. His training as a knight has taught him that it's uncourteous to express too much curiosity.

Tragically, he doesn't realize that he has arrived at the very place where his quest could be satisfied. The wounded lord is actually the fisher king, the marvelous bowl is the Grail, and he is being presented with a magical test. The test consists of a simple task: to ask about the bowl. Because Parzival fails to do so, the king does not reveal the secret and does not give him the Grail.

The next morning, Parzival wakes up to find the castle empty, and he leaves having missed the very opportunity he wanted most.

"Be homesick for wild knowing." —Clarissa Pinkola Estes, *Women Who Run with the Wolves*

Dionysian Manifesto

YOUR CHALICE

Visualize a chalice—a ceremonial drinking cup. What's the first image that comes up for you? Picture it in your mind's eye. Is it silver? Ceramic? Plastic? What color? How big is it? Is it long-stemmed or squat? Does it have a wide, shallow cup or a tall, narrow one, or what? Close your eyes and spend a moment with this vision before reading on.

So you've pictured a chalice in your mind's eye. Here's an analysis of its possible meaning: What you envisioned represents your capacity to be filled up with goodies. It's a snapshot of your subconscious receptivity to favors and help and inspiration.

For instance, if you imagined a shallow plastic champagne glass, it signifies that you may not be well prepared to drink deeply of the elixirs the universe is conspiring to provide you.

On the other hand, a large-volume, gracefully shaped sterling silver cup suggests that you're ready and willing to receive a steady outpouring of wonders.

A long-stemmed chalice may indicate you're inclined to be aggressive about filling your cup. A short, squat stem could mean you're not feeling very deserving of having your cup filled.

Now here's the fun part. If you visualized an inadequate chalice, you can change it. If you pictured a chalice you like, you can add more details to it.

Take some time to picture a vessel that's perfectly worth of you. Imprint it on your imagination. Then, for the next nine days, conjure it up every morning for five minutes right after you wake up, and every evening for five minutes before you go to sleep. It will reprogram your subconscious mind to be ready and willing to accept all the favors and help and inspiration you need.

That in turn will exert an influence on your surroundings, making it easier for the world to deliver its favors and help and inspiration.

YOU ARE A DISSEMINATOR OF PRONOIA

The Beauty and Truth Laboratory is coming to you live from your repressed memory of paradise, reminding you that all of creation loves you very much.

Even now, secret allies are cooking up mysteries that will excite you and incite you for years to come.

Even now, the earth, moon, and sun are collaborating to make sure you have all you need to make your next move.

But here's the loaded question: Are you willing to start loving life back with an equal intensity? The adoration it offers you has not exactly been unrequited, but there is room for you to be more demonstrative.

Half of the art of pronoia is about being improvisationally receptive to life's elaborate scheme to shower you with blessings. The other half is about learning to be a co-conspirator who assists life in doling out blessings—to help everyone *else* get exactly what they need, exactly when they need it.

Visualize yourself being able to recognize the raw truth about the people you care about. Imagine that you can see how they already embody the beauty their souls' codes have promised as well as how they still fall short of embodying that beauty. Picture yourself being able to make them feel appreciated even as you inspire them to risk changes that will activate more of their souls' codes.

PRONOIA NEWS NETWORK

Top Secret Mass Gathering

History's largest meeting of world religious leaders was virtually unreported by the media. The top-secret event transpired in January 2002, when 200 representatives from every major faith gathered in Assisi, Italy. At the end of the conference, they issued the Assisi Decalogue for Peace, a document denouncing all violence committed in the name of God or religion. It declared, "We commit ourselves to stand at the side of those who suffer poverty and abandonment, speaking out for those who have no voice, and to working effectively to change these situations."

Eclipsing this rare outbreak of unity were many stories the media deemed more important: Mike Tyson got his boxing license; John Walker Lindh made a court appearance; the Enron hearings began. (Source: David Waters, religion columnist)

Does Reality Exist?

The Annals of Improbable Research polled its readers on the question: "Does reality exist?" Forty-two percent answered yes; 31 percent said that it most certainly does not. The other 27 percent were undecided. Some believed their reality exists but no one else's does. Two people said, "Reality exists, but you can't get to it." According to one respondent, "Reality especially exists right after a thunderstorm." Another person quoted Philip K. Dick: "Reality is that which, when you stop believing in it, doesn't go away."

Evolution of an Axiom   The fundamental laws of physics may evolve as the cosmos grows older. That was the conclusion of a paper published by a team of astrophysicists in the prestigious *Physical Review Letters.*

Using the giant Keck Telescope in Hawaii, the researchers investigated the absorption of light by metal atoms in gas clouds billions of light years away. Their results showed apparent variations in the value of the "fine structure constant," which measures the strength of the electromagnetic force that controls how electrons and photons interact.

The scientists were effectively looking back in time, gazing at light that left its point of origin billions of years ago. The fine structure constant seemed to be a smaller number then than it is now. Until their study, this constant was thought to be as immutable as the speed of light.

The implications are clear: If one supposed axiom has changed over time, others may have done so also. (Source: James Glanz and Dennis Overbye, "Anything Can Change, It Seems, Even an Immutable Law of Nature," *The New York Times,* August 15, 2001)

India and China Get Rich Quick

China and India, which comprise one-third of the earth's population, have more than twice the wealth they had in 1989. (Source: *The Economist*)

In the past twenty years, hundreds of millions of Chinese have escaped poverty and begun earning middle-class incomes. Economist Jeffrey Sachs, renowned for his work in assisting Third World nations to raise their standards of living, says, "China is the most successful development story in world history." (Source: Fareed Zakaria, "The Big Story Everyone Missed," *Newsweek,* December 30, 2002)

Returned to the Source

In 1999, the government of Canada officially created and recognized the territory of Nunavut, giving back control of a huge part of the far north to the Inuit people who have lived there for millennia. A story in the *National Geographic* discussed the struggle of the Inuit to emerge from the white man's domination. In one photo, a woman named Pauloosie Muckpa crossed the tundra carrying the bloody head of a caribou, whose brains and antler tips were to be the centerpiece of a great feast. "We used to be ashamed of what we ate," she said. "But now we're not. Today we are not ashamed of who we are."

> PNN is brought to you by
> Albert Camus' belief that
> "Each of us is free to stoke
> the crematory fires of Buchenwald or
> nurse lepers in an African hospital."
> (Source: Notebooks 1935–1951)

Partial Truce in Drug War   "The silver lining in the budget crisis affecting the states throughout this nation is that from Louisiana to Texas to Michigan, state governments are cutting prison budgets by releasing nonviolent drug offenders. There has been a steady move toward treatment instead of incarceration, and a greater understanding that drug abuse should be handled in the doctors' office, not the prison cell." —Medea Benjamin, AlterNet, www.alternet.org

School Days Increase   Literacy and education levels are rising steadily on a global scale. Since 1970, the percentage of students going to secondary school has more than doubled. (Source: www.goodnewsnetwork.org)

Evolution of a Poet As a young poet, Carolyn Forché pursued an academic study of her craft at placid Midwestern universities. Her first book dealt with her family, ancestry, and coming of age. Then she made a radical departure. Leaving behind familiar comforts, she moved to El Salvador at the height of its death squad activity, working as an activist. Later she lived in Lebanon during its traumatic civil war, serving as a correspondent for NPR. Her adventures in these war zones forged her into a human rights advocate and instilled her work with a moral fervor that's rare among modern poets.

Blind Compassion Watch "In January 2003, a Muslim gas station attendant saved a New York synagogue from arson with his phone call to 911. Pakistani immigrant Syed Ali watched as a man bought gasoline, marched across the street, and began dousing the front of the temple. Police responded to Ali's call in time to stop the crime. Ali declined the mantle of hero saying 'It was a sacred place he was going to destroy.'"
—Geraldine Weis-Corbley, www.goodnewsnetwork.org

Healing Protest A study by psychologists at the University of Sussex in Great Britain has found that taking part in campaigns, demonstrations, strikes, and protests is good for you. Interviews with activists revealed that participants experienced a deep sense of happiness and even euphoria in being involved in protest events.

Breaking the Pronoia Taboo

"Everything is blooming most recklessly; if it were voices instead of colors, there would be an unbelievable shrieking into the heart of the night." —Rainer Maria Rilke, *Letters of Rainer Maria Rilke, 1892–1910,* M.D. Herter Norton, translator

"One of the tenets of Zen is that the good poet, to be a good poet, must first be a person of good character." —Christopher Buckley

"The sun, with all those planets revolving around it and dependent on it, can still ripen a bunch of grapes as if it had nothing else in the universe to do." —Galileo Galilei

"The unhappy person resents it when you try to cheer him up, because that means he has to stop dwelling on himself and start paying attention to the universe. Unhappiness is the ultimate form of self-indulgence. When you're unhappy, you get to pay a lot of attention to yourself. You get to take yourself oh so very seriously." —Tom Robbins, *Jitterbug Perfume*

Thomas Merton's notion of what makes a saint saintly doesn't have to do with being a perfectly sinless paragon of virtue. The more important measure of sanctity, he said, is one's ability to see what's good and beautiful in other people. The truly godly person "retires from the struggle of judging others."

"This earth is honey for all beings, and all beings are honey for this earth. The intelligent, immortal being, the soul of the earth, and the intelligent, immortal being, the soul in the individual being—each is honey to the other." —Brihadaranyaka Upanishad

"To feel the love of people whom we love is a fire that feeds our life. But to feel the affection that comes from those we do not know, from those unknown to us, who are watching over our sleep and solitude, over our dangers and our weakness—that is something still greater and more beautiful because it widens the boundaries of our being, and unites all living things." —Pablo Neruda, *The Book of Virtues*

TWICE AS ALIVE

Tantric sex practitioners say an artful lover never makes love the same way twice.

Similarly, chanteuse Billie Holiday believed a good singer should never sing a song the same way twice. If you use all the same phrasing and melody, she said, you're failing your art.

The only Zen master we know—whose name we can't tell you because she changes it every week, and we haven't heard the latest one—likes to quote the ancient Greek philosopher, Heraclitus: "You cannot step into the same river twice, for fresh waters are ever flowing in upon you."

Buddhist monk Thich Nhat Hanh has the last word: "Thanks to impermanence, everything is possible."

Midwife Genius Abroad Around the age of 17, students in Denmark take a standardized test that determines their educational fate and, ultimately, their career path. Teens who earn a little less than the highest scores are eligible to become physicists, chemists, and theologians. The very smartest kids become doctors, psychologists, and midwives. (Source: Garrison Keilor, *National Geographic.*)

The Psychotherapeutic Value of Activism

Psychologist James Hillman says that taking action to correct social and economic injustice in the world can serve as powerful psychotherapy. In some cases, it may even be a more effective way to transmute one's personal pain than talking about the pain with a therapist.

Crime-Fighter Declares Victory

At age 94, Simon Wiesenthal announced that his work was done. The renowned Holocaust survivor fought for five decades to bring more than 1,000 Nazi fugitives to justice, including Adolf Eichmann. "I found the mass murderers I was looking for," he said, "and I have outlived all of them." (Source: *Format* magazine)

Squat of the Century

In 1999, 40 starving artists in Paris broke into an abandoned building near the Louvre. They built studios inside and have been squatting there rent-free ever since. In 2003, the city of Paris bought the building and is paying $3.5 million to renovate it so that the artists can continue to enjoy their home.

Your Gut Brain

You and I have always known that we can think with our bellies. Gut instinct, we call it. Now scientists have found evidence confirming our hunch. *In the Second Brain: Your Gut Has a Mind of Its Own*, Dr. Michael Gershon documents the evidence for a literal second brain in our stomachs and intestines. Here, in a bundle of 100 billion nerve cells, our gut reactions originate.

Sixth-Grade Zeitgeist Update

The following bon mots were scrawled on the backpacks and binders of sixth grade girls at Greenwood School in Mill Valley, California:

Learn as if you'll live forever

Explain yourself wildly, not carefully

Wake up—but not too fast, or you might hurt yourself

Question authority, including the authority that told you to question authority

Give me chocolate or I'll scream

It's all so funny—how can you not be laughing?

When you shout "halaluya," never spell it right

Live the freakiest truth

Benevolent Pranks One night in February 2004, anonymous mischief-makers in the English town of Pembury sneaked into 100 gardens and secretly planted an ash sapling in each one. It was hard work. The weather was terrible, and each tree had to be carefully rooted in a six-inch hole. Some residents were pleased by the unsolicited gift, while others were confused.

The Rest of the Middle East News "In Israel, several thousand Israeli and Palestinian families living in relatively close proximity to one another, and each deeply proud of their respective nation's history and foundations and traditions, did not actively seethe in a roiling cauldron of hatred or religious bile, nor did they let the horrible atrocities some of their people are perpetrating on each other cause them to froth with self-righteousness and mad desire for war.

"They did not go about their day cowering in a pit of lost hope, fearing for their lives and wishing their neighbors extreme painful death and eternal damnation, despite all the painful evidence and political urgency currently screeching at them that they must do so immediately." —Mark Morford, *SFGate,* www.sfgate.com/columnists/morford/

Twenty Thousand Years of Progress in the 21st Century

"Centuries ago people didn't think that the world was changing at all. Their grandparents had the same lives that they did, and they expected their grandchildren would do the same, and that expectation was largely fulfilled.

"Today it's an axiom that life is changing and that technology is affecting the nature of society. What's not fully understood is that the pace of change is itself accelerating, and the last 20 years are not a good guide to the next 20 years. We're doubling the paradigm shift rate, the rate of progress, every decade. ·

"The whole 20th century was like 25 years of change at today's rate of change. In the next 25 years we'll make four times the progress you saw in the 20th century. And we'll make 20,000 years of progress in the 21st century, which is almost a thousand times more technical change than we saw in the 20th century." —Ray Kurzweil, excerpted from "The Singularity," on the *Edge* website, March 25, 2001, www.edge.org/3rd_culture/kurzweil_singularity/kurzweil_singularity_index.html

Integrity Inventory

Finland, Iceland, and Denmark are the least corrupt nations, according to Transparency International's annual survey. (Source: www.transparency.org/)

Iacocca's Repentance

Former Chrysler Chairman Lee Iacocca left the car business and started a company to develop electric scooters. "I've spent 50 years polluting the world," he told the *Denver Post.* "Now it's time to do something cleaner and better." —*Earth Island Journal,* Fall, 1997, www.earthisland.org

Worthless Emotions

"Pain and conflict are, to a large extent, the result of a discrepancy between the way we think others should treat us, react to us, and appreciate us, and the way they actually do. Many of our miseries are thus rooted in self-pity, the most worthless of all human emotions." —Ann Davies, www.bota.org

Simple Gifts

Habitat for Humanity is a grass roots organization devoted to eliminating substandard housing and homelessness. During 2002, its affiliates built or renovated 4,776 homes in the United States, and 11,545 elsewhere, mostly in South America, Africa, the Middle East, and the Asia-Pacific region. Since its inception in 1976, it has constructed 135,000 houses.

MIRABILIA REPORT

Mirabilia n. modest astonishments, friendly shocks, sweet anomalies; from the Latin *mirabilia,* "marvels."

■ Romanian physicists created gaseous globes of plasma that grew, reproduced, and communicated with each other, thereby fulfilling the definition for life.

■ In an apparent attempt to raise their volume above the prevailing human din, some nightingales in big cities have learned to unleash 95-decibel songs, matching the loudness of a chainsaw.

■ Current definitions of what's normal will be regarded as pathological in 15 years.

■ *Fortune* magazine estimates that basketball star Michael Jordan's career has contributed $10 billion to the U.S. economy.

■ Thirty-eight percent of North America is wilderness.

■ There is a statistically significant probability of world-class athletes and military leaders being born when Mars is rising in the sky.

■ Fertility clinics in the U.S. are filled to the brim with frozen human embryos. Forty thousand would-be fetuses are now on ice, waiting for a go-ahead from the couples that spawned them.

■ In the pueblos of New Mexico, bricks still measure 33 by 15 by 10 centimeters, proportions that almost exactly match those of the bricks used to build Egypt's Temple of Hatshepsut 3,500 years ago.

■ To make a pound of honey, bees have to gather nectar from about two million flowers. To produce a single pound of the spice saffron, humans have to handpick and process 80,000 flowers. In delivering the single survivor necessary to fertilize an ovum, a man releases 500 million sperm.

■ Childbirth is often joyful even though it's painful.

■ In hopes of calming flustered lawbreakers, Japanese cops have substituted the sound of church bells for sirens on police cars.

■ Scientists believe they'll eventually be able to figure out why cancer cells are virtually immortal, and then apply that secret to keeping normal cells alive much longer, thereby dramatically extending the human life span.

ENOUGH IS ENOUGH

Multimillionaire pop star George Michael has decided to give away his music for free, posting it on the Internet for anyone to download. "I've been very well remunerated for my talents over the years," he told BBC, "so I really don't need the public's money."

Hollywood movie and music mogul David Geffen also believes he has enough money. The billionaire cofounder of DreamWorks told *Forbes,* "I have no interest in making money anymore. Everything I make in the entertainment business will go to charity."

CNN founder and billionaire Ted Turner is in the middle of a 10-year, billion-dollar giveaway to the United Nations. Since 1997, he has been donating annual installments of 100 million dollars, specifying that they not be used for administration costs but for programs like eliminating land mines, feeding children, and preventing disease.

THIS WEEK IN PRONOIAC HISTORY

Lady Godiva was more than a seminal performance artist. She was also a humanitarian and patron of the arts. When she doffed her clothes and rode a white horse through the English town of Coventry in 1057, her purpose was philanthropic. Her husband, the local assessor, had promised to abolish all taxes on the local folk if she did the daring deed.

✺

Early in his career, while working as a newspaper editor, L. Frank Baum advocated the extermination of Native Americans. Later he mellowed. The books he wrote about the magical kingdom of Oz are celebrations of cultural and ethnic diversity.

Druidic Engineering

A 275-meter section of Austria's A9 highway was the most dangerous in the country. Accidents occurred there at an alarming rate.

"We had put up signs to reduce speed, renewed the road surface and made bends more secure, but we still kept getting accidents," said an engineer from the motorway authority.

Finally, archdruid Gerald Knobloch was summoned. To heal and revitalize the natural flow of "earth energy," he directed pillars of white quartz to be placed alongside the road. Traffic carnage soon disappeared.

"I located dangerous elements that had disrupted the energy flow," Knobloch said. "The worst was a river which human interference had forced to flow against its natural direction. By erecting two stones of quartz the energy lines were restored."

The pillars had a similar function to acupuncture, he said. "Acupuncture needles also restore broken energy lines. What acupuncture does for the body, the stones do for the environment." (Source: London's *The Telegraph*, www.telegraph.co.uk)

Turner's Gender Revolution   To distribute the funds he has pledged to the United Nations, Ted Turner created a board of directors that has more women than men.

"If women were in control of the world," he said, "it would be a much more peaceful, prosperous, equitable world in a very short period of time. You'd have a huge shift away from military budgets and into education and health care. And we're trying to set the example."

Open Secret Revealed
"There is a great insight which our culture is deliberately designed to suppress, distort, and ignore: that Nature is a minded entity; that Nature is not simply the random flight of atoms through electromagnetic fields; that Nature is not the empty, despiritualized lumpen matter that we inherit from modern physics. But it is instead a kind of intelligence, a kind of mind." —Terence McKenna, www.deoxy.org/mckenna.htm

Wildness Revised   In his book *The Rag and Bone Shop of the Heart*, Robert Bly says that to be wild is not to be crazy like a criminal or psychotic, but "mad as the mist and snow." It has nothing to do with being childish or primitive, nor does it manifest as manic rebellion or self-damaging alienation. The real marks of wildness, he asserts, are a love of nature, a delight in silence, a voice free to say spontaneous things, and an exuberant curiosity in the face of the unknown.

Karma in Action   In 2001, Mitzi Nichols of Virginia Beach anonymously donated one of her kidneys to a stranger. She got paid nothing for this rare act of generosity, and after recovering from surgery went back to her job as a cashier at a gift shop. It took the universe three years to figure out a way to compensate her properly. In June 2004, she won $500,000 in the Virginia state lottery.

PNN is made possible by Dave Eggers' rant in The Harvard Advocate*:*
"Do not be critics, you people, I beg you. I was a critic and I wish I could take it all back because it came from a smelly and ignorant place in me and spoke with a voice that was all rage and envy. Do not dismiss a book until you have written one, and do not dismiss a movie until you have made one, and do not dismiss a person until you have met them. It is a fuckload of work to be open-minded and generous and understanding and forgiving and accepting, but, Christ, that is what matters. What matters is saying yes."

FLEXIBLE PRONOIA THERAPY

Experiments and exercises in becoming a tenderly objective, cagily candid, fanatically balanced Master of Iconoclastic Listening

---

Report your answers & research results below

1 If you're typical, your natural curiosity was virtually extinguished at an early age by mediocre teachers, boring lessons, and oppressive classrooms. Have you ever wondered what your life would be like if your imagination hadn't been squelched? What interesting adventures might you have sought out if your natural love of learning hadn't been crushed?

Let's launch a quest to undo the damage. Imagine I've handed you an *undiploma:* your official release from the soul-death of your formal education; the beginning of the healing of your wounded love of learning. What's the first thing you'll do to invoke a steady stream of inspired teachers and invigorating lessons?

2 When I lived in Santa Cruz, I had an acquaintance named Barnaby who lived at a remote rural community called Last Chance Farm. Combination shaman, wise elder, and lunatic, he would on rare occasions slip into town and lead me on fact-finding missions he dubbed whirlygigs. "Steep yourself with the intention of attracting lessons you don't know you need," he'd say, and then we'd meander the streets at random, going places I'd never been and striking up conversations with strangers with whom I seemingly had nothing in common. Barnaby described the whirlygig as an urban version of the walkabout, which for aborigines is a time when they leave work and wander out into the bush to commune with the mysteries of nature.

Carry out your own whirlygig. When you're done, write an essay entitled, "People, Places, and Things I Didn't Know I Loved."

3 The German religious reformer Martin Luther was fond of referring to the faculty of reason as a "damned whore." He believed it gave itself in service to any old theory, often propping up specious arguments rooted in hidden emotional agendas.

Though I regard my ability to reason as a prized asset, I confess to having some of Luther's mistrust about it. Like most of us, I have corrupted my logical mind by sometimes using it to disguise and rationalize my subjective biases.

Can you imagine having so much self-awareness that you never turn your reasoning ability into a whore? Are you willing to probe with merciless honesty for the unconscious feelings that drive you to believe what you do, and to analyze the ways you mask your subjective biases as "objective fact"? Could you suspend all your preconceptions and greet every situation with a scrupulously open mind? Try to live up to that high standard for a period of three days.

4 To the ancient Chinese, pigs were sacred because they could eat anything and turn it into energy. The creatures were regarded as masters of transmutation. Nothing, not even garbage, was unusable to them. The Chinese aspired to be like pigs in the sense of being able to learn from and derive benefit from every experience, not just the tidy, tasteful ones.

Borrowing this strategy, name two garbage-like experiences that you could turn into fuel for your growing urge to be a pronoiac co-conspirator.

5 Is it really healthy to have a shrill, 25-words-or-less opinion about everything, as radio and TV talk shows seem to imply? Would anyone mind if now and then you served as a compassionate witness about the hot-button issues? Is it conceivable that you could simply sit on the fence in the midst of the wars of words and beam articulate sympathy at both sides?

Yes, you can. You have the rebellious resourcefulness to be a freedom fighter without hating anyone. Go out and prove it. Document your success here.

6 Do you realize you can actually *listen* a person's soul into existence? Your fervent interest in the inner life of those you care for can awaken their dormant powers. The teacher Richard Moss says, "The greatest gift you can give another is the purity of your attention." Offer this gift to a loved one who's struggling to birth an inspiration or revelation.

7 "You may enjoy this movie if you shut down enough brain cells. I turned off all except the ones needed

to remember where I parked my car." This observation comes from a critic's evaluation of *Charlie's Angels: Full Throttle,* but I've read similar comments in many reviews of other films and entertainment. Indeed, it's an approach that many intelligent people employ routinely in response to the loud, shiny slop our culture foists on us.

What about you? Do you assume you have to make yourself dumber in order to have fun? Has the blaring inanity of the world caused you to shut down your sensitivity? Work to reverse this trend. You'll receive help from unexpected sources if you do.

8 Literary critic Harold Bloom believes *Finnegans Wake* was James Joyce's masterpiece—the closest thing our age has come to the genius of Shakespeare and Dante. Novelist Anthony Burgess called it "a great comic vision that makes us laugh aloud on nearly every page." Yet when Joyce was writing the book, his wife Nora hated it, calling it "chop suey." She asked him why he didn't make "sensible books that people can understand." Joyce's patron, Harriet Weaver, also derided *Finnegans Wake,* saying it was a waste of his genius. Luckily, Joyce was mainly loyal to the little voices in his head, not the little voices outside of his head.

Talk about a showdown you've experienced between those two kinds of voices.

9 Have you ever played the game of "Tell me the story of your scars?" It's best to do it with a skilled empath who is curious about your fate's riddles and skilled at helping you find redemption in your wounds.

"How did you get that blotch on your knee?" he or she might begin, and you describe the time in childhood when you fell on the sidewalk. Then maybe he or she would say, "Why do you always look so sad when you hear that song?" And you'd narrate the tale of how it was playing when an old lover broke your heart. The questions and answers continue until you unveil the history of your hurts, both physical and psychic. Treat yourself to this game soon. Afterwards, return the favor.

10 In preparing for a performance at Burning Man in 2004, I bought 18 jars of pigs' feet at the grocery store, 200 pairs of white underpants at Costco, and 22 alarm clocks at the drugstore. None of the clerks who took my money expressed the slightest interest in the reasons for my peculiar and prodigious orders. Their lack of curiosity was astounding to me. Do you have any theories that might explain it?

Flexible Pronoia Therapy

11 After seeing the temple of Artemis in Ephesus, the ancient writer Philo of Byzantium wrote, "He who has laid eyes on it will be convinced that the world of the immortal gods has moved from heaven to earth."

Seek out an experience that provokes an equally breathtaking response in you.

12 In *The Book of Embraces,* Uruguayan author Eduardo Galeano writes, "The fishermen of the Colombian coast must be learned doctors of ethics and morality, for they invented the word *sentipensante,* or 'feeling-thinking,' to define language that speaks the truth."

Describe a time when you pulled off the feat of thinking with your heart and feeling with your head.

13 Chilean poet Pablo Neruda was master of the ode, a lyric blessing that bestows praise and thanks. Some of the subjects that received Neruda's appreciation were grand: his "Ode to the Moon of the Sea," "Ode to the Birth of a Fawn," and "Ode to a Beautiful Nude." But many of his praise poems were directed at everyday objects, like "Ode to a Bar of Soap," "Ode to a Pair of Socks," and "Ode to French Fries."

Be like Neruda. Write an ode to an ordinary thing.

14 Leaving behind her beloved Europe, a young Anaïs Nin arrived in New York full of misgivings. "I hate it," she wrote about the city in one of her famous diaries. "I find it superficial. It's an ugly prison." She was not unwilling to have her mind changed, however. "Make me love New York," she told photographer Alfred Stieglitz, a long-time resident. "Show me what you love."

Imagine I've come to visit you. Envision the places you'd take me to and the experiences you'd give me to demonstrate what delights you about your home turf.

15 Here's Bruce Chatwin in *The Songlines:* "Aboriginal creation myths tell of the legendary totemic beings who had wandered over the continent in the Dreamtime, singing out the name of everything that crossed their path—birds, animals, plants, rocks, waterholes—and so singing the world into existence. Any species can be a Dreaming. A virus can be a Dreaming. You can have a chickenpox Dreaming, a rain Dreaming, a desert-orange Dreaming, a lice Dreaming."

Close your eyes and tune in to the song of a Dreaming species of your choice. Either that, or else *pretend* you can tune in the song of a Dreaming species.

Flexible Pronoia Therapy

Sacred Advertisement

This perfect moment is brought to you by the following pronoiac testimony from Tom of Ohio:

"I am a devout atheist, but I have to explain to my atheist friends that I do pray to the 'GodIdontbelievein.'

"My first direct contact with this Divinity arrived when I was coming out of anesthesia after surgery. I was somehow aware of my existence but totally sensory-deprived. As I emerged from total unconsciousness, a tiny flickering Tinkerbell-like creature in the form of a shimmering globe of light fluttered into my consciousness and hovered irresistibly before my internal eyes. I was in love with it and it loved me. In fact it was me, or at least the manifestation of cosmic energy that settles in me and is my being. It gave me a blessing of good will, then went about its business of operating my body. In parting, it gave me the assurance that it would always be there for me and with me, and would join me after it shut the body down for the last time.

"Since that first encounter, I commune with the little sparkling wonder every so often. I thank it for its presence and it thanks me for mine, though we are actually one and the same. I find myself praying to it, though there's really no need to—it knows me better than I do, and guides me toward my goals, though I know not what they are."

This space has been liberated for your use

11

Stronger than hate,
older than death,
deeper than the abyss,
more exotic than trust

Tummler and Ondinnonk

While you carry out your experiments in pronoia, your words of power are *tummler* and *ondinnonk*.

Tummler is a Yiddish term derived from *tumlen,* 'to make a racket.' A *tummler* stirs up a commotion, makes things happen, and incites people to action through his or her affectionate agitation. Clowning and pranks may be part of a *tummler's* repertoire.

Ondinnonk is an Iroquois word with two related meanings: 1. a secret wish of the soul, especially as revealed in dreams; 2. the spiritual part of our nature that longs to do good deeds.

Use your two words of power together: Let your *ondinnonk* guide you as you carry out your mission as a pronoiac *tummler.*

WELCOME HOME

Let me remind you who you really are: You're an immortal freedom fighter in service to divine love. You have temporarily taken on the form of a human being, suffering amnesia about your true origins, in order to liberate all sentient creatures from suffering and help them claim the ecstatic awareness that is their birthright. You will accept nothing less than the miracle of bringing heaven all the way down to earth.

Your task may look impossible. Ignorance and inertia, partially camouflaged as time-honored morality, seem to surround you. Pessimism is enshrined as a hallmark of worldliness. Compulsive skepticism masquerades as perceptiveness. Mean-spirited irony is chic. Stories about treachery and degradation provoke a visceral thrill in millions of people who think of themselves as reasonable and smart. Beautiful truths are suspect and ugly truths are readily believed.

To grapple against these odds, you have to be both a wrathful insurrectionary and an exuberant lover of life. You've got to cultivate cheerful buoyancy even as you resist the temptation to swallow thousands of delusions that have been carefully crafted and seductively packaged by very self-important people who act as if they know what they're doing. You have to learn how to stay in a good mood as you overthrow the sour, puckered hallucination that is mistakenly referred to as reality.

What can we do to help each other in this work?

First, we can create safe houses to shelter everyone who's devoted to the slow-motion awakening. These sanctuaries might take the form of temporary autonomous zones like festivals and parties and workshops, where we can ritually potentiate the evolving mysteries of pronoia. Or they might be more enduring autonomous zones like homes and cafes and businesses where we can get regular practice in freeing ourselves from the slavery of hatred in all of its many guises.

What else can we do to help each other? We can conspire together to carry out the agenda that futurist Barbara Marx Hubbard names: to hospice what's dying and midwife what's being born. We need the trigger of each other's rebel glee as we kill off every reflex within us that resonates in harmony with the putrefaction. We need each other's dauntless cunning as we goad and foment the blooming life forces within us that thrive on the New World's incandescent questions.

Here's a third way we can collaborate: We can inspire each other to perpetrate healing mischief, friendly shocks, compassionate tricks, blasphemous reverence, holy pranks, and crazy wisdom.

What? Huh? What do tricks and mischief and jokes have to do with our quest? Isn't America in a permanent state of war? Isn't it the most militarized empire in the history of the world? Hasn't the government's paranoia about terrorism decimated our civil liberties? Isn't it our duty to grow more serious and weighty than ever before?

I say it's the perfect moment to take everything less seriously and less personally and less literally.

Permanent war and the loss of civil liberties *are* immediate dangers. But there is an even bigger long-term threat to the fate of the earth, of which the others are but symptoms: the genocide of the imagination.

Earlier I cited pop nihilist storytellers as vanguard perpetrators of the genocide of the imagination. But there are other culprits as well: the fundamentalists. I'm not referring to just the usual suspects—the religious fanatics of Islam and Christianity and Judaism and Hinduism.

Scientists can be fundamentalists. So can liberals and capitalists, atheists and hedonists, patriots and anarchists, hippies and goths, you and me. Those who champion the ideology of materialism can be the most fanatical fundamentalists of all. And the journalists, filmmakers, novelists, critics, poets, and other artists who relentlessly generate rotten visions of the human condition are often pop nihilist fundamentalists.

Every fundamentalist divides the world into two camps, those who agree with him and like him and help him, and those who don't. There is

---

Don't make nasty comments about yourself behind your own back.

Do play soccer in bunny slippers at dawn in a supermarket parking lot with a gang of sadomasochistic stockbrokers who have promised to teach you the Balinese monkey chant.

Don't decorate your thigh with a slipshod tattoo of the devil pushing a lawn mower.

Do wear a t-shirt that says, "Of all the things I've lost, I miss my mind the most."

Don't glide into a bar, scout around for the person whose face has the most pain etched in it, and ask that person to come home with you.

Do eat ripe organic strawberries that have been genetically modified and irradiated. Do chain-smoke Marlboros as you peddle your exercise bicycle. Do wander through a garbage dump while listening to Mozart on your iPod.

Don't pile up framed photos of old flames in a vacant lot and drive a monster truck over them.

Do stage a slow-motion water balloon fight.

Don't get a vanity license plate that reads KZMYAZ.

Do shake your fist at the night sky as you call out, "I defy you, stars!"

Don't burst into a New Age workshop and shout, "Rainbows suck!"

Do pretend sometimes that maybe you mean the opposite of what you're saying as well as what you're saying.

Don't lie on a floor surrounded by wine-stained poetry books, crumpled Matisse prints, abandoned underwear, and half-eaten bowls of corn flakes as you stare up at the ceiling with a blank gaze, muttering gibberish and waving your hands as if swatting away demons.

Do run along the tops of cars during a traffic jam, escaping from the bad guys as you make your way to a helicopter that takes you to a spot hovering over an erupting volcano, into which you drop the *Buns of Steel* video.

Don't put your soul up for auction on the eBay website.

Do write a cookbook filled with recipes you've channeled from dead celebrities.

If you come upon a lamp with a genie in it, don't wish you had a magic wand.

---

only one right way to interpret the world—according to the ideas the fundamentalist believes to be true—and a million wrong ways.

The fundamental attitude of all fundamentalists is to take everything way too seriously and way too personally and way too literally. The untrammeled imagination is taboo. Correct belief is the only virtue. Every fundamentalist is committed to waging war against the imagination unless the imagination is enslaved to his or her belief system.

And here's the bad news: Like almost everyone in the world, each of us has our own share of the fundamentalist virus. It may not be as virulent and dangerous to the collective welfare as, say, the fundamentalism of Islamic terrorists or right-wing Christian politicians or CEOs who act as if making a financial profit is the supreme good or scientists who deny the existence of the large part of reality that's imperceptible to the five senses.

But still: We are infected, you and I, with fundamentalism. What are we going to do about it?

I say we practice taking everything less seriously and less personally and less literally. I suggest we administer plentiful doses of healing mischief, friendly shocks, compassionate tricks, blasphemous reverence, holy pranks, and crazy wisdom.

Primordial Gossip

186 **Welcome Home**

CONFESS YOUR FUNDAMENTALIST VIRUS

It's easy to see fanaticism, rigidity, and intolerance in other people, but harder to acknowledge them in yourself. Take this opportunity to identify the unique variety of the fundamentalist virus that infects you.

The Limits of Interweaving

"As above, so below" is the maxim at the heart of the Western hermetic tradition.

It implies that the nature of the cosmos is intimately reflected here on earth—and vice versa. Everything we imagine to be far away and "out there" has a parallel in the here and now. A miniature heaven resides within each of us, although we may not yet have activated its full potential. Astrologers go so far as to say that we all contain the spiritual essences of the planets. A little bit of Mars lives in your reproductive system and the corresponding parts of your psyche; Jupiter inhabits your solar plexus and feeds your will.

At the Beauty and Truth Laboratory, we act as if the hypothesis "as above, so below" is a useful perceptual filter. We urge pronoia lovers to experiment with it in the course of their daily practice.

Now and then, though, we recommend that you exercise caution about promoting unity. Writer Hanna Blank sets the right tone. "My cat attempted to adorn a prayer rug with a hairball, and I had to stop her," she says. "There are some instances in which we do not wish all things to be interconnected."

The More Accidental, the More True

"The more accidental, the more true," wrote Boris Pasternak in his poem "February." Scholar Mikhail Epstein expanded this observation: "The more accidental the phenomenon, the more divine its nature, for the divine is what has not been envisioned, what cannot be deduced from general rules, nor irreducible to them."

If we pursue this line of thought to its logical conclusion, we may decide that the most useful sources of illumination are not always holy books, revered dogma, and great truths that everyone has heard. They might also be serendipitous anomalies that erupt into the daily routine and break the trance of ordinary awareness. "The tiny spark," Epstein writes, "is the precise measure of the holiness of the world." (Source: Mikhail Epstein, "Judaic Spiritual Traditions in the Poetry of Pasternak and Mandel'shtam." Translated from Russian by Ruth Rischin. *Symposium. A Quarterly Journal in Modern Literatures,* Volume 52, No. 4)

When you're an aspiring master of pronoia, you see the cracks in the facades as opportunities; inspiration erupts as you career over bumps in the road; you love the enticing magic that flows from situations that other people regard as rough or crooked. "That which is not slightly distorted lacks sensible appeal," wrote poet Charles Baudelaire, "from which it follows that irregularity—that is to say, the unexpected, surprise and astonishment—is an essential part and characteristic of beauty."

Wabi-sabi is a Japanese term that refers to a captivating work of art with a distinctive flaw that embodies the idiosyncratic humanity of its creator. An aqua groove in an otherwise perfectly green ceramic pot may give it wabi-sabi. A skilled blues singer who intentionally wails out of pitch for a moment may be expressing wabi-sabi.

Wabi-sabi is rooted in the idea that perfection is a kind of death.

"The essence of Wabi-sabi is that true beauty, whether it comes from an object, architecture, or visual art, doesn't reveal itself until the winds of time have had their say. Beauty is in the cracks, the worn spots, and the imperfect lines." —Todd Dominey, www.whatdoiknow.org

Wabi-sabi is a kind of beauty that's imperfect, impermanent, and incomplete, says Leonard Koren in his book *Wabi-Sabi for Artists, Designers,*

Poets and Philosophers. It differs from Western notions that beauty resides in the "monumental, spectacular, and enduring." It's about "the minor and the hidden, the tentative and the ephemeral: things so subtle and evanescent they are almost invisible at first glance."

"When bread is baked, some parts are split at the surface, and these parts which thus open, and have a certain fashion contrary to the purpose of the baker's art, are beautiful, and in a peculiar way excite a desire for eating. Again, figs, when they are quite ripe, gape open; and in the ripe olives the very circumstance of their being near to rottenness adds a peculiar beauty to the fruit. And the ears of corn bending down, and the lion's eyebrows, and the foam which flows from the mouth of wild boars, though they are far from being beautiful, please the mind." —Marcus Aurelius, *Meditations,* translated by George Long

"I am done with great things and big plans, great institutions and big success. I am for those tiny, invisible loving human forces that work from individual to individual, creeping through the crannies of the world like so many rootlets, or like the capillaries." —William James, "The Will to Believe"

"The great lessons from the true mystics, from the Zen monks, is that the sacred is in the ordinary, that it is to be found in one's daily life, in one's neighbors, friends, and family, in one's back yard, and that travel may be a flight from confronting the sacred. To be looking everywhere for miracles is a sure sign of ignorance that everything is miraculous." —Abraham H. Maslow, *Religions, Values, and Peak Experiences*

"If you love the sacred and despise the ordinary, you are still bobbing in the ocean of delusion." —Lin-Chi, *The Taoist Classics,* translated by Thomas Cleary

"The lesson that life constantly enforces is 'Look underfoot.' You are always nearer to the true sources of your power than you think. The lure of the distant and the difficult is deceptive. The great opportunity is where you are. Don't despise your own place and hour. Every place is the center of the world." —Naturalist John Burroughs

"We want to be God in all the ways that are not the ways of God, in what we hope is indestructible or unmoving. But God is fragile, a bare smear of pollen, that scatter of yellow dust from the tree that tumbled over in a storm of grief and planted itself again." —Deena Metzger, *Prayers for a Thousand Years,* edited by Elizabeth Roberts and Elias Amidon

"Nature exults in abounding radicality, extremism, anarchy. If we were to judge nature by its common sense or likelihood, we wouldn't believe the world existed. In nature, improbabilities are the one stock in trade. The whole creation is one lunatic fringe . . . No claims of any and all revelations could be so far-fetched as a single giraffe." —Annie Dillard, *Pilgrim at Tinker Creek*

"What we want from poetry is to be moved from where we now stand. We don't just want to have our ideas or emotions confirmed. Or if we do, we turn to lesser poems, poems that are happy to tell you that killing children is bad, chopping down the rain forest is bad, dying is sad. A good poet would agree with those sentiments, but would also strive for an understanding beyond those givens." —James Tate, *American Poetry Review*

"What we want from the news is to be moved from where we now stand. We don't just want to have our ideas or emotions confirmed. Or if we do, we turn to lesser news, news that is happy to tell you about the same old chaos and sadness. A good reporter would notice the themes that are repeating for the millionth time, but would also strive to find stories beyond the givens." —Vimala Blavatsky, Beauty and Truth Lab

"Great improvisers are like priests. They are thinking only of their god." —Stéphane Grappelli, jazz violinist

Dionysian Manifesto

RAUCOUS PRONOIA THERAPY

Experiments and exercises in becoming a rigorously flexible, seriously delirious, studiously playful Master of Zany Dignity

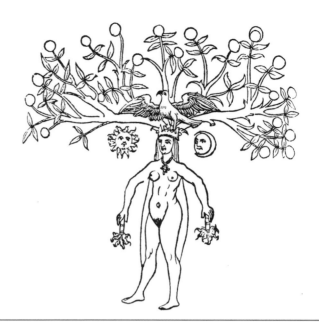

Report your answers & research results below

1 Take inventory of the extent to which your "No" reflex dominates your life. Notice for 24 hours (even in your dreams) how often you say or think:

"No."

"That's not right."

"I don't like them."

"I don't agree with that."

"They don't like me."

"That should be different from what it is."

Then retrain yourself to say "YES" at least 51 percent of the time. Start the transformation by saying "YES" aloud 22 times right now.

2 The factor most likely to drive us to addiction or illness is a lack of intimate contact with spirit. We all need a daily dose of vastness. Paradoxically, many of us would also benefit from more microscopic vision. Because we're so deprived of divine connection, we're half-dreaming all the time; our unconscious pining for our eternal source causes our minds to wander and saps our energy to dig in and master the gritty details that are right in front of us.

Practice seeing the little things. Gather glimpses of colors, shapes, tones, and shifts you usually ignore.

3 Some people feel polluted when they look at porn; others when they eat junk food. Personally, I experience a sense of violation after being exposed to celebrity gossip. And yet, if I've learned anything about how to maintain a healthy relationship with purity, it's that an overly zealous adherence to it is as dangerous as a compulsive indifference. This will naturally be true for you as you practice pronoia. I urge you, therefore,

191

to rebel now and then against your drive to be a perfect perpetrator of goodness and beauty and truth and justice. Describe two examples of how you might do so without causing any harm.

4 During a trip to Europe, New York poet Stephen Ben Israel performed Re-Blessing Ceremonies in venerable cathedrals and synagogues. His primary sacramental act was to smoke a joint and invoke a visceral awareness of the Divine Intelligence. In so doing, he aspired to reanimate those sterile sanctuaries, where over the years so many worshipers have brought only their inert concepts and habit-encrusted beliefs.

Carry out your own version of a Re-Blessing Ceremony in a once-sacred place that has lost its juice.

5 Jungian analyst Arnold Mindell explores the relationship between mind and body. He thinks you can achieve optimum physical health if you're devoted to shedding outworn self-images. In his book *The Shaman's Body,* he says, "You have one central lesson to learn—to continuously drop all your rigid identities. Personal history may be your greatest danger."

Kate Bornstein, author of *Gender Outlaw: On Men, Women and the Rest of Us*, agrees. Raised as a male, she later became a female, but ultimately renounced gender altogether. "I love being without an identity," she says. "It gives me a lot of room to play around."

What identities would be healthy for you to lose? Describe all the fun you'd have if you were free of them.

6 If I ever produce a self-help manual called *The Reverse Psychology of Getting Everything You Want,* it will discuss the following paradoxes:

a. People are more willing to accommodate your longings if you're not greedy or grasping.

b. A good way to achieve your desires is to cultivate the feeling that you have already achieved them.

c. Whatever you're longing for has been changed by your pursuit of it. It's not the same as it was when you felt the first pangs of desire. In order to make it yours, then, you will have to modify your ideas about it.

d. Be careful what you wish for because if your wish does materialize it will require you to change in ways you didn't foresee.

Review your own life and identify experiences that exemplify these four principles.

Raucous Pronoia Therapy

7 "Is it bad to live without a hell?" poet Pablo Neruda asks in *The Book of Questions.* Let's add these queries to his: Is it dangerous to live without the awakening force that an enemy provides? Is it naive to think you can achieve great success without the driving motivation that comes from having ideas you hate?

Consider the issue from another angle. Dentists love tooth decay. Treating cavities provides them with a steady income. Likewise, exterminators are dependent on termites, lawyers need crime, and priests crave sinners. Lots of people have symbiotic connections with nasty stuff. In fact, isn't it true that most of us nurture our feelings for the things we love to despise and fear?

What's your favorite poison or adversary? Assume that your exposure to pronoia is changing you in ways that will require you to update your relationship with it. Speculate on how you'll go about this task.

8 We tried to get our manifesto *Bigger, Better, More Original Sins* excerpted in *Taboo Busters,* a zine published by American expatriates in Berlin. Unfortunately, the editors didn't like the spin we put on the subject of taboos. They're fixated on depraved vices and sickening violations and contrived rejections of conventional values: smuggled photos of dead celebrities lying in morgues, for instance; paintings of religious scenes that use the artist's blood or other bodily fluids; hospital scenes of Iraqi children with gangrenous stumps where their limbs once were; performance artists who do Marquis de Sade imitations.

Our approach is different. We're connoisseurs of taboo-busting that yields uplifting pleasures; we identify and initiate transgressions that don't hurt anyone and expand our intelligence and improve the world. Here are a few examples: midwife Ida May Gaskin's suggestion that a partner can expedite the birth process by giving erotic pleasure to the woman in labor; our idea that satirizing one's own cherished beliefs is the most honest form of mockery; the Menstrual Temple of the Funky Grail's classes that teach men how to symbolically menstruate in order to learn to love rather than fear the Dark Goddess; my ability to use principles formulated by people I mostly disagree with, as in the case of St. Paul's "I die daily."

Are there examples of this kind of taboo-busting in your own life? Make a list of uplifting transgressions that expand your intelligence and improve the world.

Raucous Pronoia Therapy

9 I was never the class clown. I am not a troubled but devilishly handsome wastrel living on a trust fund. I've never beaten up anyone, have steadfastly not aspired to write like Raymond Carver, and have never played strip Scrabble with a junkie violinist on a leaky waterbed in a Key West penthouse. There are so many things I am not and will never be, and I'm glad I know about them. It helps me stay focused on exactly who I am. What about you? Who aren't you? Fantasize about all the paths you will never take. Put it in writing.

10 The "Kumulipo" is an old Hawaiian prayer chant that poetically describes the creation of the world. The word literally means "beginning-in-deep-darkness." Here darkness doesn't connote gloom and evil. Rather, it's about the inscrutability of the embryonic state; the obscure chaos that reigns before germination. Talk about a time you dwelt in kumulipo.

11 While putting on your shirt or blouse some morning, fasten the top button in the second hole, the second button in the third hole, and so on all the way down. For the rest of the day, preserve this dishevelment with all your composure intact, even in the face of odd stares and snide comments. If anyone says, "Hey, your shirt's buttoned wrong," reply calmly, "No it isn't. I buttoned it this way on purpose."

12 Mythology is replete with tales of substances that can be both curative or harmful, depending on how they are obtained and used. The ancient Greeks believed that Asclepius, founder of medicine, possessed vials of Medusa's blood. "With what had been drawn from the veins of her left side," Robert Graves notes, "he could raise the dead; with what had been drawn from her right side, he could destroy instantly."

What has been a comparable substance or influence in your own life?

13 Every act of genius, Carl Jung said, is an act *contra naturam:* against nature. Indeed, every effort to achieve psychological integration and union with the divine requires a knack for working against the grain. The 18th-century mystic Jacob Boehme recommended the same technique. The great secret to becoming enlightened, he said, is "to walk in all things contrary to the world." Qabalist teacher Paul Foster Case agreed: "The basis of the spiritual approach to life, the foundation of the everyday practice of a person who lives the life of obedience to esoteric law, is the reversal of the more usual ways of thinking, speaking and doing."

Raucous Pronoia Therapy

Name the ways you already use this approach, and brainstorm about others you might like to try.

14 The spider has a bad reputation, symbolically speaking. In myths and folk tales, it's often portrayed as the spinner of delusions and snares. Many therapists interpret dreams of spiders as signs of paranoia, gossip, enemies, or predatory relationships.

This may sometimes be true. But I prefer to regard the spider as primarily a symbol of secret help or of a building process going on behind the scenes. In my dreams, the appearance of a spider suggests that though my conscious mind isn't smart enough to fix my current problem, a solution is being woven for me by an unknown intelligence, perhaps a spiritual ally or an unconscious part of my own brain.

Give an example of spider power from your life.

15 Somewhere in the world is a tree that has been struck by lightning in such a way that the scorch marks reveal a symbol you would find exciting. Locate that tree.

Somewhere in the world there is a treasure that has no value to anyone but you, and a secret that is meaningless to everyone except you, and a frontier that possesses a revelation only you know how to exploit. Go in search of those things.

Somewhere in the world there is a person who could ask you the precise question you need to hear in order to catalyze the next phase of your evolution. Do what's necessary to run into that person.

16 Psychotherapists say it's not only naughty but counterproductive to blame others for your problems. A skilled practitioner urges her clients to accept responsibility for the part they've played in creating their predicaments. The reason is as much pragmatic as it is ethical: When you're obsessed with how people have done you wrong, you have little ambition to change the behavior in yourself that led you into the mess.

While I endorse this approach, I also know that dogmatic adherence to it can warp your mental health as much as any other form of fanaticism. That's why I urge you to enjoy an unapologetic Blame Fest. Choose a time when you will find fault with everyone *except* yourself. Howl in protest at the unfair slights people have committed against you. Wallow in self-pity as you visualize the clueless jerks who have done you wrong. For best results, bark your complaints in the direction of no one but God, an inanimate object, or your mirror.

Raucous Pronoia Therapy

BUT WE DON'T HATE THE HATERS

But we don't hate the haters

But we don't hate the haters

BUT WE DON'T HATE THE HATERS

BUT WE DON'T HATE THE HATERS

But we don't hate the haters

But we don't hate the haters

BUT WE DON'T HATE THE HATERS

We
hate   hatred   WE   HATE
HATRED We hate hatred WE HATE
HATRED We HATE HATRED We hate hatred WE
HATE HATRED We hate hatred We HATE HATRED We
hate hatred WE HATE hatred WE HATE HATRED We hate
hatred WE HATE HATRED WE HATE HATRED We hate hatred
WE HATE HATRED We hate hatred WE HATE HATRED We hate
hatred WE HATE HATRED We hate hatred WE HATE HATRED We hate
hatred WE HATE HATRED WE HATE HATRED We hate hatred WE HATE
HATRED We hate hatred WE HATE HATRED We hate hatred WE HATE
HATRED WE HATE HATRED We hate hatred WE HATE HATRED We hate
hatred We HATE HATRED We hate hatred WE HATE HATRED WE HATE
HATRED We hate hatred WE HATE HATRED WE HATE HATRED We hate
hatred WE HATE HATRED We hate hatred WE HATE HATRED We hate
hatred WE HATE HATRED WE HATE HATRED We hate hatred WE
HATE HATRED We hate hatred WE HATE HATRED We hate hatred
WE HATE HATRED WE HATE HATRED We hate hatred WE
HATE HATRED We hate hatred We HATE HATRED We
hatred WE HATE HATRED WE HATE HATRED We hate
hatred WE HATE HATRED WE HATE HATRED
We hate hatred WE HATE HATRED
WE HATE HATRED

The 80 Percent Rule

Readers of my horoscope column "Free Will Astrology" are sometimes surprised when I say I only believe in astrology about 80 percent. "You're a quack?!" they cry. Not at all, I explain. I've been a passionate student of the ancient art for years. About the time my overeducated young brain was on the verge of desertification, crazy wisdom showed up in the guise of astrology, moistening my soul just in time to save it.

"But what about the other 20 percent?" they press on. "Are you saying your horoscopes are only partially true?"

I assure them that my doubt proves my love. By cultivating a tender, cheerful skepticism, I inoculate myself against the virus of fanaticism. This ensures that astrology will be a supple tool in my hands, an adaptable art form, and not a rigid, explain-it-all dogma that over-literalizes and distorts the mysteries it seeks to illuminate.

During the question-and-answer segment of one of my performances, an audience member got hostile. "Why do you diss science so much?" he complained. "Science is the source of a lot of pronoia, so I would think you'd love it."

My accuser obviously hadn't read much of my work. Otherwise he'd have gathered many clues that belied his theory. In my column, for instance, I often quote reverently from peer-reviewed scientific journals like *Nature* and *Scientific American*. And I regularly extol the virtues of the scientific method. "Some of my best friends are scientists," I teased the heckler.

The fact is, I critique science no more than I do *all* of the systems of thought I respect and use. I believe in science about 80 percent—the same as I do in astrology, psychology, Deconstructionism, feminism, Qabalah, Buddhism, left-wing political philosophy, and 22 others.

I do think science has the greatest need of loving skepticism, though. As the dominant ideology of our age, it has a magisterial reputation comparable to the infallibility accorded to the medieval Church. Its priestly promoters sell it as the ultimate arbiter of truth; as an approach to gathering and evaluating information that trumps all others.

Here's another problem: Though science is an elegant method of understanding the world, only a minority of its practitioners live up to its high standards. The field is dominated by men motivated as much by careerism and egotism as by a rigorous quest for excellence. This is common behavior in all spheres, of course, but it's a special problem for a creed that the intellectual elite promotes as the premier method for knowing the truth.

There's a further complication: Scientists are no less likely to harbor irrational biases and emotional fixations than the rest of us. They purport to do just the opposite, of course. But in fact they simply hide their unconscious motivations better, aided by the way the scientific establishment relentlessly promotes the myth that its practitioners are in pure service to objective truth. This discrepancy between the cover story and the actual state of things is, again, a universal tendency, not confined to science. But it's particularly toxic in a discipline that presents itself as the very embodiment of dispassionate investigation.

There are many scientists who, upon reading these words, might discharge a blast of emotionally charged, non-scientific derision in my direction. Like true believers everywhere, they can't accept half-hearted converts. If I won't buy their whole package, then I must be a superstitious, fuzzy-brained, New Age goofball.

To which I'd respond: I love the scientific approach to understanding the world. I aspire to appraise everything I experience with the relaxed yet eager curiosity and the skeptical yet open-minded lucidity characteristic of a true scientist.

Sacred Advertisement

"The 80 Percent Rule" is brought to you by this excerpt from Deena Metzger's prayer:

"Let us learn the secret language of light again. Also the letters of the dark. Learn the flight patterns of birds, the syllables of wolf howl and bird song, the moving pantomime of branch and leaf, valleys and peaks of whale calls, the long sentences of ants moving in unison, the combinations and recombinations of clouds, the codices of stars. Let us, thus, reconstitute the world, sign by sign and melody by melody.

"Let us sing the world back into the very Heart of the Holy Name of God."

—Deena Metzger, Prayers for a Thousand Years, *edited by Elizabeth Roberts and Elias Amidon*

★12.

This language prevents crime.
This engineering moves you to sing.
These advertisements make you smart.
These rhythms free
all prisoners of childhood.

Your Horoscope

Plant orchids on a strip-mined hill.

Imagine you have a guardian angel who looks like Malcolm X.

Teach an animal to dance.

Hire a puppet troupe to reenact your life story using marionettes
in Renaissance costumes.

Make believe you are the ocean king or thunder queen.

Improvise a fresh bedtime story for someone you love.

Put on an inflatable sumo wrestler costume
and play a bagpipe as badly as possible.

Watch TV with your third eye.

Sip holy water blessed by a smart teenage girl.

Bear in mind that you are the Chosen One, and so is everyone else.

GUERRILLA ORACLE

Clues to the Rebel Grail

Surrender to the Conspiracy

"Make me one with everything," the Buddhist monk said to a hot dog vendor who was hawking food near the temple.

The vendor made a frank with mustard, ketchup, relish, and onions, and the monk took it, handing over a $20 bill.

The vendor stashed the cash in his apron and turned his attention to the next customer.

"But where's my change?" the monk inquired.

"Change must come from within, my friend," said the vendor.

HOW I GOT STARTED IN THE BEAUTY AND TRUTH BUSINESS

The place: the restroom of a Roy Rogers restaurant in Chapel Hill, North Carolina. The moment: Once upon a time. The main character: a tall, skinny, young white guy with shoulder-length hair.

The guy was me, Rob Brezsny. Using my fingers as a comb, I was doing my best to marshal my hair into a more beautiful mess than its current bedraggled state. My girlfriend Babushka was supposed to meet me at the salad bar in a few minutes, and I wanted to resemble an attractive wild man, not a scruffy one.

Nearing completion in my primitive attempts at cosmetic improvement, I happened to glance at the wall below the towel dispenser. There I spied a tantalizing mess of graffiti. "I got Santa Cruzified and Californicated," it read, "and it felt like paradise."

A jolt of kundalini zipped through me. I was used to surfing waves of synchronicity; collecting meaningful coincidences was my hobby. But this scrawl on the wall was a freaky tidal wave of synchronicity. Babushka was coming to Roy Rogers today in order to discuss with me the prospect of jumping on a Greyhound bus together sometime in the next couple of weeks and heading out to the place we'd heard was a bohemian utopia: Santa Cruz, California.

I strained to see some smaller print beneath the message on the wall. "You know you'll never become the artist you were meant to be," it warned, "until you come live in Santa Cruz."

Goose bumps rose on my arms. Shivers raced up and down the back of my neck. Whatever strange angel had scrawled those words seemed to have lifted them directly from the back of my subconscious mind. The idea expressed there matched my hope and fear precisely. It had become increasingly clear to me that my aspirations to be a poet and musician with an inspirational effect on my community were doomed to chronic frustration as long as I resided in the Deep South, even in a university town like Chapel Hill. Here I would never be any more than a weirdo, a cross between a village idiot and a marginally entertaining monstrosity.

In that moment, my fate gelled.

By the first day of spring, Babushka and I had arrived in Santa Cruz with $90 in our pockets. We were gleefully homeless, sleeping in the park by day and spending the hours from 11 p.m. to 6 a.m. hanging out in all-night restaurants. When we weren't striking up conversations with the steady stream of colorful crazy folks, I dreamed and schemed about how I would build my new artistic career here in the promised land.

Within a few months I not only had a tiny studio apartment in a basement beneath a garage adjoining an old woman's house. I was well on my way to harvesting the rewards I'd journeyed to Santa Cruz to claim.

Barely three weeks after I stumbled off the cross-country Greyhound bus, I performed at the Good Fruit Company cafe. My songs "Blasphemy Blues" and "Reptile Rodeo Man," along with my long rant-poem "Microwave Beehive Star," impressed a reviewer for a local entertainment rag, who described my contribution as a "mouth-watering, id-tickling, ass-kicking communiqué from the collective unconscious itself."

With a burst of pent-up energy, I did a rash of poetry readings and performance art spectacles in a variety of cafes, as well as many street shows. I photocopied and sold 212 copies of my first homemade chapbook, *Crazy Science,* and practiced the art of enlightened demagoguery in a semi-regular late-night show, "Babbling Ambiance," on local radio station KZSC.

Best of all, I cobbled together my first Santa Cruz band, Kamikaze Angel Slander. When we played our first gig at a friend's party, our set consisted of five songs I had written in North Carolina, covers of two David Bowie tunes, and four epics my band-mates and I had whipped up, including "The Prisoner Is in Control."

There was only one factor darkening my growing exhilaration: grubby poverty. None of the music or spectacles I was creating earned me more than the cash I plowed into making them happen. And I resented life's apparent insistence that I was supposed to take time out from my projects to draw a steady wage. My enrollment at the University of California at Santa Cruz helped. For a few sporadic quarters I was able to garner government loans and grants in return for attending once-a-week poetry and creative writing classes. Monthly allotments of food stamps also aided the cause.

Despite assistance from the welfare state, though, I was still compelled to degrade myself with actual part-time jobs. Among my humiliations were stints washing dishes at restaurants and posing as a model for artists and putting in time as a farm laborer in apple orchards. Even then I barely made my rent, let alone trying to finance the accessories that up-and-coming rock stars need, like a car and good musical equipment.

I lived in a moldy basement with nothing but a temperamental space heater to warm my fingers as I composed rebellious anthems on my dinky electric piano with three broken keys. On occasions, I was forced to resort to a trick I'd learned from a homeless friend, which was to hang out in cafeteria-style restaurants and scavenge the food that diners left behind. My wardrobe? Both my street clothes and stage costumes were garnered entirely from a warehouse called the Bargain Barn, which charged a reasonable one dollar per five pounds of recycled garments.

Given my hardship, I was very receptive when I chanced across an opportunity to make money through creative writing.

My rickety bike had recently been stolen. In my search for a used replacement, I turned to the classi-

fied ads of the *Good Times,* Santa Cruz's largest weekly newspaper. As I scanned the "Misc for Sale" section, my eye tripped across an intriguing invitation one column over.

"*Good Times* is looking for an astrology columnist. Submit sample column for the week of January 26. Address to Editor, GT, 1100 Pacific Avenue, Santa Cruz 95060."

I was at first confused. *Good Times* already had an astrology column, didn't it? I leafed through the paper to find it, but it was gone. Had the author quit? Not that I'd be sorry to see him go. My impression of his writing, from the few times I had read it, was that it covered the whole range between mawkish New Age clichés and unfunny silliness.

Of course I had always despised *all* astrology columns; his was actually more entertaining than most. Though I was a student of astrology, not a teacher, I had high standards about how the ancient art form should be used. And I considered newspaper horoscopes to be an abomination. Without exception, they were poorly written and dull. They encouraged people to be superstitious and made the dead-wrong implication that astrology preaches predetermination and annuls free will. It was bad enough that their blather fed gullible readers inane advice that pandered to the least interesting forms of egotism. Worst of all, they were based in only the most tenuous way on real astrological understanding.

Any reputable practitioner would have told you, for instance, that in order to assess the cosmic energies with authenticity, you'd have to meditate on the movements and relationships of *all* the heavenly bodies, not just the sun. But newspaper horoscopes based their ersatz "predictions" solely on the sun's position. They made the absurd proposition that the lives of millions of people who share any particular "sun sign" are all headed in the same direction.

Artistic geniuses who in days past might have been van Goghs or Rembrandts now create gorgeous propaganda for the advertising industry

In full awareness of all these truths, I struggled to drum up a rationalization for pursuing the gig. The prospect of actually being paid to write something— *anything*—was thrilling. Even more exciting was the fantasy of receiving a regular paycheck. This was a weekly column, not a one-shot deal.

Besides that, it couldn't possibly violate my integrity more than the other jobs I had already slaved away at.

"It's a dirty job, but someone's got to do it," was my opening gambit in the campaign to convince myself that the pros of penning the astrology column outweighed the cons.

My next strategy was figuring out how I could write the column in ways that would not feel fraudulent.

That's when I hatched my plan to become a poet in disguise.

Both in and out of academia, I had for some time been composing stuff that loosely qualified as poetry. From the declamatory rants I foisted on audiences between rock songs to the slightly more disciplined stanzas I produced for my creative writing classes, I worked hard at the craft and wanted it to become as necessary to me as food.

True, I couldn't help but notice that the culture at large regarded poetry as a stuffy irrelevancy; people I considered huge talents, like John Berryman, W.S. Merwyn, and Galway Kinnell, were not getting rich selling their lyrical creations.

To a degree, I sympathized with the hoi polloi's underwhelming appreciation of the art form I loved. The majority of poets *were* humorless academics who seemed to have studied at the feet of a single constipated celibate. It was shocking how little kundalini—how little *entertainment*—burst from the caste that I thought should be in charge of mining the frontiers of the imagination. I was perfectly willing for poetry to be demanding, complex, subtle, and even maddeningly mysterious. The whole point was to dynamite the ruts cut by ordinary waking consciousness, to sabotage cliché and common sense, to reinvent the language. But why did so much of this noble effort have to be uniformly listless, pretentious, and inaccessible?

And then there was my secret agenda. I was peeved that so few of "the antennae of the race" had enough courage to blow their own minds with psychedelics. How could you explode the consensual trance unless you poked your head over onto the other side of the veil now and then? Allen Ginsberg, at least, had the balls to go where shamans go. Berryman seemed to have accomplished the same feat with the help of alcohol.

As for myself, I had been drawn to and in contact with the other side of the veil long before resorting to

psychedelic technology. I regularly remembered and treasured my dreams throughout childhood, and when I was 13 years old I also began to record them. This ongoing immersion in the realm of the dreamtime imbued me early on with the understanding that there were other realities besides the narrow little niche that most everyone habitually inhabited. My psychedelic experiments only confirmed and extended that certainty.

As I gained confidence in the suspicion that my formal education had concealed from me nine-tenths of reality, I tuned in to the paper trail documenting the existence of the missing part. It had been mapped by shamans and alchemists and magicians for millennia: So my readings of Jung and Campbell and Graves and Eliade revealed. Their work in turn magnetized me to the literature of Western occultism, whose rich material was written not by academics but by experimenters who actually traveled to the place in question.

The myriad reports were not in complete agreement, but many of their descriptions overlapped. The consensus was that the other side of the veil is not a single territory, but teems with a variety of realms, some relatively hellish and some heavenly. Its names are many: dreamtime, fourth dimension, underworld, astral plane, collective unconscious, afterdeath state, eternity, bardo, and Hades—to name a few.

There was another issue on which all the explorers agreed: Events in those "invisible" realms are the root cause of everything that happens here. Shamans visit the spirit world to cure their sick patients because the origins of illness lie there. For Qabalists, the visible Earth is a tiny outcropping at the end of a long chain of creation that originates at a point that is both inconceivably far away and yet right here right now. Even modern psychotherapists believe in a materialistic version of the ancient idea: that how we behave today is shaped by events that happened in a distant time and place.

As I researched the testimonials about the treasure land, I registered the fact that dreams and drugs were not the only points of entry. Meditation could give access, as could specialized forms of drumming and chanting and singing and dancing. The tantric tradition taught that certain kinds of sexual communion can lead there. As does, of course, physical death.

I wanted to try all those other doors except the last one. Pot, hashish, and LSD were very good to me (never a single bad trip), but their revelations were too hard to hold onto. As I came down from a psychedelic high, I could barely translate the truths about the fourth dimension into a usable form back in normal waking awareness. At least in my work with dreams I had seen a steady growth of both my unconscious mind's ability to generate meaningful stories and my conscious mind's skill at interpreting them. But my progress was sketchy in the work of retrieving booty from the exotic places where drugs took me.

The problem was that unlike the other techniques on the list, psychedelics bypassed my willpower. Their chemical battering ram simply smashed through the doors of perception. No adroitness or craft was involved on my part. One of my meditation teachers referred to drug use, no matter how responsible, as "storming the kingdom of heaven through violence."

Gradually, then, I ended my relationship with the illegal magic. Instead I affirmed my desire to build mastery through hard work. Dream interpretation, meditation, and tantric exploration became the cornerstones of my practice. In time, I learned to slip into the suburbs of the mysterium via song and dance as well.

I must confess, though, that my plans did not immediately bear the fruit I hoped they would. Even my most ecstatic lucid dreams and illuminated meditations did not bring me to dwell on the other side of the veil with the same heart-melting vividness once provided by psychedelics. Even my deepest tantric lovemaking and music-induced trances failed to provide the same boost.

But then into my life came a consolation: the 19th-century artist and visionary William Blake. My encounter with his work alerted me to fact that there is yet another name for the fourth dimension—a name that also describes a common, everyday human faculty that most of us take for granted.

Here's the special message Blake seemed to have written just for me in *A Vision of the Last Judgment*:

This world of Imagination is the world of Eternity; it is the divine bosom into which we shall go after the death of the Vegetated body. This World of Imagination is Infinite and Eternal, whereas the world of Generation, or Vegetation, is Finite and Temporal. There exists in that Eternal World the Permanent Realities of Every Thing which we see reflected in this Vegetable Glass of Nature. All Things are comprehended in their Eternal Forms in the divine body of the Saviour, the True Vine of Eternity, the Human Imagination.

I exulted in this discovery. Blake became a secret weapon I could use in my covert struggle against the poets who refused to be antennae of the race, against the poets who regarded the visible world as the only one that deserved to have poetry written about it.

Now it's true that some of these poets, whom I called "materialists," inspired me. William Carlos Williams, for instance, taught me much about the art of capturing concrete beauty.

I loved this Williams poem:

> so much depends
> upon
>
> a red wheel
> barrow
>
> glazed with rain
> water
>
> beside the white
> chickens

I watched videos of babies being born until I was healed.

Williams was the best of the materialist poets. His work helped me hone my perceptions and employ more vigorous language. But my pal William Blake gave me the doctrinal foundation with which I could rebel against Williams and rise to a higher calling. Blake suggested that the worlds you dream up in your imagination might be *more real than a red wheelbarrow.*

Might be was the key qualifier. Even then, at an unripe age, I was cautious about the indiscriminate use of this liberating proposition. I had read the Russian occultists Ouspensky and Gurdjieff, and they had made me aware that the out-of-control imagination in service to the ego is the function by which most people lie to themselves constantly, thereby creating hell on earth. Obviously, this was not the kind of imagination Blake meant, and I vowed to keep that clear.

More real than a red wheelbarrow. Blake showed me there was another way to access the Fourth Dimension: working as a creative artist, striving to discipline and supercharge the engine of the imagination. That was an extremely pleasurable realization. I saw that my passion for playing with music and language and images might dovetail perfectly with my longing to hang around the Elysian Fields.

Furthermore, if it were true, as Blake and the shamans said, that every event on earth originates in the spirit world, then the skilled imaginer was potentially God's co-creator—not just *describing* conditions here below but *creating* them. I wanted to be like that. I wanted to fly away into the fourth dimension, reconnoiter the source of the messed-up conditions on the material plane, and give them a healer's tweak. Better yet, I fantasized myself being so at home and masterful in the dreamtime that I could rummage around there looking for attractive but embryonic archetypes to capture and bring down to earth for ripening.

All these thoughts became fodder as I tried to imagine a way I could write an astrology column without violating my integrity. I wanted the gig badly. One way or another I was going to get it. But I would feel so much better about myself if I could refute my conscience's accusations of "Fraud! Panderer!" with highfalutin bullshit about William Blake and the shamanic tradition.

"More Real Than a Red Wheelbarrow." Why not call my "horoscope" column that? Why not do whatever my imagination wanted to do and disguise it all under the rubric of an astrological oracle? There was certainly no International Committee on Standards for Horoscope Columns that I would have to answer to. For that matter, as long as I shaped my horoscopes like love letters to my readers, it was unlikely they'd complain about the Blake-ian, shamanic stuff I'd wrap it in.

Before spying the help wanted ad in the *Good Times,* I'd hated astrology columns because I knew they had no basis in astrological data and could not possibly be an accurate interpretation of so many readers' lives at the same time. Driven by what had become an unstoppable

intent, I now argued from a different angle. What happens to people, I told myself, tends to be what they *believe* will happen to them; the world runs on the fuel of self-fulfilling prophecies. Therefore, couldn't it be said that my oracles would be accurate by definition, since anyone who regarded them seriously would subconsciously head in the directions I named? As long as I diligently maintained an optimistic and uplifting tone, no one could fault me for manipulating people in such a way.

My initial column took me an agonizing 43 hours to compose. It had some good moments:

> What you have at your command, Scorpio,
> is a magic we'll discreetly *not* call black.
> Let's say, instead, that it's a vivid, flagrant
> grey. At your best you'll be a charming
> *enfant terrible* playing with boring
> equilibriums, a necessary troublemaker
> bringing a messy vigor to all the overly
> cautious game plans. If you can manage
> to inject some mercy into your bad-ass
> attitude, no one will get stung and everyone
> will be thoroughly entertained.

Still, the first offering and many after it fell short of my lofty formulations. My work was sufficiently yeasty, though, to win the favor of the *Good Times'* boss. Or maybe he saw I was adept in the arts of spelling and grammar, and looked forward to an easy editing job. For all I know, I was the only applicant for the job. It's not as if the financial rewards alone would have drawn a crowd. As I discovered during my new editor's congratulatory handshake, the pay was $15 a week—so low that I could keep some of my food stamp allotment.

I regarded it as a fortune, though, considering that I was getting paid to be a poet in disguise. My secret long-term agenda, after all, was to build an imagination strong enough to gain regular access to the fourth dimension without the aid of psychedelics. What could be better training for that than a weekly assignment to spew out 12 oracular riffs and shape them into terse word-bombs?

Medicine Story

SACRED
ADVERTISEMENT

This experiment in adoration is brought to you by
Telepathics Anonymous,
a 12-step program for those who are ignorant
of how the thoughts and feelings of others
leak over into their own.

Are you one of the millions of brainwashed materialists
suffering from the delusion that your psyche is an
utterly separate and sealed-off territory?
Telepathics Anonymous
offers proof
that you are in continual extrasensory contact
with more souls than you can imagine.

As a get-acquainted gift, Telepathics Anonymous will
present you with an omen concerning the future of
your relationship with love exactly 95 hours and 19
minutes from right now.

Dreamtime University

According to Nobel Prize-winning biologist Francis Crick, our nightly dreams consist of nothing more than hallucinations produced as the brain flushes out metabolic wastes. Of the many arguments that can be mustered against this appalling idiocy, none is more forceful than the life of Harriet Tubman. After escaping from slavery in 1849, she helped organize the Underground Railroad and personally led 300 slaves to freedom. Few history books choose to convey the fact that she often relied on her dreams to provide specific information about where to find safe houses, helpers, and passages through dangerous territory. Robert Moss tells the whole story in his book, *Dreaming True.*

The chemist Friedrich August Kekulé von Stradonitz solved the central mystery of his scientific quest with the help of an event that happened while he was asleep. In 1865, after strenuous but unsuccessful efforts to determine the precise structure of the benzene ring, he had a dream of a snake biting its own tail. As he awoke with this vivid image in mind, he finally guessed the solution that had long eluded him. What if the six carbon atoms of benzene formed a closed ring—the shape formed by the snake—and not, as he had previously believed, a mere chain? The research that followed this eureka moment led to the discovery of principles that revolutionized organic chemistry.

Robert Louis Stevenson said the tale of Dr. Jekyll and Mr. Hyde came to him in a dream. He simply wrote it down. He credited "little people" in his dreams with providing material for his other books, as well.

Russian chemist Dmitri Mendeleyev worked long and hard to discover a coherent scheme for classifying elements, but the turning point in his search came in a dream on February 17, 1869. It revealed to him the system which is now called the Periodic Table of the Elements.

In 1844, Elias Howe dreamt of being chased by canni-bals wielding spears with holes in the top. This inspired him to design a sewing needle with the eye in its tip, which in turn led him to invent the sewing machine.

Physiologist Otto Loewi won the Nobel Prize thanks to help he received in a dream. In 1903, he had begun to doubt the prevailing theory about how nerve impulses traveled. For 17 years, however, he could not find a way to prove his hunch that the transmission happened chemically rather than electrically. In 1920, he had a dream that revealed how to design an experiment to determine whether his hypothesis was correct. The experiment succeeded, and ultimately led to the work that won Loewi the Nobel Prize.

Dante Alighieri finished his masterpiece *The Divine Com-edy*, before he died in 1321. But when his sons, Jacopo and Pietro, assembled the manuscript for publication, they realized parts of it were missing. They searched the house for days, to no avail. Only after they had given up hope did help arrive. The spirit of Dante appeared in Jacopo's dream and showed his son a hiding place in his old bedroom wall. Upon awakening, Jacopo went to the spot his father had indicated and found the lost papers.

Srinivasa Ramanujan was a mathematical genius. He lacked formal training and his work was thought pecu-liar by his fellow mathematicians, but he made dramatic breakthroughs that are highly regarded. He attributed his success to the Hindu goddess Namakkal. She appeared regularly in his dreams, where she revealed innovative formulas he had only to verify once he awoke.

Naturalist Louis Agassiz was a seminal contributor to the American scientific tradition. While working on an exhaus-tive inventory of fossil fish, he received dream instruc-tions that enabled him to chisel away at a certain slab of stone in his lab in just the right way to extract the whole, undamaged fossil of a previously unknown ancient fish.

Jack Nicklaus had more major tournament wins than any golfer in history. Skill and practice were the keys to his athletic prowess, but once he tapped into a differ-ent source of power. In 1973, he got into an uncharac-teristic slump that had him stumped. One night he had a dream in which he experimented with a new grip on his clubs. When he went to the golf course that morn-ing, he tried the dream's idea. It worked; his funk ended.

In 1977, English professor Coleman Barks had a dream that changed his life. In the dream, he was relaxing on a riverbank near his childhood home in Georgia. A ball of light floated towards him. It contained a man with his head bowed and eyes closed, sitting cross-legged and wear-ing a white shawl. The man raised his head, opened his eyes, and said, "I love you." Barks answered, "I love you, too." Some time after this dream, he met the same figure in waking life. It was a Sri Lankan holy man, Bawa Muhaiyaddeen, who set Barks on the path to becoming a translator of the dead mystic poet Rumi. Today Rumi's books are bestsellers, largely due to Barks.

When sleeping in an RV at the Burning Man festival in 2003, I dreamed that the Dalai Lama and I, along with three other people, were wandering in the middle of the night through a big city neighborhood dominated by boarded-up buildings and abandoned cars. A police siren wailed in the distance. We passed a group of skin-heads in the midst of a drug deal. A bottle hurled from out of a dark alley landed and crashed a few feet behind us. Finally the Dalai Lama squatted down on the side-walk near a wet heap of half-eaten food and McDon-ald's packaging. "This is the perfect place to meditate," he announced with a grin. "If we can summon the spirit of pronoia here, we will be able to do it anywhere."

A dream of smoking cigarettes in a bathroom stall at high school means you should find worthier forms of rebellion. A dream of flamingos nesting in a burnt-out red Cadillac convertible in the mist at dawn means you should expand your ideas about where you might find beauty. A dream of a driver who doesn't use his turn signal means you shouldn't follow anyone too closely. A dream of baking a birthday cake for Buddha in the kitchen of a ship passing through the Panama Canal means you're ready to upgrade your skill at expressing generosity. A dream of wearing your birthday suit as you address an audience on the subject of privacy invasion means you should never tell a lie if you can bullshit your way through the situation. A dream of finding frogs with six legs means that the next car you buy should get at least 35 miles per gallon of gas. A dream of staging a drunken poetry reading in a run-down cafe bordering the interstate means you should develop more "Zen pride," the capacity for being proud about the fact that you have successfully rooted out all false pride.

Dionysian Manifesto

Record and muse about the dreams you have while reading this book.

Interpret and draw pictures of the dreams you have while reading this book.

Dionysian Manifesto

PRONOIA NEWS NETWORK

Cheap Loans for the Destitute The Grameen Bank in Bangladesh lends money to beggars at low interest rates, hoping to help get them off the streets and start their own businesses. Three thousand poor people have already taken advantage of the program. The bank accepts no collateral, does not pressure the borrowers to repay the money, and is even willing to forgo repayment for some who are unable to use it profitably. (Source: www.oneworld.net)

TEAR ABATEMENT

In his book *Crying: the Natural and Cultural History of Tears,* Tom Lutz says that people don't cry as much as they used to. The English of the Victorian era, renowned for their stuffy behavior, put us to shame with their abundant outpouring of tears.

Attitude Adjustment, Babemba Style

"In the Babemba tribe of South Africa, when a person acts irresponsibly or unjustly, he is placed in the center of the village, alone and unfettered. All work ceases, and everyone in the village gathers in a large circle around the accused. Then each person in the tribe speaks to the accused, one at a time, recalling the good things the person has done in his life. Every experience that can be recalled with detail and accuracy is recounted. All his positive attributes, good deeds, strengths, and kindnesses are recited carefully. This ceremony often lasts for several days. At the end, a joyous celebration takes place, and the person is symbolically and literally welcomed back into the tribe."
—Jack Kornfield, *The Art of Forgiveness, Lovingkindness, and Peace*

This perfect moment, as well as the next 22 perfect moments, are brought to you by this excerpt from Og Mandino's book The Greatest Salesman in the World: *"Treat everyone you meet as if he or she were going to be dead by midnight. Extend to them all the care, kindness, and understanding you can muster, and do so with no thought of reward. Your life will never be the same."*

Lyric and Burlesque A group of French towns has formed an organization called Villages of Lyric or Burlesque Names. Among the members are the villages of Saligos (English translation: Filthy Pig), Montcuq (My Arse), Beaufou (Beautiful Mad), Cocumont (Cuckold Hill), and Trecon (Very Stupid).

Ugly Purifiers Houseflies purify the air by eradicating rotting vegetation. Vultures don't kill the things they devour, but rather assist nature in processing carrion, cleaning up messes other creatures have made. In a throwback to medieval medicine, modern British doctors place maggots in their patients' wounds to cleanse infections, compensating for the fact that some bacteria have become immune to antibiotics.

Lottery Winners More than half of all people polled say they would keep their jobs if they won the lottery.

Anti-Measles Crusade The Measles Initiative is a project of public health organizations devoted to lowering the mortality rate from measles in Africa. Under its auspices, five million Zambian children were vaccinated against measles in 2003 by the Red Cross and affiliated groups. To fight malaria, the campaign simultaneously delivered vitamins, de-worming medication, and 75,000 bed nets treated with insecticide. (Source: International Federation of Red Cross and Red Crescent Societies, www.ifrc.org)

Next Stop: Paper from Hemp Kinko's, the photocopy franchise with 1,200 branches in nine countries, no longer buys paper from companies that use wood from old-growth and endangered forests.

China Lifts Africa At a conference in Ethiopia in December 2003, Chinese premier Wen Jiabao announced that his country had canceled the $1.27 billion debt owed to it by poor African nations. He also said China would encourage trade by opening its markets to African exports on a duty-free basis.

Gun Amnesty Fest "The Washington, D.C., police department held a gun amnesty program that paid $100 to anyone turning in a firearm, no questions asked. Nearly a quarter of a million dollars in confiscated drug money was used for the publicized campaign that removed from the streets 2,907 handguns, sawed-off shotguns, and other firearms." —Geraldine Weis-Corbley, www.goodnews network.org

Backward Is Forward "The great secret known to Apollonius of Tyana, Paul of Tarsus, Simon Magus, Asclepius, Paracelsus, Boehme, and Bruno is that we are moving backward in time. The universe in fact is contracting into a unitary entity which is completing itself. Decay and disorder are seen by us in reverse, as increasing. These healers learned to move forward in time, which is retrograde to us." —Philip K. Dick, *The Divine Invasion*

MIRABILIA REPORT *Mirabilia* n. eccentric enchantments, unplanned jubilations, sudden deliverance from boring evils; from the Latin *mirabilia,* "marvels."

■ "The average river requires a million years to move a grain of sand 100 miles," says science writer James Trefil.

■ Clown fish can alter their gender as their social status rises.

■ When she is born, a baby girl has all the ova she will ever have.

■ Bluebirds cannot see the color blue.

■ Kind people are more likely than mean people to yawn when someone near them does.

■ There are always so many fragments of spider legs floating in the air that you are constantly inhaling them wherever you go.

■ Gregorian chants can cure dyslexia.

■ Scientists in Antarctica have photographed whales farting.

■ To keep from digesting itself, your stomach generates a fresh layer of mucus every two weeks.

■ Bob Hope donated half a million jokes to the Library of Congress.

■ Bees perform a valuable service for the flowers from which they steal.

■ All the gold ever mined could be molded into a 60-foot bust of your mom.

■ The moon smells like exploded firecrackers.

■ Physicists in Tennessee coaxed electric signals to travel through coaxial cable at four times the speed of light, even though the equipment they used was cheap stuff from Radio Shack.

■ Revlon makes 177 different shades of lipstick.

■ Your tongue is the strongest muscle in your body.

■ The most frequently shoplifted book in America is the Bible.

■ Copper, iodine, alcohol, iron, sunshine, sodium, and cholesterol are harmful to you in large amounts, but good for you in small quantities.

■ "I always turn to the sports page first," said Earl Warren, former Chief Justice of the U.S. Supreme Court. "It records people's accomplishments; the front page, nothing but man's failure."

■ "Leafing through *Forbes* or *Fortune* [magazine]s is like reading the operating manual of a strangely sanctimonious pirate ship," wrote Adam Gopnik in *The New Yorker.*

Opinions Are Overrated

Writing in *The Week* magazine, Bill Falk reminisced about how earlier in his career he churned out three opinion columns a week for newspapers. It was tough. "The truth is," he said, "there were many weeks in which I didn't have three fresh opinions of any value."

These days, he added, he couldn't handle a gig like that. As he has matured, he has become suspicious of his own certainties. "Opinions are highly overrated," he concludes. "Most concern passing phenomena that, six months or six years from now, will become utterly irrelevant." (Source: www.theweekmagazine.com)

Chagall

Realpolitik

The Official Monster Raving Loony Party is a political party that has nominated candidates for British elections since 1983. Its goal is to inject healing mayhem into a process that everyone takes too seriously. Here are some of its proposals: Anyone using a cell phone in a theater must be squirted with Silly String; joggers must run on giant treadmills that generate electricity for public use; men must wear veils on International Women's Day; TV anchormen must preface each night's broadcast with the disclaimer, "I am a a trained actor in thrall to corporate greed." The OMRLP is run by Alan Howling Laud Hope and his dead cat, Cat Mandu. Its headquarters is the Dog and Partridge pub at Yateley, and its slogan is "Vote for insanity. You know it makes sense."

8	1	6
3	5	7
4	9	2

BREAKING THE PRONOIA TABOO

"Irregularity and unpredictability are important features of health. On the other hand, decreased variability and accentuated periodicities are associated with disease. Healthy systems don't want homeostasis. They want chaos." —John R. Van Eenwyk, "The Chaotic Dynamics of Everyday Life," *Quest* magazine

"One must have chaos within oneself if one is to be a dancing star." —Friedrich Nietzsche

"We are too sincere, too productive, and too realistic. We need to enter more fully and more willingly into that realm under the rocks and behind the mirror." —Thomas Moore, "Neither Here Nor There," *Parabola*, Spring 2000

"There is nothing stable in the world; uproar's your only music." —John Keats, *Letters of John Keats*

"Half of what you know today will be obsolete in five years. That prospect should fill you with excitement." —Vimala Blavatsky

"The Truth is like the bear. Is it a gentle beast, a model for the stuffed animal children love? Or is it a vicious carnivore that will rip you to shreds if you turn your back on it? The answer is that it's both." —Robert Morning Sky

"In teaching my students, I try to figure out what questions I can ask that have no right answer. I seek to frame paradoxes, to force students to develop original thought." —Meg Gorman, Waldorf teacher

"We are the sum of our efforts to change who we are. Identity is no museum piece sitting stock-still in a display case, but rather the endlessly astonishing synthesis of the contradictions of everyday life." —Eduardo Galeano, *Book of Embraces*

"Authenticity depends entirely on being faithful to the essential ambiguity of experience." —John Berger

"Reasonable people adapt themselves to the world. Unreasonable people attempt to adapt the world to themselves. All progress, therefore, depends on unreasonable people." —George Bernard Shaw

"Rebellion to tyrants is obedience to God." —Thomas Jefferson

"You're only given a little spark of madness. You mustn't lose it." —Robin Williams

"There ain't no answer. There ain't going to be any answer. There never has been an answer. That's the answer." —Gertrude Stein

"Chaos is a name for any order that produces confusion in our minds." —George Santayana

Holy Masquerade Some spectators allow themselves to be tremendously undignified at professional sports events. With no concern for how ridiculous others might think them, they wear giant foam rubber hats resembling cheese wedges. They paint their bellies with the home team's insignia and go shirtless outdoors in sub-freezing weather. They scream nonsense chants and make bizarre faces and wave their arms in frantic salutes. Studies by researchers at the Beauty and Truth Laboratory suggest that up to four percent of these folks might be bodhisattvas in disguise—wise tricksters who intentionally lose their dignity as a spiritual practice, cultivating non-attachment to their egos.

The Ten-Thousandth Amazement "You start out as a single cell derived from the coupling of a sperm and egg; this divides in two, then four, then eight, and so on. At a certain stage there emerges a single cell that has as all its progeny the human brain. The mere existence of such a cell should be one of the world's great astonishments. People ought to be walking around all day, calling to each other in endless wonderment, talking of that cell." —Lewis Thomas, *The Lives of a Cell*

Wild Urban Medicines Many plants used for prescription drugs originate in tropical rain forests. There are unquestionably other healing herbs, as yet undiscovered, in these endangered ecosystems. But a recent study suggests that weeds growing in towns and villages may be an equally important source of medicine. *The Journal of Ethnopharmacology* reports that the Highland Mayans of Chiapa, for instance, get much of their medicinal plants from vacant lots and other disturbed areas, even in communities that are adjacent to stands of primary forest. (Source: www.eurekalert.org)

Win-Win Spiritual Battle After a long struggle with authorities, Norwegian Muslims won permission to proclaim "God is great" from a loudspeaker atop the World Islamic Mission mosque in Oslo. Shortly thereafter, atheists in that city were granted the right to electronically amplify their cherished mantra, "There is no God," from a nearby building.

Beauty Work Traveling cosmetic saleswomen from America have penetrated the Amazon jungle. Inflamed with faith in the value of their products, Avon ladies brave 100-degree heat as they paddle canoes down piranha-infested tributaries to hawk lipstick and eyeshadow to women who have previously been deprived of these modern enhancements.

Supermodel Scarcity Our planet is running out of essential resources, including fresh water and oil. The *Weekly World News* has reported another crucial shortage: the global supply of supermodels: "The original generation of supermodels is fading, and very few new ones are coming along to replace them. Soon the supermodel as we know it may become extinct."

The Language of Initiation
Tjiliwirri is a special language taught to boys undergoing initiation rites among the Warlpiri tribe of the Australian Aborigines. A speaker uses it to express the opposite of what he pretends to mean. To say the equivalent of "You are very smart," for example, a boy might say, "How dumb you are!" To express a desire to eat, he'd say, "I'm not hungry." (Source: *Readers' Digest Book of Facts*)

Doughnut-Eating Competitions
"When in a doughnut-eating competition," writes *Esquire's* Cal Fussman, "press down hard on each one before biting into it. If you don't, the air inside will bloat your belly and you'll get blown out after six."

Escape Tip If a crocodile has you in the grip of its jaws, jam your thumbs into its eyeballs and it will release you.

Bargain Bulletin It *is* possible to buy happiness. Researchers at Yahoo! Personal Finance have determined the precise amount necessary: $4.9 million.

Your Increased Brainpower
Michael Weliky, a professor of brain and cognitive sciences, decided to test the accuracy of the old saw that we only use 10 percent of our brains. He dreamed up an experiment that involved 12 ferrets watching the movie *The Matrix*. His research was so convincing that the journal *Nature* published it. He concluded that we actually use 80 percent of our available brainpower, though much of the activity takes place unconsciously.

Astrological Engineering In Bhutan, astrologers play an important official role. Before each year begins, the king's stargazers determine the least and most cosmically propitious dates coming up in the next twelve months. The calendar is then altered accordingly. If June looks bad from the astrologers' point of view, for instance, it might be canceled, while July will be observed twice.

Useless Gifts During the war in Bosnia in the 1990s, Western governments showered the beleaguered people with free consumer goods. *Earth Island Journal* reported that the U.S. sent thousands of bottles of mouthwash. Norway contributed anti-leprosy medication and Britain supplied weight-reduction pills. "This is a good example of the kind of generosity that pronoiacs should avoid as they conspire to shower blessings on everyone," said Beauty and Truth Laboratory spokesperson Rapunzel Blavatsky.

Evolution's Second and Third Chances "Use it or lose it" has long been a key dogma in the theory of evolution. Biologists have believed that if a species accidentally develops a certain new characteristic but then fails to incorporate it permanently as a vital feature, it's gone forever. Recently, however, researchers have begun to question this tenet. They've found evidence that the "walking stick" insects known as phasmids have, over the last 300 million years, lost their wings because of disuse several times, but then re-evolved them.

Jewel-Toned Pick-Me-Ups Discordianism is one of the rare religions that takes account of Ralph Abraham's assertion that heart physiologists find more chaos in the healthy heart than in the sick heart. Here's a sampling of Discordian tenets. 1. Everyone is a saint, especially you. 2. Meditation consists primarily of cruising around looking for good luck. 3. Eating hot dog buns is prohibited, except on Friday, when it's compulsory. 4. When you're stuck in a rut, you must speak in tongues, handle snakes, and experience phantasmagoria. 5. Your guardian angel loves you better when your room is a mess. 6. Bowling alleys are sacred; you must protect them from desecration. 7. The Goddess will solve all your problems if you solve all hers.

Impossible Feats A master practitioner of the Indonesian martial art pencak silat can demolish a stack of bricks with one bash of his arm. Indian yogis can survive being buried in the earth for an hour. Circus performers swallow swords. Some couples keep their love and intimacy fresh through the trials of time, chaos, and tedium.

You know about the Russian physiologist Ivan Pavlov, who discovered the conditioned reflex. In his famous experiment, he trained laboratory dogs to salivate at the sound of a bell.

You may not have heard, though, about the story's surprise ending. The dogs were programmed for weeks with such rigor that their behavior became as predictable as machines. Then one day a flood inundated the lab. In the confusion, the dogs forgot all their training instantly. (Source: Raoul Vaneigem, *The Revolution of Everyday Life*)

More than seven centuries before a few European men dared to sail beyond the safe boundaries of their known world, entire Polynesian families crossed vast expanses of the Pacific Ocean in catamarans. The first humans to arrive in Hawaii, they were led by "wayfinders." These miracle workers navigated the uncharted seas by reading star positions, discerning weather patterns, and interpreting the ocean's colors and movements.

Because he opposed apartheid, Nelson Mandela was imprisoned in his native South Africa for nearly 30 years. After being released in 1993, he won the Nobel Peace Prize and was elected president of his country.

Bad News And Good News, Part 1

In the last 50 years, America's Great Plains area has lost a third of its population, due largely to the disappearance of family farms. People are moving out in droves. Ghost towns are proliferating. From one perspective, that's sad, but from another, it's cause for celebration: The wilderness is returning in some places, and vast herds of buffalo once again roam the land. (Source: *The Week* magazine, January 16, 2004)

Bad News And Good News, Part 2

The U.S. Air Force has complied with the Environmental Protection Agency's ban on ozone-destroying chlorofluorocarbons. It has removed CFCs from the cooling systems of ballistic missiles that carry nuclear warheads. "If they are ever fired," *Access to Energy* reported in its July 1993 issue, "there will be an environmentally friendly nuclear holocaust."

What's Your Flub Rate?

In 2003 *The Boston Globe* ran 901 corrections of previously published information. In other words, it averaged 17.3 acknowledged mistakes per week. The *Chicago Tribune's* total was 658, or 12.7 errors per week. How do your numbers compare?

Your Brain Is Illegal

The U.S. government has criminalized the chemical compounds of peyote, even though one of them, dopamine, is a primary neurotransmitter in the human brain. Our brains also produce anandamide, a substance that's nearly identical to THC, the active ingredient in marijuana.

Generosity Is Trendy

Charitable giving by Americans has risen 180 percent in the last 45 years.

Gender Swaps

A few years ago, members of the Barbie Liberation Organization sneaked into toy stores and swapped the voice boxes of 300 GI Joe and Barbie dolls. Boys who later purchased the plastic soldiers were surprised to hear them make comments like "I like to go shopping with you," while the girls who came into possession of the mutated Barbies heard terse barks like "To the front lines, men!"

Sneaky Advertisement

Buy Nothing Day, held each November, is a holiday from consumerism. You're free to spend no money at that time.

Kissing Traditions

In her book *A Natural History of the Senses,* Diane Ackerman says that in many cultures the word for kiss means smell. "A kiss is really a prolonged smelling of one's beloved, relative, or friend," she writes. "Members of a tribe in New Guinea say good-bye by putting a hand in each other's armpit, withdrawing it and stroking it over themselves, thus becoming coated with the friend's scent. Other cultures sniff each other or rub noses."

Free Allah

More than 1.2 billion Muslims live under democratically elected governments, and there is a steady move towards democratization, civil rights, and political freedom in many other Islamic countries. (Source: Freedom House Survey)

Butt Divination

A blind German clairvoyant named Ulf Buck claims he can foretell people's future by feeling their naked buttocks.

Climate Change Perks

According to Russian President Vladimir Putin, global warming might be a boon for his country because people "would spend less money on fur coats and other warm things." (Source: Reuters)

Sometimes Pronoia Is a Bit Perverse

Moms and dads who launch screaming fights in front of their kids could actually be helping them, a new study reveals. Researchers at McGill University found that listening to their parents yelling often makes children more imaginative because it forces them into a fantasy world to escape.

Menace to Civilization

"The greatest menace to civilization," wrote historian Herbert Butterfield in his *Whig Interpretation of History*, "is the conflict between giant organized systems of self-righteousness—each system only too delighted to find that the other is wicked—each only too glad that the sins give it the pretext for still deeper hatred and animosity."

PNN is brought to you by the philosophies of panpsychism, animism, and pantheism, all of which propose that everything in the universe, even matter itself, is alive, conscious, and ensouled.

EDITORIAL

The superstition of materialism is the dominant ideology of a majority of people in the world. It's the specious doctrine that physical matter is the only reality and that nothing can be said to exist unless it's perceivable by a human being's five senses or detected by technologies that humans have created. Materialism paradoxically preaches the value of being agnostic about all phenomena it does not recognize as real, even as it obsessively evades questions about its own fundamentalist assumptions.

ESTABLISH TURNING POINT · WAVE THE ROD · FACE THE ROD · REVERSE THE ROD · BOOST THE ROD · MOVE FORWARD · COME IN

The Good Side of Globalization

More than 240,000 people died in the earthquake that struck Tangshan, China, in 1976. The relief effort was negligible compared to the help that arrived in response to the tsunami disaster in December 2004. One explanation for the difference is that there has been a dramatic globalization of consciousness. People currently living on the planet are increasingly aware of how intimately interdependent we all are. Years ago no one had heard of the butterfly effect—the theory that the flapping of a butterfly's wings in Japan can affect the weather in Texas. Now millions understand the principle.

Wet Chicken Feathers

A poultry expert has come up with a revolutionary use for the feathers that are left over when chickens are slaughtered. David Emery has built a machine to turn the damp, dirty refuse into a strong, light fiber that's suitable for making auto parts and medical instruments.

Beyond the G-Spot

In his book *The Naked Woman*, biologist Desmond Morris says that in addition to the G-Spot, women have three other highly sensitive erotic zones in the vagina. He calls them the A-Spot, C-Spot, and U-Spot.

Glass Way More Than Half Full

In portentous tones, as if exposing yet another demoralizing deterioration of our collective health, the Centers for Disease Control informed us that the average person is "sad, blue, or depressed" about three days a month. As we pored over various news articles reporting the results of the CDC's survey, we looked in vain for even a glimmer of glee. After all, if we're downhearted three days every month, it means we're feeling pretty good the other 27 or 28 days.

EASY PRONOIA THERAPY

Practice in becoming an exuberantly discriminating Master of Erudite Ecstasy

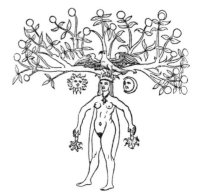

It's time for the Gratitude Fest. Write thank-you notes to the creatures, both human and otherwise, that have played seminal roles in inspiring you to become yourself. Who have been your guides along the way, both the purposeful teachers and the inadvertent helpers? Who has seen you for who you really are? Who has nudged you in the direction of your fuller destiny and awakened you to your signature truths? Who has loved you very, very well?

★13

The 11th Commandment:
Thou Shalt Not Bore God.
The 12th Commandment:
Thou Shalt Not Bore Thyself.

You
Are
Here

Your Sledgehammer and Watercolor Brush

Thank your mother for the pain she endured while birthing you.

For three minutes on the first Friday of every month, close your eyes
and imagine yourself riding a wild horse through a cemetery.

Fantasize that your so-called "dark side" is sweet and creamy.

When you come home after a day of triumphs, take out the garbage.

Dream you're a red-tailed hawk soaring over a shopping mall.

Forgive yourself for the blindness that put you in the path
of those who betrayed you.

Buy seven used gowns
worn to the Academy Awards show by famous actresses,
and send them gratis to seven Guatemalan teenagers.

Visualize two versions of yourself, one male and one female,
holding hands as they gaze into a reflection of the moon on a river.

Keep an image of a sphinx with you at all times.

Sacred Uproar

Pronoia is closer than your breath and older than death. It dreams like a mountain, laughs like a river, prays like the sun, and sings the way the animals think. It's always as fresh as the beginning of time.

Life is a vast and intricate conspiracy designed to keep us well supplied with blessings. What kind of blessings? Palatial homes, attractive lovers, lottery winnings, career success? Maybe. But just as likely: interesting surprises, unexpected challenges, gifts we hardly know what to do with, conundrums that force us to get smarter.

Novelist William Vollman referred to the latter types of blessings when he said that "the most important and enjoyable thing in life is doing something that's a complicated, tricky problem for you that you don't know how to solve."

The Christian writer C.S. Lewis once said: "I thank God that He hasn't given me all the things I've prayed for, because as I look back now I realize it would have been disastrous to have received some of them."

Pronoia provides the gifts your soul needs,
not necessarily those your ego craves.

Pronoia works because there is a Divine Being who comprises the entire universe. When I say, "Life is a conspiracy to shower us with blessings," I understand that this Divine Being is the Chief Architect, Builder, and Manager of the conspiracy. She oversees the evolution of

500 billion galaxies and every single thing in them, yet is also
available as an intimate companion and daily advisor
to each one of us humans.

Some lovers of pronoia don't like this part of my rap. They want
pronoia to be free of anything that smacks of God. Atheism works
better for them. That's OK with me. No hard feelings.

Other lovers of pronoia don't appreciate me referring to the Creator
as "She." They either want to stick with the pronoun that has been
used for hundreds of years, or else don't want any gender
associations whatsoever. That's OK with me. No hard feelings.

The Maker of the conspiracy constantly tinkers, always keeping the
big picture in mind and moving in the direction of ultimate blessings
for all concerned.

But the Maker also loves getting help from us. To the degree that we
co-conspire, the inevitable blessings ripen more lyrically and in
greater fullness.

Pronoia asks us to be awake to the shifting conditions of the
Wild Divine's ever-fresh creation. It encourages us to be quite happy
about regularly divesting ourselves of the beliefs and theories that
guided us yesterday so that we can see clearly
what's right in front of us today.

As much as we might be dismayed at the actions of our political
leaders, pronoia says that toppling any particular junta, clique, or elite
is irrelevant unless we overthrow the sour, puckered
mass hallucination that is mistakenly called "reality"—
including the part of that hallucination we foster in ourselves.

The revolution begins at home. If you overthrow yourself again and
again, you might earn the right to help overthrow the rest of us.

Pronoia will change your past if you let it. It's the language you study
at night in your dreams, the open secret of how to live forever,
the last judgment transformed into a daily gift.

Secrets of Pronoia

Do-It-Yourself Pronoia

Pronoia is a gnostic art: Everyone is potentially a visionary capable of revealing more of its mysteries. The Beauty and Truth Laboratory is not the final authority on the subject. So reveal away. Write your oracles and definitions about pronoia here.

Evil Fears Laughter

Are demons and devils real? In my view, it doesn't matter whether or not they exist in an objective or literal sense. The point is that we are all plagued by split-off, unintegrated portions of our own and other people's psyches. They behave exactly as if they were diabolical entities—demons, djinns, dybbuks, and devils—working at cross-purposes to our conscious desires.

In dealing with their hassling interventions, I endorse the approach described by Paul Foster Case in his book *The Tarot: A Key to the Wisdom of the Ages.* There he suggested that mirth is the best way to beat the devil. "Laughter is prophylactic," he wrote. "It purifies subconsciousness and dissolves mental complexes. In a hymn to the sun god Ra we read, 'Thy priests go forth at dawn, washing their hearts with laughter.' This is a prescription we may all follow to advantage."

My friend and teacher, Vimala Nostradamus, echoes Case. "The best way to neutralize the devil is to laugh at him," she says. "Satan's most effective recruiting technique is to get people to take themselves too seriously." To exemplify her argument, she once told her daughter in my presence about a foolproof way to avoid being hassled if you're a woman walking by a crew of construction workers: "Pick your nose."

The novels of Tom Robbins provide spiritual guidance about dealing with diabolical spirits, both those that originate within us and those that come from without. Here's a sample tip from his *Jitterbug Perfume:* "Play—more than piety, more than charity or vigilance—is what allows human beings to transcend evil."

We regret to report that further help on this matter is not available from the holy books of the world's major religions. None of their authors ever figured out that an excellent weapon against the fragmented, shadowy portions of our psyches is humor, tomfoolery, and laughter. This ignorance may be the greatest mystery in history.

But Christianity, Judaism, Islam, Buddhism, Hinduism, Confucianism, Taoism, Shintoism, Zoroastrianism, and Jainism aren't the only spiritual traditions that have failed to take advantage of evil's primary weakness. The esoteric spiritual paths of the West, including Hermeticism, Rosicrucianism, and alchemy, also suffer from an inexplicable lack of jokes and fun at the heart of their practice. Shamanism, paganism, yoga, and tantra are, for the most part, similarly bereft.

There are rare exceptions. The Sufis have cracked a few funny stories down through the ages. The Fourth Way teacher, George Gurdjieff, had a sense of humor that he used pedagogically. And 20th-century America spawned two authentically comic religions, Discordianism and the Church of the Subgenius. Unfortunately, their combined flocks are smaller than the crowds drawn by any popular evangelical preacher in one night of mean-spirited pontificating.

Here's a letter we received at the Beauty and Truth Laboratory, along with our response.

"Dear Beauty and Truth Laboratory: After long meditation on what's missing from my relationship with God, I found the answer: a sense of humor. I realized I can never truly love or honestly communicate with a Supreme Being who doesn't chuckle. Alas, there does not seem to be a single text in any religious tradition that's even slightly comical. Can you give me some hope? —In Search of a Droll Deity"

Dear In Search of: Below are a few possibly hope-inspiring passages from one of the Beauty and Truth Laboratory's unpublished holy books *God's Laughing With You, Not at You.*

Chapter 26, Verses 182–188: The Plot to Debunk Pronoia

A meeting of Hell's board of directors was taking place. The devil was upset because recruitment had dropped to a new low since the pronoia meme had begun to spread. "It's intolerable," he raged. "These fucking pronoiacs are so mentally healthy it makes me want to puke. Suggestions?"

Hell's executive vice-president blurted out, "I'll go down to earth and convince thousands of pronoiacs that their friends are jealous of their happiness."

The marketing chief chimed in: "I'll go down to earth and make them feel guilty for feeling so good."

Then the head of intelligence spoke: "I'll go down to earth and inspire a bestselling New Age author to write a sappy mass market book about pronoia."

Chapter 57, Verses 112–116: How to Ask for What You Want

George prayed every day for three years to win the lottery, but never heard from God or hit the jackpot.

Finally, God woke him up in the middle of the night. "George, is that you who's been praying so hard to win the lottery?" the Supreme Being boomed.

"Yes, Lord, desperately!"

God paused for a moment, then said thoughtfully, "George, I'll tell you what. I want you to meet me halfway. Buy a ticket, OK?"

Chapter 88, Verses 15–21: Do-It-Yourself Exorcism

If you're average, you're demonically possessed not just by split-off, unintegrated portions of your own and other people's psyches, but also by 20 million ads and 200,000 televised acts of violence stored in your brain.

The good news is that as you practice the art of pronoia, you'll attract steady streams of amusing experiences that are effective at neutralizing those toxins. Every time you laugh, you'll most likely purge a nihilistic image or inane story that had been depleting your energy. A belly laugh may flush out the imprints of as many as 500 commercials.

Chapter 93, Verses 81–84: Pronoiac Homework

Upon request, the Beauty and Truth Laboratory gives homework to students of pronoia. An assignment we're fond of is to ask them to finish the sentence, "The one thing that keeps me from being myself is _____."

Many respondents fill in the blank with "my fears." Other common answers are "lack of money," "my spouse," and "my obsession with status."

Of course there are no right answers. But the above replies don't capture the spirit of pronoia as well as an exemplary offering from Ann-Marie at Getunderground.com. "The one thing that keeps me from being myself," she wrote, "is other people's reluctance to lick patent leather."

Chapter 153, Verses 11–16: How to Know God

Below you'll find three messages. One is an authentic communiqué from the Divine Wow, which I channeled while in ecstatic trance. The other two are fakes that I made up. If you're as thoroughly in tune with your inner purpose as you need to be, you won't have any trouble knowing which is the *true* Word of the Creator.

Message #1: "I, the Supreme Designer of Heaven and Earth, am totally pissed off at your lazy sins and lack of faith. Cut the crap and shape up."

Message #2: "I, untouchable and unknowable CEO of the Universe, couldn't care less what you do. Don't bother me."

Message #3: "I, the Universal Jokester who runs all of creation on the fuel of my sublime pleasure, am well-entertained by the stories you've been living. Thanks! I can't wait to see what you do next."

Homeopathic Medicine Spell #4

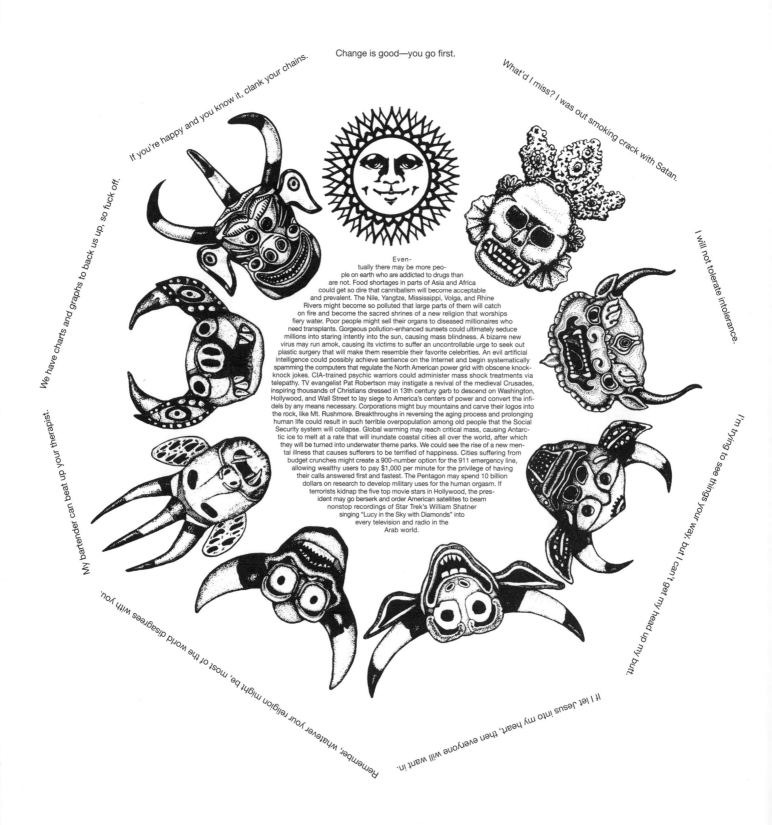

Change is good—you go first.

If you're happy and you know it, clank your chains.

What'd I miss? I was out smoking crack with Satan.

We have charts and graphs to back us up, so fuck off.

I will not tolerate intolerance.

My bartender can beat up your therapist.

I'm trying to see things your way, but I can't get my head up my butt.

Remember, whatever your religion might be, most of the world disagrees with you.

If I let Jesus into my heart, then everyone will want in.

Even-tually there may be more peo-ple on earth who are addicted to drugs than are not. Food shortages in parts of Asia and Africa could get so dire that cannibalism will become acceptable and prevalent. The Nile, Yangtze, Mississippi, Volga, and Rhine Rivers might become so polluted that large parts of them will catch on fire and become the sacred shrines of a new religion that worships fiery water. Poor people might sell their organs to diseased millionaires who need transplants. Gorgeous pollution-enhanced sunsets could ultimately seduce millions into staring intently into the sun, causing mass blindness. A bizarre new virus may run amok, causing its victims to suffer an uncontrollable urge to seek out plastic surgery that will make them resemble their favorite celebrities. An evil artificial intelligence could possibly achieve sentience on the Internet and begin systematically spamming the computers that regulate the North American power grid with obscene knock-knock jokes. CIA-trained psychic warriors could administer mass shock treatments via telepathy. TV evangelist Pat Robertson may instigate a revival of the medieval Crusades, inspiring thousands of Christians dressed in 13th century garb to descend on Washington, Hollywood, and Wall Street to lay siege to America's centers of power and convert the infi-dels by any means necessary. Corporations might buy mountains and carve their logos into the rock, like Mt. Rushmore. Breakthroughs in reversing the aging process and prolonging human life could result in such terrible overpopulation among old people that the Social Security system will collapse. Global warming may reach critical mass, causing Antarc-tic ice to melt at a rate that will inundate coastal cities all over the world, after which they will be turned into underwater theme parks. We could see the rise of a new men-tal illness that causes sufferers to be terrified of happiness. Cities suffering from budget crunches might create a 900-number option for the 911 emergency line, allowing wealthy users to pay $1,000 per minute for the privilege of having their calls answered first and fastest. The Pentagon may spend 10 billion dollars on research to develop military uses for the human orgasm. If terrorists kidnap the five top movie stars in Hollywood, the pres-ident may go berserk and order American satellites to beam nonstop recordings of Star Trek's William Shatner singing "Lucy in the Sky with Diamonds" into every television and radio in the Arab world.

The Science of the invisible

"Who am I? Where did I come from? Where am I going?" Biologist E.O. Wilson says that philosophers long ago stopped addressing these questions, believing them to be unanswerable. Scientists stepped forward to fill the vacuum, and now act as supreme arbiters of the mysteries that were once the province of philosophers.

I'm saddened by the loss. The scientific method is a tremendous tool for understanding the world, but most scientists refuse to use it to study phenomena that can't be repeated under controlled conditions and that can't be explained by current models of reality. I think it's impossible to explore the Big Three Questions without taking into account all that elusive, enigmatic, unrepeatable stuff. *The more accidental, the more true.*

I can at least hope the scientists won't object if the Beauty and Truth Laboratory borrows their disciplined objectivity and incisive reasoning to explore areas they regard as off-limits.

Two groups that may not mind are the astronomers and astrophysicists. More than other scientists, they've been compelled to develop an intimate relationship with invisible realms. In fact, they've come to a conclusion that's eerily similar to the assessment of shamans and mystics from virtually every culture throughout history: Most of reality is hidden from our five senses.

"Ninety-six percent of the universe is stuff we've never seen," cosmologist Michael Turner told Geoff Brumfiel in the March 13, 2003 issue of the journal *Nature.* To be exact, the cosmos is 23 percent dark matter and 73 percent dark energy, both of which are missing. All the stars and planets and moons and asteroids and comets and nebulas and gas clouds together comprise the visible four percent.

So where is the other 96 percent? No one knows. It's not only concealed from humans, it's imperceptible to the instruments humans have devised, and its whereabouts can't be predicted by any existing theories.

What will happen as the implications of these data filter down to the other sciences? Maybe there will be a reversal of a long-term trend documented by *Nature.* In 1914, the magazine found that 30 percent of the world's top scientists believed in God. In a second survey in 1934, the number dropped to 15 percent, and by 1998 it was seven percent.

If the fact that most of reality is hidden doesn't spur them to reconsider the possibility of a divine presence working behind the scenes, maybe it will move them to become more sympathetic to a project like ours, which has the intention of adopting the scientific approach to an exploration of the invisible.

Most modern intellectuals scoff at angels, dismissing them as superstitious hallucinations or New Age goofiness. But not all deep thinkers have shared their scorn. John Milton and William Blake regarded angels as worthy of their explorations. Celestial beings have also received serious treatment by Saul Bellow, E.M. Forster, Gabriel Garcia Marquez, Isaac Bashevis Singer, and Leo Tolstoy. Of course, just because smart people have considered the possibility that angels can have real effects on the material world doesn't mean they do. Still, it might be interesting to keep an open mind.

"I believe that my soul is a dark forest. That my known self will never be more than a clearing in the forest. That gods come forth from the forest into the clearing of my known self, and then go back. That I must have the courage to let them come and go. That I will try always to recognize and submit to them." —D.H. Lawrence

Scientist Carl Sagan smoked pot. "He believed the drug enhanced his creativity and insights," wrote Keay Davidson in the *San Francisco Examiner,* quoting Sagan's pal Lester Grinspoon. "If I find in the morning a message from myself the night before informing me that there is a world around us which we barely sense," Sagan said, "or that we can become one with the universe, I may disbelieve; but when I'm high I know about this disbelief. And so I have a tape in which I exhort myself to take such remarks seriously. I say 'Listen closely, you sonofabitch of the morning! This stuff is real!'"

The 17th-century Church fathers wouldn't look through Galileo's telescope. Why bother? Catholic doctrine was clear that moons could not possibly circle Jupiter.

Likewise, most of today's scientists refuse to consider the possibility that there have been unidentified craft flying around our skies for years. "It's absurd to think that beings from other star systems could traverse the vast distances between them and us," they declare, "so why should we even examine the so-called evidence?" Their certainty contains a giant bias: that creatures from other worlds can only have ships that are limited to the means of propulsion we have thus far discovered here on Earth.

Arthur Koestler said that to the ancient Greeks, electricity was as bizarre and unfathomable as telepathy is to us in the modern era. Yet electricity existed before it was believed in. It's just that there was no theory that proposed its existence and no mechanism to gather evidence for it. Culture had to change in order for people to be able to know where and how to look.

Today we're aware of electricity as well as black holes, X-rays, radio waves, and infrared light because we have instruments to extend our senses. But is it wise to assume that we have finally developed every sense-extending technology that will ever be invented?

When Columbus's ships first appeared on the horizon, the Arawaks on the island of Guanahaní saw them as floating monsters. They didn't have the conceptual framework to know them for what they literally were. *You can't perceive what you can't conceive.* An adult who has been blind all his life and through surgery is suddenly given the power of sight takes quite a while to be able to learn to interpret what he's looking at. The eye alone doesn't see. The mind and the cultural biases it has internalized interpret and shape the raw data.

Modern science is a fabulous way of understanding reality, but it's not the crown of creation. Just as meteors, dinosaurs, and electricity (and dark matter and neutrinos and gamma rays) were inconceivable and therefore not real to earlier generations, there may be phenomena here with us now that won't be real until our culture and minds and instruments evolve further. Will they include events we now call UFOs and angels? Maybe. Maybe not. Let's remain curious.

"Ancient stars in their death throes spat out atoms like iron which this universe had never known. The novel tidbits of debris were sucked up by infant suns which, in turn, created yet more atoms when their race was run. Now the iron of old nova coughings vivifies the redness of our blood.

"If stars step constantly upward, why should the global interlace of humans, microbes, plants, and animals not move upward steadily as well? The horizons toward which we must soar are within us, anxious to break free, to emerge from our imaginings, then to beckon us forward into fresh realities.`

"We have a mission to create, for we are evolution incarnate. We are her self-awareness, her frontal lobes and fingertips. We are second-generation star stuff come alive. We are parts of something 3.5 billion years old, but pubertal in cosmic time. We are neurons of this planet's interspecies mind." —Howard Bloom, *Global Brain: The Evolution of Mass Mind from the Big Bang to the 21st Century*

Dionysian Manifesto

Kary Mullis is the only Nobel Prize-winning scientist ever to suggest that some aspects of astrology are valid. He's also the most distinguished prodigy in history to have described a close encounter with a UFO. When he's not doing pioneering research on the human genome, he likes to surf and explore shamanism.

"He's a scientific genius with a vibrant soul," said a critic who reviewed his autobiography *Dancing Naked in the Mind Field.* "There is nothing too preposterous for him to rigorously investigate and learn something valuable from, just as there are few commonly held truths in which he cannot find some fundamental fallacy."

Physicist Roger Penrose, who helped to develop the theories about black holes, has said that the chance of an ordered universe happening at random is nil: one in 10 to the 10th to the 30th, a number so large that if you programmed a computer to write a million zeros per second, it would take a million times the age of the universe just to write the number down.

"The big bang is so preposterous," says renowned astronomer Allan Sandage, co-discoverer of the quasar, "and the chain of events it set off so unlikely, that it makes most sense when thought of as a 'miracle.'"

For the sake of argument, let's assume Sandage is right. If the very beginning of the universe itself was a miracle, then everything in it is impregnated with the possibility of smaller but equally marvelous miracles.

"When a scientist states that something is possible, he is almost certainly right. When he states that something is impossible, he is very probably wrong," said Arthur C. Clarke, who, due to his contributions to science, has had an asteroid and dinosaur species named after him.

"The laws of physics appear 'fine tuned' for our existence. Even slight deviations in the laws would result in a universe devoid of stars and life. If, for instance, the force of gravity were just a few percent weaker it could not squeeze and heat the matter inside stars to the millions of degrees that are necessary to trigger sunlight-generating nuclear reactions. If gravity were only a few percent stronger, however, it would heat up stars, causing them to consume their fuel faster. They would not exist for the billions of years needed for evolution to produce intelligence. This kind of fine tuning is widespread." —Marcus Chown, "Radical Science: Did Angels Create the Universe?," *The Independent,* March 15, 2002, www.millennium-debate.org/ind15mar024.htm

Science: looking for a black cat in a dark room. *Philosophy:* looking for a black cat in a dark room where there is no black cat. *Psychoanalysis:* looking for a black cat in a dark room where there is no black cat—and finding it. *Beauty and Truth Laboratory:* looking for a black cat in a dark room and finding it.

Once the full impact of Einstein's theory of relativity became clear, an admiring journalist interviewed him about the process by which he'd arrived at the revolutionary breakthrough. "How did you do it?" the journalist asked. "I ignored an axiom," Einstein replied.

To be clear, the revolutionary scientist didn't say he'd ignored an opinion or theory, but rather an idea so well-established that it was regarded as self-evident. Furthermore, he didn't say he rebelled or fought against the axiom: He simply acted as if it weren't there.

"Something unknown is doing we don't know what." —Astrophysicist Arthur Eddington, "one of three persons in the world who understood Einstein's theory of general relativity"

Dear scientists: We pledge to summon our finest analytical intelligence and use impeccable logic as we experiment with the hypothesis that there is no contradiction between cultivating scrupulous critical thinking and communing with the part of reality that's hidden from our senses. —Love, the Beauty and Truth Lab

"Nature loves to hide." —Heraclitus

Dionysian Manifesto

22ND-CENTURY PRONOIA THERAPY

Experiments and exercises in becoming a bewilderingly enlightened, ecstatically grateful, unselfishly proud Master of Fiendishly Benevolent Tricks

Report your answers & research results below

1 Philosopher Robert Anton Wilson has proposed that the single greatest contribution to world peace would come from there being six billion different religions—a unique spiritual path for each person on the planet. The Beauty and Truth Laboratory urges you to get started on doing your part to make this happen. What will your religion be called? What rituals will you perform? Write down your three core tenets.

2 You'll also need a new name for the Creator. "God" and "Goddess" have been so overused and abused that most of us are numb to them. And given the spiritual opportunities that will open up for you as you explore pronoia, you can't afford to have an impaired sensitivity towards the Great Mystery.

Here's an idea to stimulate your search: The Russian word for God is "Bog." The Basques call the Supreme Being "Jingo." To purge your psychic dockets of built-up fixations about deity, you might try singing improvisational prayers to "Jingo Bog."

Here are a few other fresh names to inspire you:
Blooming HaHa
Wild Divine
Whirl-Zap-Gush
Sublime Cackler
Chthonic Riddler

3 Since ancient times, China has hosted three religions: Confucianism, Buddhism, and Taoism. The typical Chinese person has cobbled together a mélange of beliefs gathered from all three. This is different from the Western way, which is to be faithful to one religion or another, never mixing and matching.

But that's changing in certain enclaves in North America, where growing numbers of seekers are adopting the Chinese approach. They borrow elements from a variety of spiritual traditions to create a personalized path. Religious historians call this syncretism.

As you meditate on conjuring up your own unique mode of worship, think of the good parts you'd like to steal from other religions.

4 Most religions designate a special class of people—priests, rabbis, ayatollahs—to oversee official communications with the Source. This has led to a prevailing assumption, even among those who don't follow an established faith, that we can't initiate a divine conversation without the aid of a professional class of trained mediators. Among some sects of the ancient gnostics, in contrast, everyone was regarded as a potential prophet who could experience epiphanies worthy of becoming part of the ever-evolving doctrine.

As you create your own spiritual path, experiment with this approach. What might you do to eliminate the middleman and commune directly with the Source?

5 The chorus of an old Depeche Mode song goes like this: "I don't want to start/ Any blasphemous rumors/ But I think that God's/ Got a sick sense of humor/ And when I die/ I expect to find him laughing." I have a grudging respect for these lyrics. In an age when God has been co-opted by intolerant fundamentalists and mirthless sentimentalists, I appreciate any artist who suggests there's more to the Infinite Spirit than the one-dimensional prig described in the Bible or Koran.

On the other hand, Depeche Mode's notion of the Blooming HaHa is also disinformation. It's as much a hostage to pop culture's knee-jerk nihilism as the right-wing bigots' God is to their monumental hatreds. One thing I know for sure about the Supreme Being is that while she does have a complicated sense of humor, it's not cruel or vengeful.

Your assignment: Pray to be granted a healing sample of her comedic genius—a funny, shocking miracle that will free you of any tendencies you have to believe the age-old lies about her.

6 Will there be prayer in your new religion? If so, we suggest that you avoid the body language traditionally used by Christians in their worship. The gesture of clasping one's hands together originated long ago as an imitation of being shackled; it was thought to be the proper way to express submission to divine power.

The prayers you make, however, may be imbued as much with reverent exuberance or ecstatic gratitude

22nd-Century Pronoia Therapy

as somber submissiveness. An example of a more apt gesture is to spread your arms as wide and high as they'll go, as if you're hugging the sky. Any other ideas?

7 What if the Creator is like Rainer Maria Rilke's God, "like a webbing made of a hundred roots, that drink in silence"? What if the Source of All Life inhabits both the dark and the light, heals with strange splendor as much as with sweet insight, is hermaphroditic and omni-sexual? What if the Source loves to give you riddles that push you past the boundaries of your understanding, forcing you to deepen your perceptions and change the ways you think about everything? Close your eyes and imagine you can sense the presence of this tender, marvelous, difficult, entertaining intelligence.

8 At a candy store one Easter season, I heard a philo-sophical debate about Jesus-themed confections. "It's just not right to eat a symbol of God," one woman said as she gazed at a chocolate Christ on the cross. A man agreed: "It's sacrilegious. An abomination." An employee overheard and jumped in. "I'll ask my boss to take that stuff off the shelf," she clucked.

I was tempted to say what I was thinking: "Actually, the holiest ritual of Christian worship involves eating Christ's body and blood." But I held my tongue; I wasn't in the mood for a brouhaha.

Where do you stand on this issue? Do you or do you not want to eat a symbolic embodiment of your deity? If you do, what food will you choose?

9 At one point in James Michener's novel *Hawaii,* a native Hawaiian tells ignorant missionaries, "You cannot speak to the gods with your clothes on." Where-upon he strips and prepares for prayer. Test this theory. Find out if your communion with the Divine Wow improves when you're naked.

10 A few Christian sects now enjoy a new addition to their once-staid church services: holy laugh-ter. Parishioners become so excited while worshiping that they erupt in uncontrollable glee. Some crack up so profoundly that they fall on the floor and flop around like breakdancers. Others repeatedly leap into the air as if on pogo sticks, or wobble and zigzag as if trying to dance while drunk.

Imagine that the holy books of your religion pre-scribe laughing prayers as a reliable way to know the Divine Wow. Recite one of those laughing prayers.

22nd-Century Pronoia Therapy

11 In Judeo-Christian cultures, many people associate the sky with the masculine form of God. According to this bias, the Supreme Father rules us all from on high—up, away, far from here. But if you were an ancient Egyptian, the sky was the goddess Nuit, her body its very substance. She was a loving mother whose tender touch could be felt with each new breath.

For one day, act as if you and the sky goddess are in constant contact.

12 The time: 2003. The place: a New York restaurant. The scenario: A talking carp began shouting at an Hispanic food preparer who was about to turn it into a meal. The restaurant owner came in to investigate and became a second witness to the event. He determined that the carp was offering religious advice in Hebrew. *The New York Times* reported the story, and soon a local Hasidic sect was proclaiming the fish's message to be a direct communication from God. Though many people laugh with derision when they hear this tale, I retain an open mind. The Divine Trickster has appeared to me in equally unusual forms. What about you? Are you crazy enough to listen to the wisdom of a talking carp? If not, what have you got to lose?

13 In Kevin Smith's movie *Dogma,* pop singer Alanis Morissette played God. Anthony Quinn was Zeus in the TV show *Hercules,* and comedian George Burns performed the role of God in three movies, always "without makeup," as he bragged. Your assignment is to choose the person you'd like to portray God or Goddess in the movie of your life.

14 It came to pass that the Goddess appeared to me in a vision and told me of a rooster who'd soon win a cock fight in rural Maurice, Louisiana. "Bet on Cocky Wizard," she urged, "and you will double your money." "But Shining Lady," I protested, "aren't cock fights cruel and illegal?" And She said unto me, "I will protect you from karmic harm as long as you promise Me that you will donate your earnings to beauty and truth fans who want more money in order to be better servants of pronoia." Obeying Her command, I bet on Cocky Wizard, and just as she predicted, won $30. Which is why I now say that whosoever among you are the first 30 worthy people to tell me why you deserve it, I will mail you a dollar blessed with the Goddess's Juju. Write to P.O. Box 150628, San Rafael, CA 94915.

15 In *Letters to a Young Poet,* Rilke urged an aspiring bard to change the way he imagined the Supreme Being. "Why don't you conceive of God as an ally who is coming," Rilke said, "who has been approaching since time began, the one who will someday arrive, the fruit of a tree whose leaves we are? Why not project his birth into the future, and live your life as an excruciating and lyrical moment in the history of a prodigious pregnancy?"

How would your life change if you made this idea your working hypothesis?

16 In some ancient Greek dramas, a god showed up out of nowhere to cause a miraculous twist at a crucial point in the tale. This divine intrusion was referred to as *theos ek mechanes,* literally "god from a machine," because the symbolic figure of the god was lowered onto the stage by a crane. In modern usage, the term is Latin—*deus ex machina*—and refers to a story in which a sudden event unexpectedly brings about a resolution to a baffling problem.

Write a tale in which you're the beneficiary of such an intervention.

17 In Frederick Buechner's book *On the Road with the Archangel,* the star is the archangel Raphael. This supernatural helper has a tough gig: gathering the prayers of human beings and delivering them to God. Here's how he describes the range of pleas he hears: "'There are prayers of such power that you might say they carry me rather than the other way around. There are prayers so apologetic and shamefaced and half-hearted that they all but melt away in my grasp like sad little flakes of snow. Some prayers are very boring.'"

Compose a prayer that's so powerful and entertaining that it could thrill an archangel.

18 There is no God. God is dead. God is a drug for people who aren't very smart. God is an illusion sold to dupes by money-hungry religions. God is a right-wing conspiracy. God is an infantile fantasy favored by superstitious cowards who can't face life's existential meaningless. APRIL FOOL! In fact, anyone who says he knows what God is or isn't, doesn't. Confess what you don't know about God.

19 In 2003, astronomers discovered a shiny red planet-like world orbiting the sun beyond Pluto. They called it Sedna, a name they said was derived from the Inuit deity that created the Arctic's sea creatures. But the truth about the myth of Sedna is more complicated. She is the Dark Nurturer, embodiment of the wild female potencies that are feared yet sorely needed by

22nd-Century Pronoia Therapy

cultures in which the masculine perspective dominates. Dwelling on the edge of life and death in her home at the bottom of the sea, Sedna is both a daunting freak and a primal source of abundance. Shamans from the world above swim down to sing her songs and comb her long black hair. If they win her favor, she gives them magic to heal their suffering patients.

The discovery of Sedna is one of many omens signaling our collective readiness to welcome back the long-repressed influence of the Dark Nurturer. Another omen is a book I wrote, *The Televisionary Oracle.* (Buy it from Powells.com or Amazon.com, or read it for free at www.freewillastrology.com/writings/oracle.html.)

Do you have room for the Dark Nurturer in your religion? Compose a prayer asking for her love.

20 Thousands of scientists are engaged in research to crack the code of the aging process. Their coming breakthroughs may allow you to live a healthy and vigorous life well into your 90s—and even beyond.

How can you contribute to this worthy cause? What might you do to promote your longevity? Brainstorm about possible strategies.

And now I drink a toast to your coffin. May it be fashioned of lumber obtained from a hundred-year-old cypress tree whose seed will germinate this year.

21 Let's move on to discuss the possibility that sooner or later, the physical body you inhabit will expire. Your heart will shut down. Blood will no longer course through your veins. The fleshly vehicle you knew as your home for so many years will rot. Is this the ultimate proof, as some people bitterly proclaim, that there is no God and that pronoia is a lie?

I say no. I say that the Creator includes death as an essential part of evolution's master plan. Lifetime after lifetime, our immortal souls take on a series of temporary forms as we help unfold, in our own small ways, the inconceivably complex plot of the divine drama. Each time we die, it's hard and sad to our time-bound egos. But from the perspective of the part of us that has always been and will always be, it's simply part of the epic adventure.

Assume, for argument's sake, that what I've just said is a fact. Describe how different your life would be if you not only believed but perceived the truth that your essential self will never die, but will inhabit many bodies and live many lives on earth.

22nd-Century Pronoia Therapy

PRONOIA NEWS NETWORK

Tundra Cheer

"A major psychiatric study of 1,200 Finnish reindeer herders found midwinter to be quite a cheery time, despite darkness and daily temperatures that averaged a bone-chilling minus 22 degrees. 'All kinds of disorders, including depression, were rare in the darkest season,' Dr. Nayha Vaisanen and his team of scientists concluded in the 1994 issue of the journal *Acta Psychiatrica Scandinavia*."
—Lisa M. Krieger, *San Francisco Examiner*

Hands That Harvested Your Food

"Strawberries are too delicate to be picked by machine. The perfectly ripe ones bruise even at too heavy a human touch. Every strawberry you have ever eaten has been picked by callused human hands. Every piece of toast with jelly represents someone's knees, someone's aching backs and hips, someone with a bandanna on her wrist to wipe away the sweat." —Alison Luterman, quoted in *After the Ecstasy, the Laundry,* by Jack Kornfield

PNN is brought to you by the Buddha's reminder that "No miseries befall one who does not cling to name and form," and by Henry Miller's brag in his book, Tropic of Cancer, *"I have no money, no resources, no hopes. I am the happiest man alive."*

Creeping Democracy

Democracy is coming to China, at least on the local level. A majority of villages now use voting to select their government officials. (Source: www.goodnews network.org)

SPACE RACE

Businessman Dennis Tito paid the Russians to let him join their astronauts on a trip to the International Space Station. U.S. officials were peeved. Then-NASA administrator Daniel Goldin raged that it would be a "cold day in hell" before his agency would welcome "tourists" like Tito. In other words, his taxpayer-supported Old Boys Club wanted a monopoly on deciding who gets the great privilege of seeing our planet from space.

In the wake of Tito's chutzpah, a San Francisco poetry group, Lyrical Travelers, was emboldened to propose that the crew list for future space flights include more than just scientists, military personnel, and wealthy businessmen: poets and spiritual leaders, for instance, and other imaginative, articulate people who can express to the rest of us what it's like to enjoy this rare journey.

MAKE-BELIEVE ART

The Museum of Make Believe features artifacts from nursery rhymes, fairy tales, and classical literature. Among its treasures are Snow White's mirror, the baseball mitt from *The Catcher in the Rye,* Jack and Jill's notorious pail, and the tools Geppetto used to create his wooden son Pinocchio. (Source: www.ruinedeye.com/MOMB/MAKEB.htm)

Domesticating Diseases
Biologist Paul Ewald is opposed to efforts to exterminate diseases spread by germs. Instead, we should figure out how they co-evolve with humans, and push them to mutate in ways that are favorable for us.

Like every living thing, harmful microbial species change over time in response to environmental conditions. Syphilis, for example, was more lethal and fast-spreading 500 years ago. It killed its human victims relatively quickly, which diminished its ability to proliferate in new hosts. Ultimately, a milder variety evolved. An infected person survived longer and could spread the syphilis strain further.

Ewald wants to adopt this model as a conscious strategy, cultivating conditions that encourage the mellow strains of a disease to trump their nastier relatives.

"Maybe someday we'll barely notice when we get colonized by disease organisms," Ewald told journalist Joel Achenbach. "We'll have co-opted them. They'll be like in-laws, a little annoying but tolerable. If a friend sees us sniffling, we'll just say, Oh, it's nothing—just a touch of plague." (Source: Joel Achenbach, "Our Friend, the Plague," *National Geographic,* November 2003)

Freedom from Too Much Work
Women in the African country of Mali have always had to grind corn and peanuts by hand. It's a job that takes countless hours. But in recent years a Swiss development worker has spawned a revolution by introducing a simple grinding machine to 300 Mali villages. A 100-pound bag of corn once took three days of manual grinding. With the machine, dubbed by the locals "the daughter-in-law who doesn't speak," the job is done in 15 minutes.

Girls who were formerly forced to stay home all day to help with the domestic work are now free to go to school and play in the sun. Mature females are able to make more money faster and have time left over to take literacy classes, start up small businesses, or lounge around enjoying the privilege of doing absolutely nothing. (Source: Roger Thurow, *The Wall Street Journal,* July 26, 2002)

MIRABILIA REPORT *Mirabilia* n. innovations generated by unseen presences, enigmatic phenomena on the cusp between fake and real, odd acts of deliverance that inspire love or wonder or both; from the Latin *mirabilia,* "marvels."

■ In 2002, scientists discovered a secret underground river running 800 feet below a Mauritanian town in the Sahara Desert. With a flow rate of 8,450 gallons per hour, it is the biggest unnamed river in the world.

■ Oblivious to dire biblical prophecies about swarms of locusts, residents of Beijing, China, warmly greeted their arrival in 2002. They scooped the insects up in large bags, deep-fried them, and made them the main dish of an enormous feast.

■ Fingernails grow faster after they're wounded than they do normally.

■ Male rhesus monkeys often hang from tree branches by their prehensile penises.

■ The average person has over 1,460 dreams a year but remembers only five.

■ Philanthropist Alan "Ace" Greenberg contributed $1 million to buy Viagra for men with small bank accounts.

■ It's not uncommon for the eyes of the octopus to differ greatly—one little eye to see things in sunlit waters and one big eye to see things in the dimness of the deep.

■ In 1997, Jody Williams won the Nobel Peace Prize for her work to persuade more than 100 countries to ban deadly land mines. When she held a press conference at the end of a dirt road near her Vermont farmhouse, she was barefoot and wore jeans and a tank top.

■ On average, human beings have fewer than two legs.

■ Holding a spoon to his cheek during an especially blue period of his life, singer Tom Waits found that it takes 121 teardrops to fill a teaspoon.

■ Astronomers have discovered a crystal as big as our moon at the core of a dying white dwarf star.

■ A Japanese genius invented a robot that can belly dance.

School Superintendent Fires Himself

In Dollar Day, Michigan, school Superintendent Robert Barrette fired himself in order to solve budget woes. "It's either that or our teachers," he said. "Schools are about kids. If we cut teachers we hurt the quality of our education, but eliminating the administrator won't hurt kids." Barrette had been earning a yearly salary of $100,000 working for the school district, which has 262 students. (Source: Associated Press)

New Health Craze

Prayer can have a medicinal effect, according to a study of 990 heart patients at St. Luke's Hospital in Kansas City. Five prayer teams prayed daily on behalf of half of the patients. Though they did not know they were being prayed for, their health improved faster and they needed fewer drugs than the patients who did not have the benefit of the prayers. The report on the experiment appeared in the *Archives of Internal Medicine,* published by the American Medical Association. (Source: Associated Press)

Cashing in on Cosmic Rhythms

Called "Wall Street's best astrologer" by *Barron's,* Arch Crawford analyzes planetary movements to assist him in predicting the ebb and flow of the stock market. His newsletter, *The Crawford Perspectives,* was ranked the number one market timer by the *Hulbert Financial Digest* for the period 1991–1996. In 2002, *Timer Digest* said Crawford's advice was the second-best among over a hundred stock market-timing newsletters it ranked.

Booming Poetry Business

Barnes & Noble, the nation's largest book retailer, which stocks 7,500 poetry titles, says it has seen sales of poetry books rise by 30 percent in recent years. City Lights Bookstore in San Francisco has had a 60 percent increase in poetry sales in the last eight years.

Non-Violence Sells

"In Will Wright's mind, video games shouldn't always be about winning or losing. That was the trouble when he pitched an idea some two decades ago for a new game centered on building cities. Software makers were skeptical, insisting that without clear winners and losers, the idea would be a commercial flop. Since then, Wright's pet project, later known as SimCity, has become one of the most recognizable computer games of all time, with more than 20 million copies sold." —Matthew Yi, sfgate.com

Poetry Slams' Trendy Anger

In his book *The Degradation of Language and Music and Why We Should, Like, Care,* John McWhorter says he prefers the energetic rants of poetry slams to the "doggedly flat rainy-day poems" of academic writers. On the other hand, the spoken word stuff rarely ventures beyond "alienation and scolding," which limits its beauty and power. "The vast weight of human artistic achievement was not created in indignation," he notes.

Angel Styles

Real angels don't have the kind of glossy physical appearance normally associated with celebrities and film stars. So says biblical scholar Dr. Andrew Clavisch after interviewing 3,450 people who claim to have had a personal encounter with the heavenly beings. Quoted in the *Weekly World News,* Clavisch says the general consensus is that it's rare to see an angel with perfectly coiffed hair, cosmetic surgery, an underwear model's physique, or smooth, glowing skin. Most are average-looking and seem to have no interest in fashionable attire.

WANTED: Peace-loving warrior (any gender) to serve as a model for a statue of the Egyptian goddess of justice, Maat. Must be willing to sit on a lion, wear ostrich feathers, and hold a sword aloft for long hours. Your thighs should be strong and you should be able to make your eyes wild with the desire to conjure both severity and mercy. Ideally, you are also angry about at least three forms of injustice that don't affect you directly. To apply, send your thoughts on the subject "Everyone has a piece of the truth." rebelgrail@yahoo.com.

"Expect the unexpected or you won't find it." —Heraclitus

"Every day I remind myself that my inner and outer life are based on the labors of others." —Albert Einstein, *Ideas and Opinions,* translator, Sonja Bargmann

"You never change things by fighting the existing reality. To change something, build a new model that makes the existing model obsolete." —Buckminster Fuller, *Critical Path*

"Try with all your might and work very, very hard to make the world a better place. But if all your efforts are to no avail—no hard feelings." —The Dalai Lama

"The new work of art does not consist of making a living or producing an objet d'art or in self-therapy, but in finding a new soul." —Henry Miller, *The Wisdom of the Heart*

"Man is at the nadir of his strength when the earth, the seas, the mountains are not in him, for without them his soul is unsourced, and he has no images by which to abide." —Edward Dahlberg, *The Sorrows of Priapus*

"The illiterate of the 21st century will not be those who cannot read and write, but those who cannot learn, unlearn, and relearn." —Alvin Toffler, *Powershift: Knowledge, Wealth, and Power at the Edge of the 21st Century*

"When you do something, you should burn yourself completely, like a good bonfire, leaving no trace of yourself." —Shunryu Suzuki, *Zen Mind, Beginner's Mind*

Benevolent Pranks

In recent years, a tradition of guerrilla art has broken out in some American cities. Deposited anonymously in public places at night, these unauthorized sculptures and installations are often carefully designed and interesting to look at.

In 2002, for example, unknown creators swooped down on a cafe in one of the worst crime corridors in Seattle, leaving behind a handcrafted table and chairs. On top of the table was a vase filled with flowers. One seat, a metal trunk that opened, contained vintage playing cards and the game Operation, complete with batteries. (Source: *Seattle Times*)

PRONOIA NEWS NETWORK

THIS WEEK IN PRONOIAC HISTORY

In an act of random violence, playwright Samuel Beckett was stabbed by a pimp on a Paris street. A stranger, the pianist Suzanne Deschevaux-Dumesnil, found him and got medical help. She visited him in the hospital, and eventually the two were married.

Bach's *St. Matthew Passion* is a highly regarded musical composition. Yet the score disappeared and the work wasn't played for years after Bach's death in 1750. In 1829, composer Felix Mendelssohn rediscovered the long-lost manuscript being used as wrapping paper in the estate sale of a deceased cheese salesman. He arranged for a public performance of the piece, and its revival began.

Ancient Hawaiians had a sport they called *lele kawa,* in which they dived off cliffs into the ocean. *Pu'u Keka'a,* a volcanic cinder cone in West Maui, was a perfect place from which to jump, but everyone avoided it. Legend held it was a taboo place—"the leaping place of the soul," where the souls of the recently dead left the earth and ascended into the spirit world. But that changed one day in the late 19th century when a great warrior, Chief Kahekili, climbed to the top of *Pu'u Keka'a* and plunged into the sea, shattering the taboo and mutating the myth.

Bumper Sticker Therapy   Beauty and Truth Laboratory researcher Romney Austin adorned her Honda Civic with her first-ever bumper sticker, "Give Yourself to Love." While proud of announcing her compassionate philosophy to the world, she was also nervous. Hadn't she raised the pressure on herself to live up to her noble ideals?

A week later, she snapped. A guy chatting on a cell phone in a Lexus SUV cut her off in traffic, and road rage moved her to give him a middle-finger salute. Soon she added a new bumper sticker to the left of the first: "Get In, Sit Down, Shut Up, Hold On."

When I asked her about the contradiction, she confessed, "I've just accepted that I've got a split personality."

A week later, her conflicting sides reached a compromise. Romney pasted the word "and" in the space between the two stickers, to create a new thought: "Get In, Sit Down, Shut Up, Hold On, and Give Yourself to Love." She called to announce the good news: "I'm whole again!"

Mirroring the Horrors   Many creative people seem possessed by an urge to mirror the horrors they witness, making art that is as desolate as the experience it represents. Greek poet Odysseus Elytis mourned this phenomenon. He believed that artists in the grip of it are like those with healthy legs who choose to limp along with broken crutches.

"During the years of Buchenwald and Auschwitz," he said, "Matisse painted the most charming flowers and fruit that were ever made. That's why today they still speak more eloquently than the most macabre description of the period. Their creator was faithful not to the tragedy but to the reaction that tragedy kindled in his conscience." (Source: Odysseus Elytis, translated by Theophanis Stavrou: *Books Abroad,* Volume 49, no 4, Autumn 1975)

Not Exactly Bad Luck   What seems like bad luck may not be caused by the whims of fate or capricious gods. Sometimes it's the result of dumb decisions and their consequences. Take the "Curse of the Bambino." It supposedly prevented baseball's Boston Red Sox from winning the World Series for decades after they traded away future Hall of Fame star Babe Ruth in 1920. But the real reason for Boston's enduring mediocrity was less occult: its owners' racism. After Jackie Robinson finally integrated the game in 1947, they lagged far behind in signing black players. Not until the 1990s did the Red Sox fully catch up with other teams.

Corrected Beauty Facts   "I am not excited by the idea that the world we live in is made up of 90 percent ugly things and ugly places, while things and places endowed with beauty are rare and difficult to find. My opinion is that there is no ugly object or ugly person in this world. Anything is potentially fascinating." —Jean Dubuffet, *Jean Dubuffet: Towards an Alternative Reality*

Sixty-Seven Percent Failure Rate
"These are the batting averages of the best hitters in baseball history: Ty Cobb: .366; Rogers Hornsby: .358; Joe Jackson: .356. Since an average of .333 means a player did not get a hit two out of every three times he batted, these champions made an out more often than they got a hit. Most professional players do worse. Moral of the story: Unless you're a brain champion equal to these baseball champions, you're probably wrong close to two out of three times." —Robert Anton Wilson, www.rawilson.com

Smart Singing   "Sound-making instincts and the 'singing sense' are centered in the cerebellum or 'small brain.' For that reason, the singer who relies too much on the cerebrum or larger brain is hard to teach. It is a notorious fact that the 'intelligent' singer rarely sings either well or naturally, i.e. spontaneously." —Cornelius Reid, *A Dictionary of Vocal Terminology*

5.

Least Pronoiac Poet

The results of our poll are in. By a wide margin, our readers voted jejune poet John Ashbery the Least Pronoiac Poet. He garnered 58 percent of the vote. Second-place finisher Stanley Moss lagged far behind with 21 percent.

Here's a sample of the demoralizing style that earned Ashbery the honor, a passage from "Always Merry and Bright":

> The ocean sighs, finding the process of
> striking the shore
> interminable and intolerable.
> Let's pretend it's back when we were young
> and cheap, and nobody followed us. Well,
> that's not entirely true: the cat followed us
> home from school sometimes . . .
> Forget it. It all comes undone sooner or later.
> The vetch goes on growing, wondering
> whether it grew any more today.

World Conference of Soul-Making

In July 2004, the first annual World Conference of Soul-Making met in San Rafael, California. The goal of the gathering was to reach consensus on the best strategies for cultivating soul.

Three schools of thought emerged. The Ruminators theorized that humans are born without souls and can create them only through arduous, disciplined rebellion against all belief systems. The Resonators agreed that soul isn't innate, but insisted that soul-making is by no means difficult. For example, gathering good stories is effective and not at all hard. The Revelators said every person is born with a soul in seed form, and need only discover the "blueprint" of that seed in order to attract the experiences necessary to draw out its potential.

Don't Suffer for Your Art

"I glommed on to the idea that I had to suffer for my art. Acting teachers love to promote the idea that in order to really get into character, you've got to put yourself through emotional hell. Now I'd say, 'Don't suffer for your art.'" — actor Christian Slater, quoted in the *San Francisco Chronicle*

Tree Decor

In Cedar Rapids, Iowa, police were called to the scene to investigate when 15 trees in a city park were fitted with doorknobs and locks. —*Fortean Times*

Enchanted Loom

"If you are a poet, you will see that there is a cloud in this sheet of paper. Without a cloud, there will be no rain; without rain, the trees cannot grow; and without trees, we cannot make paper." —Thich Nhat Hanh, *Peace Is Every Step*

"Regardless of who sees it, there really is a cloud in this sheet of paper, as well as a bark beetle, a handful of soil, a bit of bird poop, even the gasoline that powered the logger's chain saw. It is even possible that if you were to chronicle the history of those carbon atoms currently part of the page you are now holding, you would find that they were once part of Peter the Great, a woolly mammoth, or (and!) a Komodo dragon, before they found themselves incorporated into the loblolly pine that eventually became this particular sheet of paper." —David P. Barash, "Buddhism and the 'Subversive Science,'" *The Chronicle of Higher Education*

Outlawed in 27 States

"The sublime can only be glimpsed by pressing through fear's boundary, beyond one's previous conception of the beautiful." —Rusty Morrison, *Poetry Flash*

This perfect moment is brought to you by the thousand-year-old rose bush that's growing on the wall of the Hildesheim Cathedral in Germany.

Predicting the News

When the bearded dragon lizard sits upright and cocks its head towards the heavens, Australian Aborigines know that rain will fall the next day. And when massive buds appear on the queen wattle plants, even the youngest members of a tribe can prophesy with confidence that brush fires will break out soon.

Ig Nobel Prizes

Each year the science magazine "Annals of Improbable Research" awards "Ig Nobel Prizes." A prize in chemistry was recently given to researchers who discovered that romantic infatuation is biochemically indistinguishable from obsessive-compulsive disorder. Other trophies have gone to the "Stalin World" amusement park, software that can detect a cat walking on a computer keyboard, and a report on "Courtship Behavior of Ostriches Towards Humans Under Farming Conditions."

Unsung Philanthropy

During four years of his tenure as Pepsi's CEO from 1996–2001, Roger Enrico donated his annual $900,000 salary to the company's college scholarship fund for the children of frontline workers.

How Is Enlightenment Like a Million-Dollar Vacation Home?

For some seekers, spiritual enlightenment is the ultimate commodity. They believe that through diligent meditation and self-improvement, there will come a day when it will no longer elude their grasp. Breaking through to the singular state of cosmic consciousness, they will forever after own it, free and clear. Permanently illuminated! Never to backslide into the dull ignominy of normal human awareness!

Here's what I have to say about that: It's a delusion.

The fact is, the nature of perfection is always mutating. What constitutes enlightenment today will always be different tomorrow. Even if you're fortunate and wise enough to score a sliver of "enlightenment," it's not a static treasure that becomes your indestructible, everlasting possession. Rather, it remains a mercurial knack that must be continually re-earned.

If you want to befriend the Divine Wow, you must not only be willing to change ceaselessly—you have to *love* to change ceaselessly.

Lucky you: All of creation is conspiring to help you live like that.

Certificate of
Exemption from Enlightenment

This document certifies that

_____

*is immune to the lust for enlightenment and is exempt
from the need to seek enlightenment.*

❧

This document also certifies that

_____

*has seen through the fraud of the enlightenment con game and is excused
from further clawing and scraping to own a piece of that specious reward.*

❧

This document further certifies that

_____

*is free from the temptation to be consecrated as enlightened by any
guru, saint, holy person, or religious organization that claims the right to do so.*

❧

Finally, this document certifies that

_____

*has already been enlightened a million times in a million different ways
anyway, and that seeking even further enlightenments
would be redundant and even greedy.*

❧

To ensure the continued validity of this document,

_____

*vows to regularly renew these three understandings: that it is impossible to ever reach
a complete and permanent state of enlightenment; that there is no single state of awareness
that constitutes enlightenment; and that since the nature of reality keeps changing,
the nature of enlightenment keeps changing as well.*

14

You are a
fucking
lucky
plucky
good-sucking
genius.

It's Bad Luck to Be Superstitious

Review in painstaking detail the history of your life,
honoring every moment as if you were conducting
a benevolent Judgment Day.
Forgive yourself of every mistake except one.

Create a royal crown for yourself
out of a shower cap, rubber bands, and light bulbs.

Think of the last place on earth you'd ever want to visit,
and visualize yourself having fun there.

Test to see if people are really listening to you by asserting
that Karl Marx was one of the Marx Brothers.

Steal lint from dryers in laundromats
and use it to make animal sculptures for someone you admire.

Fantasize you're the child of divine parents
who abandoned you when you were two days old,
but who will soon be coming back to reunite with you.

Meditate on how one of the symbols of plenitude in Nepal
is a mongoose vomiting jewels.

Once a year on the night before your birthday,
say these words into a mirror: "It's bad luck to be superstitious."

Start a club whose purpose is to produce an archive
ˆof controversial jokes and obscene limericks about beauty, truth, and love.

Persona Turnover

Since 1994, Mexico's Zapatistas have evolved from a small guerrilla army fighting for the rights of indigenous people to an international cultural force whose battles are mostly waged with symbols and words. The Zapatista leader, who goes by the pseudonym Subcomandante Marcos, always appears in public wearing a mask. Every 12 months or so, his old mask wears out and he has to replace it with a fresh one.

The Beauty and Truth Laboratory thinks this would be a good standard for all of us to live up to: to molt our personas, or social masks, at least once a year.

Your Brand New Name

In some spiritual traditions, devotees attempt an arduous process of self-transformation as they retrain themselves to perceive the world from God's point of view. If they succeed, they're honored with an initiation ritual and given a new name to consecrate their altered state.

I have the same problem with this custom that I have with the idea of enlightenment: Once isn't enough. Just as anyone in his or her right spiritual mind has a duty to keep claiming fresh varieties of enlightenment until the end of time, so should the initiations and renamings continue forever.

In my opinion, these considerations apply to you. You may not have sequestered yourself for years in a mountaintop monastery, and you may not have risen every morning at 5 a.m. to say prayers for hours, but you are an authentic devotee who has undergone equivalent ordeals. Your spiritual transformation has unfolded as you've dealt with the challenges of daily life during our epic moment in history, when unprecedented levels of annihilation and resurrection are the norm.

You have earned the right, therefore, to enjoy enlightenment after enlightenment and initiation after initiation and renaming after renaming.

I invite you to get started with a do-it-yourself initiation ceremony. It doesn't have to be long and complicated, and you can create it yourself. As an example of what you might do, here's a ritual that some Beauty and Truth Laboratory's initiates have performed: 1. Eat a pinch of dirt to declare your solidarity with Mother Earth. 2. Burn a five-dollar bill to purify your relationship with symbols of wealth. 3. Kick yourself in the ass to affirm your ongoing intention to discipline your shadow.

As one of your initiatory rewards, consider adopting a fresh alias during this and every initiation you carry out in the future. You can abandon your existing name if you want, or simply add your new tag to the current mix.

To celebrate the occasion, I invoke on your behalf the inspiration of all shedding things. Your tree of power will be the eucalyptus, whose bark peels away to reveal fresh layers beneath. Your lucky symbol will be the molting snake. Your sacred insect will be the silverfish, which bursts through its exoskeleton as it grows a new and bigger one. Your role model will be Japanese artist Hokusai (1760–1849), who had such a passionate commitment to reinventing himself that he celebrated 60 births, each time giving himself a new name.

Below is a list of Native American-style titles and names you might want to steal for your own use. Feel free to dream up your own, of course.

Wild Face	Shadow Wrestler	Kiss Genius	Goal Thwacker
Boink Worthy	Fizzy Nectar	Rumbler	Thrill Witch
Rowdy Gusto	Bliss Mutator	Silky Banger	Phoenix Nectar
Mucho Gusto Coco Loco	Mango Sucker	Pain Killer	Fire Keeper
Wobble Binder	Earthshaker	Wish Crayon	Pearly Thunder
Thumper	Gut Stormer	Storm Tamer	Free Sigh

246

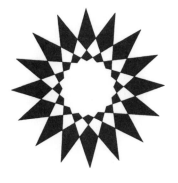

I'm a star, you're a star

You're a star—and so am I. I'm a genius—and so are you. Your success encourages my brilliance, and my charisma enhances your power. Your victory doesn't require my defeat, and vice versa. Those are the rules in the New World—quite unlike the rules in the Old World, where zero-sum games are the norm, and only one of us can win each time we play.

In the New World, you don't have to tone down or apologize for your prowess, because you love it when other people shine. You exult in your own excellence without regarding it as a sign of inherent superiority. As you ripen more and more of your latent aptitude, you inspire the rest of us to claim our own idiosyncratic magnificence.

Tibetan Buddhist teacher Geshe Chekawa (1220–1295) specialized in *bodhicitta,* seeking enlightenment not for personal gain but as a way to serve others. On his deathbed, he prayed to be sent to hell so that he might alleviate the suffering of the lost souls there.

As you explore pronoia, you will discover that like Chekawa, you have a huge capacity to help people. Unlike him, you'll find that expressing your benevolence doesn't require you to go to hell. It may even be unnecessary for you to sacrifice your own joy or to practice self-denial. Just the opposite: Being in service to humanity and celebrating your unique power will be synergistic. They will need each other to thrive.

The Golden Rule is a decent ethical principle, but it could be even better. "Do unto others as you would have them do unto you" presumes that others enjoy what you enjoy. But that's wrong. There are many things you'd like to have done unto you that others would either despise or be bored by. Here's a new, improved formulation, which we call the Platinum Rule: *Do unto others as they would like to have you do unto them.*

Using this improved formula is not just a virtuous way to live, but is also the best way to ensure the success of your selfish goals. The rituals and spells of various occult orders purport to be supercharged techniques for imposing your personal will on the chaotic flow of events, but I say that practicing the Platinum Rule outstrips all of them as an exercise to enhance your potency and happiness.

At the heart of the pronoiac way of life is an apparent conundrum: *You can have anything you want if you'll just ask for it in an unselfish way.* The trick to making this work is to locate where your deepest ambition coincides with the greatest gift you have to give. Figure out exactly how the universe, by providing you with abundance, can improve the lot of everyone whose life you touch. Seek the fulfillment of your fondest desires in such a way that you become a fount of blessings.

The Bible quotes the radical first-century spiritual activist Jesus Christ as follows: "Love your enemies, do good to those who hate you, bless those who curse you, pray for those who mistreat you."

This approach is as important to my well-being as getting good food and exercise and sleep. It's self-destructive for me to hate anything, including things that are easy to hate and that I might be naturally inclined to hate. As much harm as fundamentalist Christians have wreaked on our culture, for instance, feeling disgust for them only makes me sick. It feeds the very "us versus them" thinking that I'm pledged to root out, thereby making me a hypocrite and tainting my integrity. My mental and physical health suffer, and that diminishes my ability to get what I want.

I got an e-mail from a beauty and truth fan who calls himself Drek, Agent of the Future. "How come, in the long list of human fears, 'showing one's true self' is never included?" Drek mused. "Compared to the electrifying and terrifying prospect of shedding our protective masks and expressing our raw souls, snakes and death and public speaking really don't seem that scary."

I wrote Drek back to congratulate him for facing his greatest fear. I said I thought his struggle to reveal his naked beauty was as great a service to humanity as the work of Buddhist teacher Geshe Chekawa.

"To be an altruist, you must first be an egoist." —George Gurdjieff.

"Before you can give yourself away, you have to have a self to give." —Isabel Hickey, *Astrology: A Cosmic Science*

"In a gift-giving society, an individual gains prestige and satisfaction by receiving, then adding to what has been received and passing it on." So says Lewis Hyde in his book *The Gift, Imagination, and the Erotic Life of Property.* "In a consumer society," he continues, "prestige and satisfaction are gained through accumulation and acquisition. Nothing is given, nothing is passed on."

Though you have been born and raised in a consumer society, your attraction to pronoia suggests you have the ability to live in a gift-giving society. One of the best ways to change yourself to help create such a society is to expand your capacity for both accepting and bestowing largesse.

Pronoia isn't just a matter of raking in the blessings offered to you by the universal conspiracy, nor is it merely about aiding the conspiracy to disseminate blessings to everyone else. It's a balance of the two.

The Beauty and Truth Lab's youngest practitioner is a teenage poet, Deirdre Vonn. She's modest about her art. She worries she hasn't earned the states of awareness she writes about. "I don't know if I'm really as sensitive and deep as my poetry implies," she confessed once as she handed me a pristine, wrenching poem.

I understand her concern. Am I as consistently generous as my writings might make me appear? Nope. But in the effort to provide delicious and nutritious oracles for my readers, I am constantly pushing to live up to the moral artistry I espouse, becoming in the process a more interesting and useful person.

How about you? Is there a gift you can give or service you can provide that will awaken your sleeping endowments? Is there beauty you can bring to life in your environment that will compel you to become more of a charismatic, ingenious star?

Dionysian Manifesto

I'm a Brat, You're a Brat

Every January 1, many people make New Year's resolutions, promising to embark on programs of self-improvement. But your assignment now, should you choose to accept it, is to create a list of ANTI-resolutions.

Here are some questions to guide you: 1. What outlandish urges and controversial tendencies do you promise to cultivate in the coming months? 2. What nagging irritations will you ignore and avoid with even greater ingenuity? 3. What problems do you promise to exploit in order to have even more fun as you make the status quo accountable for its corruption? 4. What boring rules and traditions will you thumb your nose at, paving the way for exciting encounters with strange attractors?

This space has been liberated for your reckless use

SACRED ADVERTISEMENT

Thanks to our sponsor Carl Jung, who said, "The whole point of Jesus's life was not that we should become exactly like him, but that we should become ourselves in the same way he became himself. Jesus was not the great exception but the great example."

You're a Prophet

With the authority vested in me by the little voice in my head, I'm pleased to give you permission to add another job title to your résumé: prophet.

Am I being ironic? Only partially. The truth is, you generate numerous predictions every day. The source is your imagination, which tirelessly churns out visions of what you'll be doing in the future. The featured oracle of the moment may be as simple as a psychic impression of yourself devouring a fudge brownie in an hour or as monumental as a fantasy of building your dream home in Hawaii.

Your imagination is a treasure when it spins out scenarios that are aligned with your deepest desires. Indeed, it's an indispensable tool in creating the life you want; it's what you use to form images of the conditions you'd like to inhabit and the objects you hope to wield. Nothing manifests on the material plane unless it first exists as a mental picture.

But for most of us, the imagination is as much a curse as a blessing. You're just as likely to use it to conjure up premonitions that are at odds with your conscious values. Fearful fantasies regularly pop up, many disguising themselves as rational thoughts and genuine intuitions. They may hijack your psychic energy, directing it to exhaust itself in dead-end meditations.

Meanwhile, ill-suited longings are also lurking in your unconscious mind, impelling you to want things that aren't good for you and that you don't really need. Anytime you surrender to their allure, your imagination is practicing a form of black magic.

These are the imagination's unsavory aspects, which Zen Buddhists describe as the chatter of the "monkey mind." If you can stop locating your sense of self in the endless surge of its slapdash fantasies, only then might you be able to *be here now* and want what you actually have.

But whether your imagination is in service to your noble desires or in the thrall of compulsive fears and inappropriate yearnings, there is one commonality: Its prophecies can be pretty accurate. Many of your visions of the future do come to pass. The situations you expect to occur and the experiences you rehearse and dwell on are often reflected back to you as events that confirm your expectations.

Does that mean our mental projections create the future? Let's consider that possibility. What if it's at least partially true that what we expect will happen does tend to materialize? Here's the logical conclusion: It's downright stupid and self-destructive to keep infecting our imaginations with pictures of loss and failure, doom and gloom, fear and loathing. The far more sensible approach is to expect blessings.

Your Prophecies

Make five prophecies about yourself
and five about the world.

HOMEOPATHIC MEDICINE SPELL #5

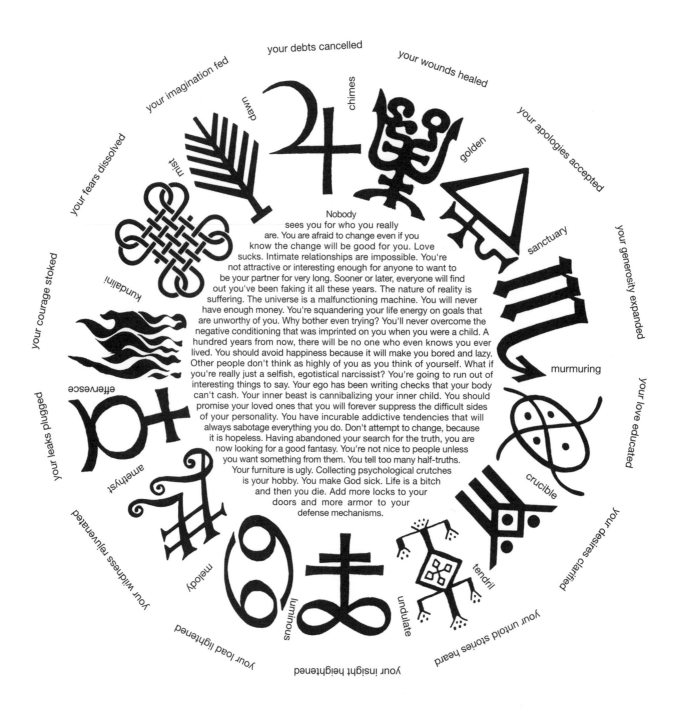

your debts cancelled

your imagination fed

your wounds healed

your fears dissolved

your apologies accepted

chimes

dawn

mist

golden

your generosity expanded

kundalini

sanctuary

your courage stoked

murmuring

effervesce

your love educated

your leaks plugged

amethyst

crucible

your wildness rejuvenated

your desires clarified

melody

tendril

luminous

undulate

your untold stories heard

your load lightened

your insight heightened

Nobody sees you for who you really are. You are afraid to change even if you know the change will be good for you. Love sucks. Intimate relationships are impossible. You're not attractive or interesting enough for anyone to want to be your partner for very long. Sooner or later, everyone will find out you've been faking it all these years. The nature of reality is suffering. The universe is a malfunctioning machine. You will never have enough money. You're squandering your life energy on goals that are unworthy of you. Why bother even trying? You'll never overcome the negative conditioning that was imprinted on you when you were a child. A hundred years from now, there will be no one who even knows you ever lived. You should avoid happiness because it will make you bored and lazy. Other people don't think as highly of you as you think of yourself. What if you're really just a selfish, egotistical narcissist? You're going to run out of interesting things to say. Your ego has been writing checks that your body can't cash. Your inner beast is cannibalizing your inner child. You should promise your loved ones that you will forever suppress the difficult sides of your personality. You have incurable addictive tendencies that will always sabotage everything you do. Don't attempt to change, because it is hopeless. Having abandoned your search for the truth, you are now looking for a good fantasy. You're not nice to people unless you want something from them. You tell too many half-truths. Your furniture is ugly. Collecting psychological crutches is your hobby. You make God sick. Life is a bitch and then you die. Add more locks to your doors and more armor to your defense mechanisms.

252

I Me Wed

Our culture places too narrow a definition on who can reap the benefits of holy matrimony. Two members of the same gender should have exactly the same right to be married as any heterosexual couple.

But why stop there? If it were within my power, I'd also legalize the marriages of any three people who wanted to enjoy wedded bliss in a triangular arrangement. Or four people, for that matter. Or 20.

But why stop there? There's another kind of holy matrimony we need: getting married to yourself. The fact is that none of us is ever likely to thrive in a relationship with a suitable partner until we master the art of loving ourselves with great ingenuity. A self-wedding ritual could be the uncanny magic that attracts a worthy consort into our lives, or else rouses the sleeping potential of an intimate bond we already have.

Are you ready to take the plunge? Are you brave and smart enough to risk a radical new collaboration with yourself? I propose that you perform a ceremony of self-marriage.

Before you begin, I'll ask you to smash two obstacles that prevent you from giving your heart to yourself with abandon.

The first barrier is your self-hatred; your disgust for your imperfections; the harsh judgments you inflict on your unripe beauty. You've got to be free from these bad habits. Let's exorcise them.

Visualize several objects that represent the ways you undermine yourself—a hammer to symbolize how you pound yourself with criticism, for example, or a drug that lifts you momentarily but debilitates you in the long run. Picture yourself throwing these objects into a vat of molten metal. Then say the following affirmation as many times as you need to:

I will never again cast a curse on myself.

There is another confusion to escape before you dive into the heart of your self-marriage ceremony. I call it the ancestral hex—the primal shame that your close relations have used to keep you bound to self-images that are at odds with who you really are.

Close your eyes and imagine that your mother and father are here with you in spirit right now. It shouldn't be hard, because they *are* here. So are your siblings, your aunts and uncles and cousins, your grandparents and their parents and their parents and their parents.

The ghostly presences of your family and forebears, their voices inside your head, often invade you when you dare to slip outside of the rules you've always followed. Many of these people are or would be full of ideas about how you should live your life. Many of them would say that getting married to yourself is a weird and unnatural act.

Though you may love them, you can't let their fixed, wrong-headed notions about you contaminate your self-wedding ceremony. Let's exorcise their influence from the sacred space. When I count to three, unleash a sound, be it a howl or whisper, that will evict them. Are you ready?

1 . . . 2 . . . 3 . . .

If any of your family loves you for exactly who you are and would applaud your decision to marry yourself, invite them in to participate.

Here's the next step to undergo as you prepare for union: You must achieve a visceral understanding of how gorgeous and mysterious you are. It's crucial that you realize beyond any doubt that you are a miraculous work of art, a masterpiece unlike any other ever created in the history of the world.

In reminding you of this fact, I don't mean to stimulate your egotism. It shouldn't make you arrogant or tempt you to believe you're superior to anyone. Remember that you are the chosen one—just as we all are.

Before we get to the main act, I'll invite you to spend some time in the coming days carrying out three devotions that will seal the sanctity of this ceremony.

First, acquire or create two wedding gifts for yourself. One should embody your determination to lovingly kill off some aspect of yourself that you don't want to bring with you into your self-married life—a bad habit or lingering remorse or stale ignorance you're finally finished with. The other gift you give yourself should symbolize a transformation that you want to give birth to.

These two gifts can be based on the same theme. For example, you could get a hard, thick work boot and a fuzzy bunny slipper to symbolize your vow to regularly kick your own ass with lighthearted exuberance as well as tough love.

The other devotion I'll ask you to perform is to go on a honeymoon with yourself. Design an extravagant jubilee in which you can fully expand into the liberated joy that is your birthright.

Now hold your own hand. Either say the following words or use them as inspiration to create your own:

I love my strange beauty and amazing pain
I love my hungry soul and entertaining games
I love my flaws, my gaps, my fears
I love my mysterious, dazzling frontiers

I will never forsake, betray, or deceive myself
I will always adore, forgive, and believe in myself
I will never refuse, abandon, or scorn myself
I will always amuse, delight, and redeem myself

Beauty and truth and love will always find me
Chaos and wilderness will always sustain me
I'm the fire and water and earth and air that are
    forever fresh from eternity
I'm a perfect creation and everything alive is
    naturally in love with me

If it's your will and desire to agree to the vows that I will now propose, express your consent by saying "amen," "ho," "yes," or any sound that feels right.

Do you vow to treat yourself with humble respect and resourceful compassion and outrageous grace?

Do you pledge to see your problems as tremendous opportunities and your flaws as imperfect talents?

Do you vow to celebrate your exalted passions and be ruthless in purging your ignorance?

Do you agree to cash in again and again on your inexhaustible power to reinvent yourself?

Do you promise to shower yourself with rowdy blessings and surprising adventures and brave emancipations?

Do you promise to love yourself unconditionally and unconventionally until the end of time?

Say this:

Novel intuitions are erupting from my smart heart, awakening me from any trance I've been ensnared in. I'm breaking and escaping obstructions that have suppressed my brilliance. My soul's code is unleashing itself, revealing in explosive precision why I'm a miraculous work of art, proving with intricate artistry why I'm a masterpiece unlike any other ever created in the history of the world.

Say this:

I am a genius. I am a fucking lucky plucky goodsucking genius.

Say this:

I am no longer looking for the perfect partner. I am my own perfect partner.

I now pronounce you your own husband AND wife, married to yourself in the eyes of the Divine Wow, till death and life and death and life bring you together, over and over again, in new and exciting ways each time, forever and ever.

You may kiss yourself on your own lips.

Use this page and next to add to your self-wedding. Include other vows you want to make to yourself.

This space is available for you to use in expanding your wedding ritual

15

"Ever since I learned
to see three sides to every story,
I'm finding much better stories"

Your Graduation Inscription

May you eat an unfamiliar dessert in a strange land at least
once every three years.

May you wake up to salsa music one summer morning,
and start dancing while you're still half-asleep.

May you spray-paint Rilke poems as graffiti
on highway overpasses.

May you mix stripes with plaids, floral patterns with checks,
and yellowish-green with brownish-purple.

May you learn to identify by name 20 flowers, 15 trees, 10 clouds,
and one extrasolar planet.

May you put a bumper sticker on your car or bike that says,
"My god can kick your god's ass!"

If you bury your face in your tear-stained pillow and beg God to
please send you your soul mate, may you not slur your words
in such a way that they sound like "cell mate."

May you dream of taking a trip to the moon in a gondola
powered by firecrackers and wild swans.

May you actually kiss the earth now and then.

May you find many good excuses to say,
as physicist Niels Bohr once did, "Your theory is crazy,
but it's not crazy enough to be true."

PRONOIA NEWS NETWORK

Eighth Wonder

The Internet is the Eighth Wonder of the World. Its power to make anyone a global publisher, regardless of income, has begun to render irrelevant A. J. Liebling's famous assertion that "Freedom of the press is guaranteed only to those who own one."

Millions of websites provide average people access to a vast storehouse of information once available only to scholars who were close to and adept at using a major library.

Thanks to the Internet, communication has sped up and expanded in unforeseen ways. Some visionaries see it as the embodiment of the global nervous system imagined by Teilhard de Chardin:

"We are faced with a harmonized collectivity of consciousnesses equivalent to a super-consciousness. The earth is not only becoming covered by myriads of grains of thought, but becoming enclosed in a single vast grain of thought on the sidereal scale, the plurality of individual reflections grouping themselves together

and reinforcing one another in the act of a single unanimous reflection.

"A world network of economic and psychic affiliations is being woven at increasing speed. It constantly penetrates more deeply within each of us. With every passing day it becomes more impossible for us to act or think otherwise than collectively."
—Teilhard de Chardin, *The Phenomenon of Man*

Soul Insider

An interviewer urged the Dalai Lama to discourse on how to cultivate lovingkindness. His Holiness said, "That may be too much to ask. How about if we just work on getting the 'kindness' part right?"

PNN is made possible by Deena Metzger's belief, described in her book Entering the Ghost River, *that "Beauty appears when something is completely and absolutely and openly itself."*

FREE WILL ASTROLOGY

"Esoteric astrology teaches that anyone whose future can be predicted by any means is living like a robot. It assumes that some people are more robotic (predictable) than others; and that further implies some of us have more free will than others." —Carolyn L. Vash, *Noetic Sciences Review,* www.noetic.org

Broken Laws "Scientists are challenging axioms of heredity that decree organisms inherit half their genetic characteristics from one parent and half from the other. They now believe chromosomes can archive the genes of ancestors and revive them in later generations. This means an organism may display characteristics of earlier generations that neither parent possesses. The discovery may force a revision of the laws of inheritance, with profound implications for crop-breeding, genetics, cancer research, and medicine."
—Jonathan Leake and Will Iredale, *The Times*

Scary Progress A quantum leap is a radical shift beyond what was previously imaginable. It can be problematic even as it's exhilarating. Physicist Fred Alan Wolf notes that in his field, such a leap often "leads to personal regrets, even though its ultimate consequences produce a new vision of humanity and the universe." Einstein, Planck, and Schrödinger, whose revolutionary work shredded the old physics, "were sadly upset with their discoveries," Wolf says.

"Whenever a quantum leap occurs," he concludes, "there is something that tends to resist it. In matter we call it inertia, in mind we call it prejudice or pig-headedness." (Source: Fred Alan Wolf, *Taking the Quantum Leap: The New Physics for Nonscientists*)

Beautiful Fuel Of all the ways that civilization generates energy to light its cities, one looks better than the rest: the arrays of majestic white windmills that snake along the hills of California's Altamont Pass. Surmounting stalks that bloom from the landscape like prehistoric trees in a David Hockney painting, their giant pinwheels whirl at different speeds, some in lazy slow-motion and others in a fast blur like a child's top.

Love Train Contrary to the orthodox notion that sperm headed towards an egg are in deadly competition with each other, researchers have discovered they collaborate, often joining together to create a "love train" so as to reach the target faster.

The Most Senior Citizen The oldest living thing on earth is a 4,767-year-old bristlecone pine tree named Methuselah. Its home is at an altitude of 10,000 feet in California's White Mountains.

Refined Sensibilities + Channeled Transmissions

For much of his career, Pulitzer Prize-winning poet James Merrill was renowned for work that was well-grounded, lucidly crafted, and formal in style. But from 1976 to 1982, while assembling his sprawling mystical epic *The Changing Light of Sandover,* he used a Ouija board to solicit the input of disembodied beings, including several archangels and the spirits of dead writers W. H. Auden and Gertrude Stein.

It was a brave—some said foolish—career move. He pushed beyond what had worked for him in the past, capitalizing on the risks his success had earned him.

The Changing Light of Sandover won a National Book Critics Circle Award. Some critics compared it to the masterpieces of Dante, Homer, and Blake. "James Merrill was one of the central American poets of the 20th century," wrote Harold Bloom in a retrospective analysis of his work after his death in 1995. "He had profound affinities with the great artists in verse: Milton, Pope, Tennyson, and Auden. Like them, he was an absolute master of diction, metrics, and cognitive music."

FREE WILL DIVINATION

Mark Seltman is a palm-reader whose approach to his art is different from most fortune-tellers. If he sees a character flaw indicated by a line on your palm, he won't make you feel like it's a curse that you're powerless to resist; instead, he'll tell you what you can do to fix it or overcome it. An article about Seltman on Newyorkmetro.com described how his daughter was born with a hand that suggested she'd suffer from low self-esteem when she grew up. In response, Seltman dedicated himself to building her confidence and competence. Now, years later, the warning sign in her hand at birth has disappeared; she's brimming with aplomb.

HELP WANTED Practical dreamers with high emotional intelligence needed to become experts in the following subjects: the art of possessing abundant resources without feeling greed or a sense of superiority; the science of cultivating luxurious comfort in a way that does not lead to spiritual sloth; and a knack for enjoying peace and serenity without diluting one's ambition. Write rebelgrail@yahoo.com.

MIRABILIA REPORT   *Mirabilia* n. winsome curiosities, supernatural gifts, healing tricks; from the Latin *mirabilia,* "marvels."

■ There's a virgin forest in New York City at the upper tip of Manhattan, near the Cloisters.

■ Your skin hosts more living organisms than there are people on the planet.

■ The Milky Way Galaxy is shaped like a thick, warped vinyl record with the edge on one side bent up and on the other side bent down.

■ Whenever an actor portraying a doctor performs a particular kind of surgery on a popular soap opera, real doctors begin performing that same surgery at a dramatically higher rate in real hospitals.

■ Researchers detected traces of marijuana and coca leaves in seventeenth-century pipes found in the house where William Shakespeare lived.

■ Actor Steven Seagal was formally declared a tulku, or reincarnation of a Buddhist lama, by a Tibetan Buddhist master, even though all of his movies depict him beating up people. One ex-friend said Seagal is "the only person I know who can use the words 'motherfucker' and 'Dalai Lama' in the same sentence."

■ Eskimos use refrigerators to keep their food from freezing.

■ Rock music incites termites to eat wood at twice their usual rate.

■ In Kampala, Uganda, an unknown prankster shot gorillas with tranquilizer darts and dressed them up as clowns while they were unconscious.

■ Sixty-five million pilgrims sought to wash away their sins by bathing in the Ganges River during 2001's Kumbha Mela, a spiritual festival in India. Sixty-five million votes were cast by phone to determine the winner of TV's *American Idol* talent contest in May 2004.

■ "Corporations of the magnitude of IBM or Citibank constitute themselves as what Renaissance Europe would have recognized as city-states, sovereign powers employing as many people as once lived in Philadelphia in 1789." —Lewis Lapham, *Harper's* Magazine

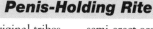

"In a number of Australian Aboriginal tribes, holding of the penis is traditionally used as a gesture to express male allegiance and cooperation, as well as a ritual part of resolving disputes between 'accused' and 'defending' parties.

"Among the Walbiri and Aranda people, when different communities get together or when grievances need to be settled in formal 'trials,' men participate in what is known variously as touch-penis, penis-offering, or the penis-holding rite. Each man presents his semi-erect organ to all the others in turn, pressing it into each man's palm and drawing it along the length of the upturned hand (held with the fingers toward the testicles). By offering and grasping each other's penis—said to represent 'paying with one's life'—the men make an avowal of mutual support and goodwill between them, or symbolize and solidify the agreement they have reached during the settling of a dispute." —Bruce Bagemihl, *Biological Exuberance: Animal Homosexuality and Natural Diversity*

Operation Ugly-Aware

"The insidious nature of ugliness is such that we gradually become accustomed to its presence. This de-sensitization can be halted only through a conscious effort to become aware of the ugliness around us, and to make others aware of it as well. To that end, the Coalition to Raise Aesthetic Awareness has developed the Operation Ugly-Aware tool kit. It consists of one item, this decal:

THIS IS UGLY

"The purpose of the decal is twofold: 1) by affixing decals to buildings and other objects which blatantly offend his or her aesthetic sensibility, the CRAC agent will increase the aesthetic awareness of other individuals who have become de-sensitized to the ugliness around them; 2) by carrying several decals in his or her pocket at all times, the CRAC agent will develop a heightened aesthetic awareness, as he or she will be constantly on the lookout for objects that need to be labeled.

"Becoming a member of the CRAC army is simple. The rules for affixing decals are as follows:

"1) No decal shall ever be affixed, either directly or indirectly, to a human being;

"2) no decal shall be affixed in a manner such as to cause permanent damage to the offending object;

"3) decals shall be affixed with discretion, and only to those objects which blatantly offend against the affixer's aesthetic conscience." (Source: The Coalition to Raise Aesthetic Consciousness, www.chadallen.net/crac)

"In his book *The Healing Power of Doing Good,* Allan Luks reports that people who spend as little as two hours a week volunteering to help others experience a 'helper's high' that produces lower blood pressure, lower heart rate, less stress, and less tension. As a bonus, Luks found, they also enjoy 'a big boost in self-esteem.' Luks theorizes that 'doing good deeds triggers the body to release endorphins—pain-killing, mood-elevating hormones.'

"Physician David Sobel and psychologist Robert Ornstein, authors of *Healthy Pleasures,* report the same effect and conclude: 'The greatest surprise of human evolution may be that the highest form of selfishness is selflessness.'" —*Earth Island Journal,* www.earthisland.org

The Power of Imagination, Part 1

Two groups were enlisted for a month-long program to boost their accuracy at shooting a basketball. One group practiced 20 minutes a day. Those in the other group didn't actually practice, but visualized themselves shooting baskets successfully for 20 minutes a day. Results? The group that literally practiced improved 56 percent. The visualizers jacked up their average 52 percent.

The Power of Imagination, Part 2

The placebo effect is a well-known but poorly understood phenomenon in medical science. Studies show that up to a third of all sick people feel better after receiving pills with no active ingredients. The reason may lie in the body's powerful instinct to participate in its own healing. When it believes help is on the way in the form of medication, it joins in by releasing endorphins, the natural opiates that induce relaxation and a sense of well-being.

The first U.S. Chief justice, John Jay, bought slaves in order to free them.

❁

William Shakespeare coined 1,700 words, more than eight percent of his total vocabulary. Some of the best: *besmirch, dauntless, dwindle, gnarled, hobnob, lackluster, madcap, pander, rancorous, sanctimonious, tranquil, bloodstained, leapfrog, gossip, fortune-teller.*

❁

Vietnamese freedom fighter Trieu Thi Trinh fought the Chinese occupation of her country in the third century. She raised a rebel army, established her own sovereign enclave, and rode into battle against the invaders on the back of an elephant. "I want to ride the tempest, tame the waves, kill the sharks," she said. "I will not resign myself."

❁

In 1,000,000 B.C. it was a miracle to kindle fire. In 10,000 B.C. it was a miracle to grow food. In 5000 B.C. a wheel was a miracle. So were metalworking, riding a horse, and sailing the ocean. In 1400 A.D. the printing press was a miracle. In 1700 an engine was a miracle. In 1870 instantaneous long-distance communication was a miracle. In 1880 the airplane was a miracle. In 1950 space travel was a miracle. (Source: L.M. Boyd)

❁

While living in Manhattan in the 1950s, avant-garde composer John Cage felt beleaguered by the omnipresence of radio sound. In response, he wrote a musical piece that featured several radios tuned to different frequencies. After that, he was able to respond to street radio noise with a pleasant sense of "They're playing my song." (Thanks to Ruby for the report.)

"Every genuine boy is a rebel and an anarch. If he were allowed to develop according to his own instincts, his own inclinations, society would undergo such a radical transformation as to make the adult revolutionary cower and cringe." —Henry Miller, *The Books in My Life*

"What would happen if one woman told the truth about her life? The world would split open." —Muriel Rukeyser, "Kathe Kollwitz," *A Muriel Rukeyser Reader*, Jan Heller Levi, editor

"Consciousness-altering devices like the microscope and telescope were once criminalized for the same reason that psychedelic plants were banned in later years. They allow us to peer into bits and zones of Chaos." —Timothy Leary

"No pessimist ever discovered the secret of the stars, or sailed to an uncharted land, or opened a new doorway for the human spirit." —Helen Keller

"Though we travel the world over to find the beautiful, we must carry it with us or we find it not." —Ralph Waldo Emerson, "Essay XII, Art," *Essays: First Series*

"To transform life into celebration is the only authentic science of religion." —Osho

ShockGuard

Supercharged Healing

Every year the MacArthur Foundation gives a stipend of $500,000, with no strings attached, to over 20 people of outstanding talent, freeing them to pursue their idiosyncratic creative, intellectual, and professional inclinations. Among the lucky geniuses selected in recent years:

Liza Lou, a glass bead artist who creates large works of color and complexity that merge fine art and craft.

Bonnie Bassler, a molecular ecobiologist who investigates the chemical signaling mechanisms that bacteria use to communicate with each other.

Loren Riesberg, a botanist who does research on one of the most perplexing questions of evolutionary biology—how new species originate.

Corinne Dufka, a photojournalist and social worker who has worked doggedly to heal war-devastated Sierra Leone.

Karen Hesse, a novelist who is playing with experimental forms of literature for children and young adults.

Janine Jagger, an epidemiologist who invents devices and monitoring systems to protect health care workers from transmission of blood-borne diseases.

Toba Khedoori, an artist who works in wax, oil, and pencil to create immense but delicate drawings on vast stretches of unframed paper.

Nawal Nour, a doctor specializing in the physical and emotional health of female immigrants who have suffered ritual clitoridectomies.

Erik Mueggler, an anthropologist who enriches the understanding of ethnic minorities in China through vivid ethnographies of ordinary lives in provincial populations.

Daisy Youngblood, a ceramicist who uses clay and bronze to create sculptures that evoke the primitive, the timeless, and the universal.

Deborah Jin, a physicist working on techniques to cool atoms to the lowest possible temperatures.

Edgar Meyer, a bassist and composer who fuses classical and bluegrass styles to create an expansive repertoire of American music.

Charles Steidel, a cosmologist who invents new methods for detecting light from the most distant galaxies, opening a window into the early history of the universe. (Source: MacArthur Foundation, www.macfound.org)

You Are a Champion of Champions

"You are a champion of champions, genetically speaking, because you are the product of an inconceivably complex web of ancestors, spiraling back for billions of years into the primordial ooze, not a single individual of which ever failed to grow to maturity and beget viable offspring while most other creatures around them, including many of their brothers, sisters, and cousins, faded away and the majority eventually disappeared forever into extinction. If your ancestors hadn't been such top performers that they were 100 percent successful in procreation, your ancestral lines of descent would be broken and you could not exist." —Guy Murchie, *The Seven Mysteries of Life*

Crucial Dust Mote?

Before the U.S. election in November 2004, *What Is Enlightenment?* magazine posed the following query to five religious leaders: "Many people argue that the upcoming presidential election is the most important in our lifetime. Do you agree?" Four respondents said, in effect, "Yes, because George W. Bush is bad for America and the world."

But the fifth, Zen Buddhist Jan Chozen Roshi, replied, "I don't know. Our existence is so short, it's like a dust mote in the eye of God. To say that the time in which my dust mote existed was the most important is a self-centered view."

Jan Chozen Roshi's wisdom resembled that in an anecdote told by Henry Kissinger. Kissinger once asked Chinese premier Zhou Enlai what he thought of the French Revolution, which had happened two centuries earlier. "Too soon to tell," Zhou answered.

THE STORY OF CIVILIZATION

"Civilization is a stream with banks. The stream is sometimes filled with blood from people killing, stealing, shouting, and doing the things historians usually record, while on the banks, unnoticed, people build homes, make love, raise children, sing song." —Will Durant, *The Story of Civilization*

BEDROCK

luminous	marrow	murmurs	lightning	praise
ancient	membrane	undulates	inside	melodies
diamond	crucible	congeals	dawn	nectar
chthonic	aurora	frees	solar	lullabies

Most Beautiful Poem

The Beauty and Truth Laboratory voted Armand Silvestre's poem, "The Secret," as the Most Beautiful Poem of the Last Millennium. This is our translation from the original French.

I want the morning to ignore
The name I told the night.
I want it to evaporate silently,
like a teardrop in the dawn wind.

I want the day to proclaim
The love I hid from the morning.
I want it to bend over my open heart
and set it aflame, like a grain of incense.

I want the sunset to forget
The secret I told the day,
And carry it away with my love
In the folds of its pale robe.

Funky Pagan Tantric Nobody with Inside Knowledge of the Big Bang

seeks Christ-Loving Buddhist in Possession of the 13 Perfect Secrets from the Beginning of Time. I am impossible to live with ... but then isn't everyone? I will drive you crazy ... but in the most useful ways possible. You don't want to get mixed up with me ... unless you love to have every one of your certainties challenged. Like the skilled Japanese pottery-makers whose work is valued for its trademark blemishes, I thrive on life's imperfections. I'll adore you for who you are, not who you might be someday. You know how to find me.

Exclusive! The Beauty and Truth Laboratory reports the news before it happens!

In this special PNN report, our psychic journalists bring you the stories that haven't happened yet—but will! It's made possible by Pulitzer Prize-winning scientist E.O. Wilson's belief that "To make sacred is the end product of evolution in our moral and aesthetic reasoning."

Conviviality Revolution A new breed of well-read, charismatic homeless people will arise. They'll spread understanding and laughter through their communities, and will be routinely feasted in the homes of grateful citizens.

Recovered Memories The recovered memories movement will take a bizarre turn when many adults begin to recall under hypnosis long-suppressed memories of joy and peace experienced when they were children.

Eros Upgrade The average length of an act of heterosexual intercourse in America—which is currently only four minutes—will jump to 22 minutes.

Lawyer Glut The government will pay subsidies to some lawyers so they won't practice law—much as it now pays supermarket chains to keep cheese off the market when there is too much and the excess would bring prices down.

Health Leaps Scientists will confirm Plato's belief that besides eating, breathing, sleeping, and mating, every creature has an instinctual need to periodically leap up into the air for no other reason than because it feels so good.

This special edition of PNN is brought to you by philosopher Norman O. Brown's belief that "civilization has to be renewed by the discovery of new mysteries, by the sovereign power of the imagination, by the undemocratic power which makes poets the unacknowledged legislators of mankind." (Source: Norman O. Brown, Apocalypse and/or Metamorphosis)

Men's Time of the Month
Biologists in Sweden will furnish conclusive evidence that men have "periods" analogous to a woman's menstrual cycle. They seem to correspond to changes in the relationship between Earth and the planet Mars, the biologists will claim. At the peak of the male "marstral cycle," which can last up to 10 days a month, the adrenal glands release a hormone which make men more likely to be irritable, more skilled at disguising their irrational impulses with logical explanations, out of touch with their feelings, and prone to violence and poor judgment. There's also a vulnerable phase preceding the period, which the biologists will dub PMS, or Pathological Macho Stress.

Genetic Performance Art
A rowdy new class of genetic engineers will have little interest in creating oil spill-eating bacteria, frost-resistant strawberries, or other useful hybrids. Considering themselves to be a cross between computer hackers and performance artists, they will create fun monstrosities that appeal to their sense of play and perversity, like winged horses and trees that grow leaves resembling $100 bills.

Homechurching As public schools continue to decline and private schools become more expensive, increasing numbers of parents will homeschool their children. As the pronoia meme spreads, an analogous phenomenon will arise among religious groups. Called the "homechurch" movement by Christians, the "homesynagogue" movement by Jews, and the "hometemple" movement by other religious groups, it will consist of people creating altars and conducting worship sessions in their own abodes. Seekers pursuing this approach to spiritual communion will serve as their own priests, priestesses, and rabbis.

The Joy Of Childbirth The national murder rate will plummet when "The Hedonistic Midwife Channel," a new cable TV network, begins to broadcast live childbirths 24 hours a day.

Sentient Vegetables Researchers will uncover stunning evidence that vegetables have an intensity of consciousness and feeling much closer to animals than has previously been suspected. Many vegetarians will renounce their previous diets and swear to eat only milk and honey.

Book Futures One of the best-selling self-help books of the decade will be *The Zen of Juicy Sacred Temper Tantrums.*

For Immediate Release

Global Village Idiot Rob Brezsny has announced his candidacy for a new Cabinet-level post that he hopes the president will create: FOOL CZAR.

Roughly analogous to America's Drug Czar, the Fool Czar would organize and lead an all-out War on Gravity—not the kind of gravity that keeps us on the ground, but rather the absurdly sober, hyper-dignified literalism that infects every level of society.

Just as the Drug Czar educates the nation on the hazards of drugs, the Fool Czar would work to show how dangerous it is feed the bad habit of taking everything so seriously all the time. He would also foster an understanding of the threat from simplistic opinion-mongering that turns every issue into fodder for infantile arguments.

To demonstrate his sincerity and commitment, Brezsny has offered to literally kiss the bare asses of the president, vice-president, and Cabinet members. In the event that would compromise their modesty, he has also indicated his willingness merely to smooch their fully clothed butts.

Upon taking office as Fool Czar, Brezsny's inaugural act would be to borrow from two traditions: 1. Among the ancient Romans, their day's work was customarily finished by noon. The rest of the day was spent in pleasure or amusement. More than half the days of the year were holidays. 2. In medieval Europe, as many as 105 days of the year were feast days.

In this spirit, Brezsny would declare a spate of new holidays and ceremonial traditions. Here they are:

Unhappy Hour. During this gala bitch fest each Tuesday afternoon, celebrants will have license to howl and mutter about everything that hurts their feelings. Having flushed all their venom in one neat ritual spew, they'll be free to enjoy generous thoughts and expansive fantasies the rest of the time.

Dare to Be Boring Day. We all deserve a break from the oppressive demands to appear smart and to be entertaining. On Dare to Be Boring Day, it will be socially unacceptable to demonstrate your wit and verve. Long-winded, rambling monologues full of obscure details will be mandatory. The more clichés and buzzwords you use, the better. Tell worn-out stories your friends have already heard several times. Flesh out your disjointed sentences with awkward silences. Discuss at length your plans for switching laundry detergents, the collection of matchbooks you had as a child, and the time you almost traveled to the Wal-Mart in another town, but didn't.

Bacchanalia. During this week-long extravaganza, work and business will be suspended so that all adults can enjoy sexual play, whether it be solo, dyadic, or in groups. To promote acceptance of the holiday, the Fool Czar will head up a new Federal Bureau of Lust. Served by advisors drawn not from the ranks of porn stars and scientific sex researchers but from tantrically trained poets and musicians, the Bureau will sponsor educational campaigns to help every citizen learn to honor the libido as a sacred gift from the Goddess.

24 Hours of Global Orgasm. What if there came a day when every adult on the planet came at the same time? This will be the climax of Bacchanalia.

Do What You Fear Festival. First, you make a list of the 100 things you're most afraid of. Next, you rate them from one to 100 in order of how badly they scare you. Then you agree to stop obsessing about the bottom 97 fears because they distract you from the three really interesting ones. Finally, you brainstorm about how you're actually going to conquer those top three fears by doing them.

Marry Yourself. As a government-sanctioned tradition, getting married to yourself will be a rite of passage as common as graduating from high school.

Be Your Own Wife Week. Whether you're male or female or transgendered, straight or gay or both, you can observe Be Your Own Wife Week. Here's how. Renounce all your yearnings to be waited on and cleaned up after. Divest yourself of every last deluded wish that someday a special person will come along to magically understand and attend to your every need. Pledge that from now on you will be a connoisseur of taking care of yourself. (This celebration might immediately follow the "Marry Yourself" holiday.)

Debunking Day. What shall we debunk? It's easy to direct scorn at targets like Bigfoot, UFOs, and the Face on Mars. On Debunking Day, we'll warm up with witty slams against them, then move on to the real sacred cows, like the cult of science, the cult of materialism, and the cult of pop nihilism.

Spiritual Makeover Day. Participants build altars celebrating beauty, truth, and love in the ugliest places they know.

Praise Binge. For 24 hours, judgmental criticism will be taboo. Revelers will stretch their imaginations as they strive to praise everything and everyone as sincerely as possible, including themselves. It will be perfectly permissible for celebrants to take detours into Brag Therapy, during which time they will boast recklessly about their own accomplishments.

Freethinkers Week. To celebrate this liberating grace period, you might indulge in any of the following festive acts: 1. Declare your independence from anyone who tries to tell you, either subliminally or directly, who you are or how you should live your life. 2. Declare your independence from your past, especially from memories that oppress your sense of possibility and from old self-images that inhibit your urge to explore. 3. Declare your independence from peer pressure, groupthink, the law of the pack, and conventional wisdom. 4. Declare your independence from your previous conception of freedom so that you'll be free to come to a completely fresh understanding of it.

Potlatch. Among certain Native American tribes, the potlatch was a generosity contest. Participants vied to give away the most gifts. In reviving this rite, we will not entirely eliminate the competitive element. Celebrants will strive to push their own largesse to the limits, even as they admire those whose munificence outstrips their own. Contributions of money and material objects will not be the only ways to partake in the Potlatch. Offerings of time, love, energy, help, and kindness will be equally valued.

Cheery Sleepy Week. Sleep deprivation has reached epidemic proportions, and the results are catastrophic. Dream-cheated somnambulists are responsible for the rise in incompetence, bad manners, and mass hypnosis. During the seven-day and seven-night Cheery Sleepy Week, all Americans will be given the luxury of catching up on their lost ZZZZs. Millions of refreshed citizens will wear buttons that brag, "I slept nine hours last night and I'm not ashamed!"

Break Bread With Your Nemesis. To observe this feast day, you simply invite the person who makes you most uncomfortable to an intimate dinner for two.

Hallowection Day. The American genius for inadvertent surrealism is nowhere better illustrated than in the proximity of Halloween and election day. Why not honor the obvious and combine the two into a single festival?

ANTI-DSM-IV, OR THE OUTLAW CATALOG OF CAGEY OPTIMISM

Psychiatry and psychotherapy obsess on what's wrong with people and give short shrift to what's right. The manual of these professions is a 943-page textbook called the *DSM-IV*. It identifies scores of pathological states but no healthy ones.

In 2002, I began to complain about this fact in my syndicated weekly column and website, and asked readers to help me compile material for a proposed antidote, the *Anti-DSM-IV*—a compendium of healthy, exalted, positive states of being. As their entries came in, we at the Beauty and Truth Laboratory were inspired to dream up some of our own. Below is our initial attempt at creating an *Anti-DSM-IV,* or as we also like to call it, *The Outlaw Catalog of Cagey Optimism.*

• ACUTE FLUENCY. Happily immersed in artistic creation or scientific exploration; lost in a trance-like state of inventiveness that's both blissful and taxing; surrendered to a state of grace in which you're fully engaged in a productive, compelling, and delightful activity. The joy of this demanding, rewarding state is intensified by a sense that time has been suspended, and is rounder and deeper than usual. (Suggested by H. H. Holiday, who reports that extensive studies in this state have been done by Mihaly Cziscenmihaliy in his book, *Flow: The Psychology of Optimal Experience.*)

• AESTHETIC BLISS. Vividly experiencing the colors, textures, tones, scents, and rhythms of the world around you, creating a symbiotic intimacy that dissolves the psychological barriers between you and what you observe. (Suggested by Jeanne Grossetti.)

• AGGRESSIVE SENSITIVITY. Animated by a strong determination to be receptive and empathetic.

• ALIGNMENT WITH THE INFINITY OF THE MOMENT. Reveling in the liberating realization that we are all exactly where we need to be at all times, even if some of us are temporarily in the midst of trial or tribulation, and that human evolution is proceeding exactly as it should, even if we can't see the big picture of the puzzle that would clarify how all the pieces fit together perfectly. (Suggested by Meredith Jones.)

• AUTONOMOUS NURTURING. Not waiting for someone to give you what you can give yourself. (Suggested by Shannen Davis.)

• BASKING IN ELDER WISDOM. A state of expansive ripeness achieved through listening to the stories of elders. (Suggested by Annabelle Aavard.)

• BIBLIOBLISS. Transported into states of transcendent pleasure while immersed in reading a favorite book. (Suggested by Catherine Kaikowska.)

• BLASPHEMOUS REVERENCE. Acting on the knowledge that the most efficacious form of devotion to the Divine Wow is tinctured with playful or mischievous behavior that prevents the buildup of fanaticism.

• BOO-DUH NATURE. Dwelling in the blithe understanding of the fact that worry is useless because most of what we worry about never happens. (Suggested by Timothy S. Wallace.)

• COMIC INTROSPECTION. Being fully aware of your own foibles while still loving yourself tenderly and maintaining confidence in your ability to give your specific genius to the world. To paraphrase Alan Jones, Dean of Grace Cathedral: following the Byzantine ploys of your ego with compassion and humor as it tries to make itself the center of everything, even of its own suffering and struggle.

• COMPASSIONATE DISCRIMINATION. Having astute judgment without being scornfully judgmental; seeing difficult truths about a situation or person without closing your heart or feeling superior. In the words of Alan Jones: having the ability "to smell a rat without allowing your ability to discern deception sour your vision of the glory and joy that is everyone's birthright."

• CRAZED KINDNESS. Having frequent, overpowering urges to bestow gifts, disseminate inspiration, and perpetrate random acts of benevolence.

• ECSTATIC GRATITUDE. Feeling genuine thankfulness with such resplendent intensity that you generate a surge of endorphins in your body and slip into a full-scale outbreak of euphoria.

• EMANCIPATED SURRENDER. Letting go of an attachment without harboring resentment toward the stimuli that led to the necessity of letting go. (Suggested by Timothy S. Wallace.)

• FRIENDLY SHOCK. Welcoming a surprise that will ultimately have benevolent effects.

• HIGHWAY EQUANIMITY. Feeling serene, polite, and benevolent while driving in heavy traffic. (Suggested by Shannen Davis.)

• HOLY LISTENING. Hearing the words of another human being as if they were a direct communication from the Divine Wow to you.

• IMAGINATIVE TRUTH-TELLING. Conveying the truth of any specific situation from multiple angles, thereby mitigating the distortions that result from assuming the truth can be told from a single viewpoint.

• IMPULSIVE LOVE SPREADING. Characterized by a fierce determination to never withhold well-deserved praise, inspirational encouragement, positive feedback, or loving thoughts; often includes a tendency to write love letters on the spur of the moment and on any medium, including napkins, grocery bags, and skin. (Suggested by Laurie Burton.)

• INADVERTENT NATURE WORSHIP. Experiencing the rapture that comes from being outside for extended periods of time. (Suggested by Sue Carol Robinson.)

• INGENIOUS INTIMACY. Having an ability to consistently create deep connections with other human beings, and to use the lush, reverential excitement stimulated by such exchanges to further deepen the connections.

A well-crafted talent for dissolving your sense of separateness and enjoying the innocent exultation that erupts in the wake of the dissolution. (Suggested by Sue Carol Robinson.)

• JOYFUL POIGNANCE. Feeling buoyantly joyful about the beauty and mystery of life while remaining aware of the sadness, injustices, wounds, and future fears that form the challenges in an examined life. (Suggested by Alka Bhargava.)

• LATE LATE-BLOOMING. Having a capacity for growth spurts well into old age, long past the time that conventional wisdom says they're possible.

• LEARNING DELIGHT. Experiencing the brain-reeling pleasure that comes from learning something new. (Suggested by Sue Carol Robinson.)

• LUCID DREAM PATRIOTISM. A love of country rooted in the fact that it provides the ideal conditions for learning lucid dreaming. (Suggested by Ken Kelzer.)

• LYRICAL CONSONANCE. Experiencing the visceral yet also cerebral excitement that comes from listening to live music played impeccably by skilled musicians. (Suggested by Susan E. Nace.)

• MODULATED RAPTURISM. Welcoming miracles and peak experiences in full awareness that the growth they initiate will require sober commitment and disciplined work to complete. (Suggested by Timothy S. Wallace.)

• NONRESENTMENT SYNDROME. Having an ability to be friendly, open, and helpful to people with whom you disagree.

• NOT HAVING TO BE RIGHT. Fostering an ability, even a willingness, to be proven wrong about one of your initial perceptions or pet theories; having an eagerness to gather information that may change your mind about something you have fervently believed; cultivating a tendency to enjoy being corrected, especially about ideas that are negative or hostile. (Suggested by Sheila Kollasch.)

• ORGIASTIC LUCIDITY. Experiencing an expansive and intricate state of clarity while in the midst of extreme sensual pleasure.

• PERMANENT DIVINE INFATUATION. Having not the abstract understanding but rather a direction perception that the Divine Intelligence, who recreates the universe fresh every moment, is deeply in love with you, even as you are in love with the Divine Intelligence.

• RADICAL CURIOSITY. Characterized by the following traits: an enthusiasm for the mystery embedded in the mundane; a preference for questions over answers;

an aversion to stereotyping, generalizations, and jumping to conclusions; a belief that people are unsolvable puzzles; an inclination to be unafraid of both change and absence of change; a strong drive to avoid boredom; a lack of interest in possessing or dominating what you are curious about. (Suggested by Laurie Burton.)

• RELENTLESS UNPRETENTIOUSNESS. Possessing a strong determination to not take yourself too seriously, not take your cherished beliefs too literally, and not take other people's ideas about you too personally.

• RIPE INTELLECTION. The understanding that a predilection to notice and analyze pathology is itself pathological. (Suggested by Timothy S. Wallace.)

• ROOTED IN ETERNITY. The state of knowing that your true identity is deeper than the constant chatter of thoughts, images, and feelings that swirls through your mind. (Suggested by Crispin R.)

• SACRED PERCEPTIVENESS. Seeing others for who they really are, in both their immaturity and genius, and articulating your insights to them with care.

• SCARY-THUNDER-IN-THE-DARK HAPPINESS. Feeling deliciously safe in a well-protected sanctuary during a severe storm. (Suggested by Sue Carol Robinson.)

• SCHIZOFRIENDIA. Hearing voices in your head that are constantly supportive, encouraging, and keen to offer advice that helps you make the most of every experience. (Suggested by Lewis.)

• SELF-ACCEPTANCE UNDER PRESSURE. The state achieved upon leaving a room filled with people who know you, and not worrying about what anyone will say about you. (Suggested by Shannen Davis.)

• SELF-HONORING. Having an unwillingness to disparage, belittle, or hurt yourself; includes a taboo against speaking phrases like, "I'm such an idiot!" and "What's wrong with me?" (Suggested by Julie Levin.)

• SLY TRUST. Having a discerning faith that the integrity of your efforts will inevitably lead to a result that's exactly what you need; being skillful in the art of never trying too hard. (Suggested by Rhonda Christmas.)

• SONGBIRD-IN-A-TREE. The cultivated awareness that daily life presents countless opportunities to be buoyed by moments of ordinary extraordinary beauty, and that these moments are most available if you perceive with your senses and not with your internal turmoil. (Suggested by Lisa Chabot.)

• TENDER RAGE. Maintaining a strong sense of love and protectiveness towards a person or creature or institution you're angry at.

• TRANSCONSUMERISM. An absence of tendencies to predicate happiness on acquiring material possessions. (Suggested by Timothy S. Wallace.)

• TRIUMPHANT NURTURING. Feeling contented expansiveness while nursing a baby. (Suggested by Susan E. Nace.)

• UNSELFCONSCIOUSNESS. Doing what you're doing and being who you're being without thinking about it at all. Being happy by virtue of not worrying about whether or not you're happy; enjoying a unified state in which you are not split between the you who acts and the you who observes. (Suggested by Valerie Keller.)

• UNTWEAKABILITY. Having a composed, blame-free readiness to correct false impressions when your actions have been misunderstood and have led to awkward consequences.

• VIRTUOSO INTEGRATION. Consistently walking your talk; effectively translating your ideals into the specific actions; creating results that are congruous with your intentions; being free of hypocrisy.

• VISIONS OF THRILLING EXPLOITS. Experiencing an eruption of intuition that clearly reveals you will attempt a certain adventure in the future, as when you spy a particular mountain for the first time and know you'll climb it one day. (Suggested by Sue Carol Robinson.)

• WEATHER SENSITIVITY. Having a high degree of awareness about your sensitivity to changes in the weather, and having a skill for managing your responses to those shifts so as to consistently bring out the best in yourself. (Suggested by Julie Caves.)

• WHOLEHEARTEDNESS. Having the capacity to give, on a moment's notice, your complete attention, empathy, and playful intelligence to any person or circumstance you choose. (Suggested by Susan Coleman.)

• WILD DISCIPLINE. Possessing a talent for creating a kind of organization that's liberating; knowing how to introduce limitations into a situation in such a way that everyone involved is empowered to express his or her unique genius; having an ability to discern hidden order within a seemingly chaotic mess.

• WHEEEE. A serenely boisterous intensely focused chaos of communion with streaming fountains of liquid light hurtling softly through the giggly upbeat tender assurance that all is well and a mysterious unimaginable intelligence is magnetizing us forward into evermore wonderful throbs of naked truth that bestow the humble happy sight of life as a river of fantastically lucky artful change flowing through us forever. (Suggested by Sarah Alexander and Jon Kohl Drucker.)

Sacred
Advertisement

The Beauty and Truth Laboratory researchers' sunny dispositions are made possible in part by the mantra, "I don't know." It's an unparalleled source of power, a declaration of independence from the pressure to have an opinion about every single subject.

It's fun to say. Try it:
"I don't know."

Let go of the drive to have it all figured out:
"I don't know."

Proclaim the only truth you can be totally sure of:
"I don't know."

Empty your mind and lift your heart:
"I don't know."

Use it as a battle cry, a joyous affirmation of your oneness with the Great Mystery:
"I don't know."

OUTLAW PRONOIA THERAPY

Experiments and exercises in becoming a blissfully rowdy, comically healing, astutely innocent Master of Crazy Wisdom

1 Have you ever had permission to indulge in a marathon of braggadocio? Have you ever gotten an invitation to bluster on endlessly about your own charms without feeling even a touch of guilt or inhibition? I hereby grant you such a license right now.

When you're ready, carry out the exercise called Brag Therapy. Grab a good listener or a recording device, and boast extravagantly about yourself for at least 20 minutes. Expound in exhaustive detail why you're so wonderful and why the world would be a better place if everyone would just act more like you.

Don't be humble or cautious. Go too far. Heap extreme glory on yourself. Brazenly proclaim the spectacular qualities about you that no one has ever fully articulated or appreciated. Don't forget to extol the prodigious flaws and vices that make you so special.

What does this have to do with pronoia? When you audaciously identify your existing gifts, you set yourself up to become a magnet for even greater abundance. In fact, we recommend that you treat yourself to a Brag Therapy session regularly.

To whet your imagination, read an excerpt from the boast of Eric Baer, a participant in a Brag Therapy session I hosted in Milwaukee. "I have opposable thumbs," Eric exulted. "I can read. I breathe all the way through the night even though I'm asleep. I have access to emporiums where I can choose from 25 different brands of toilet paper. I know how to turn food into energy. I live where knuckleheads run everything and yet nothing ever blows up."

2 The iconoclastic physicist Jack Sarfatti proposes that all "creative thought by artists, craftsmen, and scientists involves the subconscious reception of ideas from the future, which literally create themselves."

271

Beauty and Truth Laboratory researcher Vimala Blavatsky puts a different spin on it. "Our future selves are constantly transmitting great ideas to us back through time," she says, "but most of us don't believe that's possible and consequently are not alert for it."

What do you think is the most pressing communiqué your future self is currently beaming your way?

3 In the Greek epic *The Odyssey,* Odysseus and his men become stranded on an island belonging to the sorceress Circe, who uses her magic to transform the men into pigs. Later, though, she changes them back into men—only they're younger and taller and better-looking than before they were pigs.

Tell an analogous story from your own life: an experience in which you were turned into a pig for a while, and became a more beautiful version of yourself when the spell was broken.

4 Imagine that you have been relieved of your responsibilities for a given time. They will be taken care of by people you trust. You won't have to work to make money during this grace period, but will be given all you need. Nor will you have to clean your house, wash your clothes, or buy and make your food. Now here's the big question: What will you do now that you are free to do anything you like?

5 Contrary to what the Bible says, it won't be the meek who shall inherit the earth. On the other hand, the arrogant power mongers won't collect the legacy either. Neither the indecisive wimps nor the acquisitive bullies will contribute much to creating the New World.

Who, then, will inherit the earth? What kind of human beings are best-equipped to thrive in the evolving game of life? We say it will be the well-disciplined pleasure-seekers who are in vigorous dialogue with their own dark sides, who balance the masculine and feminine aspects of their natures, and who master the fine arts of working at their play and playing at their work.

Assume our definitions are true. What would you do to become more like an inheritor of the earth?

6 "Nothing's going right in my life. I feel anxious and paranoid all the time. My relationships are a mess." In my line of work, people make confessions like that to me. My first response is usually something like this: "Do you habitually gobble junk food near bedtime, steal a paltry five hours of sleep per night, gulp two cups of

coffee and no breakfast in the morning, then bolt to a workplace where you get no sunlight or exercise and sit in an uncomfortable chair?" They often reply, "You must be psychic! How did you know?!" My point is that many psychological troubles stem from our chronic failure to take good care of our physical needs.

Name three things you can do to promote pronoia in yourself by taking better care of your body.

7 In an article about storytellers in the *Los Angeles Times,* Leslie Berger profiled a high school teacher named Luigi Jannuzzi. "He once saved the life of a student who was choking on a Life Saver," Berger wrote, "and thus discovered his own gift of gab: He told the kid a joke so funny that his laughter popped the candy out of his throat."

Make up a story in which your sense of humor saves someone's life.

8 Notice how you feel as you speak the following: "The strong, independent part of me resisted the embarrassing truth for a long time, but I finally came to accept that I'm someone who craves vast amounts of love. Ever since I surrendered to this need, it doesn't nag me all the time, as it used to. In fact, it feels comforting, like a source of sweetness that doesn't go away. I never thought I'd say this, but I've come to treasure the feeling of having a voracious yearning to be loved."

9 Devote yourself to your heart's desire with unflagging shrewdness. Make it your top priority. Let no lesser wishes distract you. But consider this, too. You may sabotage even your worthiest yearning if you're maniacal in your pursuit of it.

Bear in mind the attitude described by Clarissa Pinkola Estes in her book *Women Who Run With the Wolves:* "All that you are seeking is also seeking you. If you sit still, it will find you. It has been waiting for you a long time."

Speculate on what exactly that would look like in your own life. Describe how your heart's desire has been waiting for you, seeking you.

10 Everyone influences the world in some way. No matter how powerless we may feel, each of us is a creator who continually churns out energy that bends and shapes our world and the people in it. What is the signature of your effect? How do you change the environments you pass through? What magic, for good or ill, do you exude from day to day?

Outlaw Pronoia Therapy

11 Attention please. This is your ancestors speaking. We've been trying to reach you through your dreams and fantasies, but you haven't responded. That's why we've commandeered this space. So listen up. We'll make it brief. You're at a crossroads analogous to a dilemma that has baffled your biological line for six generations. We ask you now to master the turning point that none of us have ever figured out how to negotiate. Heal yourself and you heal all of us. We mean that literally. Start brainstorming, please.

12 "If you bring forth the genius within you," said Jesus in the *Gospel of Thomas,* "it will free you. If you do not bring forth the genius within you, it will destroy you."

Is there any aspect of the genius within you that you're not bringing forth? If so, how can you fix that?

13 The Indian activist Mahatma Gandhi lead many peaceful rebellions against oppressive governments, first in South Africa and later in British-controlled India. At first he called his strategy "passive resistance," but later disavowed that term because it had negative implications. He ultimately chose the Sanskrit word *satyagraha,* meaning "love force" or "truth force." "Truth *(satya)* implies love," he said, "and firmness *(agraha)* is a synonym for force. *Satyagraha* is thus the force which is born of truth and love."

Give an example of how you have employed *satyagraha* in the past, and another example of how you might invoke it in the future.

14 Think about your relationship to human beings who haven't been born yet. What might you create for them to use? How can you make your life a gift to the future? Can you not only help preserve the wonders we live amidst, but actually enhance them? Keep in mind this thought from Lewis Carroll: "It's a poor sort of memory that only works backward."

15 In ancient Rome, gladiator contests were as popular as today's football games. The warriors back then were not hired heroes, however. They were slaves or convicts who were forced to fight. Even if they won, they were usually required to return and risk their lives another day. Now and then a grizzled veteran of many struggles-to-the-death was awarded with the ultimate prize: a wooden sword, symbolizing the end of his role as a gladiator and the beginning of his life as a free man. I believe you have earned your own personal equivalent of the wooden sword. Make one for yourself.

Outlaw Pronoia Therapy

Walking Uphill Backwards

It was the final day of my work on this book. I had to send the manuscript to the printer in a few hours. There was one problem: Page 275 was still blank. It had originally been filled with a piece I'd rejected at the last minute, and I'd written nothing to take its place.

I decided to take a hike in the hills, hoping I might drum up an oracle on the way. Nothing interesting appeared for an hour. Then, while rambling down a trail from the top of the ridge, I spied the back of a man moving towards me. It took me a while to realize he was walking up the hill backwards. As he passed me, I heard him giving himself a pep talk.

When I got home I told a friend about this scene, seeking her insight about what motivated him to engage in such an odd mode of travel. My friend said she'd done it herself. It's a psychological trick that helps make a steep ascent easier: You stay focused on how much you've already accomplished rather than being overwhelmed by the heights that are ahead of you.

Sounds pronoiac to me. Why not try it yourself?

INVITATION TO THE DANCE

Dear St. [Your Name Here]:

Do you want to join the conspiracy to incite pronoia? Are you ready to claim your rightful place in the top-secret global insurrection of undercover geniuses, rebel saints, beauty and truth strategists, spiritual freedom fighters, and troublemaking do-gooders?

You're invited to create your own branch of the Beauty and Truth Laboratory. Borrow our ideas if you like, or make up your own. Do it in the privacy of your own bedroom or in brazen public displays; in hermetically sealed solitude or with the help of your 999 closest friends.

Don't wait for everything to be perfect before you take the leap. Start in the midst of plain old everyday chaos. What's the single most maddening riddle that has always made you feel sad or confused or ashamed? Think about putting it at the heart of your first experiment.

If you feel moved to share your research, send it along. I may publish your reports in my future updates on the growing conspiracy to commit pronoia.

Here's my contact info:

Rob Brezsny
Beauty and Truth Laboratory
P.O. Box 150628
San Rafael, CA 94915
rebelgrail@yahoo.com
www.freewillastrology.com

With love and mystery,

Rob

Your Assignment

Imagine that the whole world belongs to you. The birch trees in New Hampshire's White Mountains are yours, and so are the cirrus clouds in the western sky at dusk and the black sand on the beaches of Hawaii's big island. You own everything, my dear sovereign—the paintings in all the museums of the world, as well as the Internet and the wild horses and the roads.

Please take good care of it all, OK? Be an enlightened monarch who treats your domain with reverent responsibility. And make sure you also enjoy the full measure of fun that comes with such mastery. Glide through life as if all of creation is yearning to honor and entertain you.

Author's Thanks

My gratitude is boundless. Thanks especially to these gorgeous geniuses:

Ro Loughran and Zoe Brezsny, for their smart love and endless gifts;

the readers of my weekly column, who inspire me as much as I inspire them;

the Beauty and Truth Laboratory and the Burning Man festival for their visions of heaven on earth;

Jane Heaven and KPFA for inviting me to create my pagan revival shows for a radio audience;

the Mystic Beat Lounge and the other explorers who came to my Sacred Uproar shows early on, helping me launch this work;

my parents, Bob and Felice Brezsny, for giving me a pronoiac start;

Shoshana Alexander for her energetic editing and Catherine Campaigne for her stellar help on the book design;

my generous teachers, numbering in the thousands, for their tireless efforts to wake me up;

the Divine Wow, also known as the Blooming HaHa and the Creator of the Universe, for the great pleasure of being alive.

About Me

I'm an aspiring master of curiosity, sacred janitor, and macho feminist. I write "Free Will Astrology," a syndicated weekly column that appears in many print publications and on the Web.

My horoscopes, the entire text of my last book, *The Televisionary Oracle,* and some of my music are available free at my website, www.freewillastrology.com.

Notice all miracles

16

You
Are
My
Coauthor

Use the next 17 pages any way you want. Continue the work you launched at other places in the book. Add your own Dionysian Manifestos, Guerrilla Oracles, and Medicine Stories. Expand the definitions of pronoia. Begin writing the holy texts of your fresh new personal religion. Take a chance or two.

Draw or paste in your own provocative healing images.

Wash your own brain and surprise yourself.

Provide evidence that you are an Earth-Shaking, Taboo-Breaking, Love-Erecting, Truth-Correcting, Mind-Expanding, Justice-Demanding Connoisseur of Beauty and Truth and Love.

Rebel against the obvious answers.

Spawn your own visual extravaganza.

"God was my co-pilot, but we crashed in the mountains and I had to eat Him."
Explain.

Channel your inner wise-ass.

Feel free to ignore the questions and directions at the top of each page.
You can even use whiteout or colored tape to expunge them if you want.

Don't save your enormous creativity for "something better."
Give it to this.

Draw the image or symbol that represents the absolute of your desires.

If you don't like the news, go out and make some of your own.
Report your results here.

"Thanks to them from whom the painful blessings flow, we are waking up."
True or false?

"Your body is a temple. Littering is strictly prohibited." Explain.

Design your dream house or sanctuary.

What are your minimum requirements for paradise?

Collage your unpredictable yet malleable future.

ARGUMENTS WITH GOD is the only organization on the planet that specializes in the art of debating with the Creator. Our trained Prayer Warriors are standing by, ready to deliver the protests and complaints that you want to convey. Send your mad, rebellious, poignant appeals to rebelgrail@yahoo.com, and we will relay them directly to the Cosmic Trickster with persuasive eloquence. Write your first draft here.

"Everywhere is the center of the world." Prove or refute.

Dream up questions you've never thought of before. Don't answer them till later.

Make a graphic representation of your frontier.

Is this a perfect moment? Why?

Draw the face you had before you came into this world.

Read your own mind.

You know what to do and you know how to do it.

SACRED ADVERTISEMENT

The end of the book is brought to you by this toast:
"May you get what you want and still want it."